73

DINERS, DRIVE-INS AND DIVES

the funky finds in flavortown

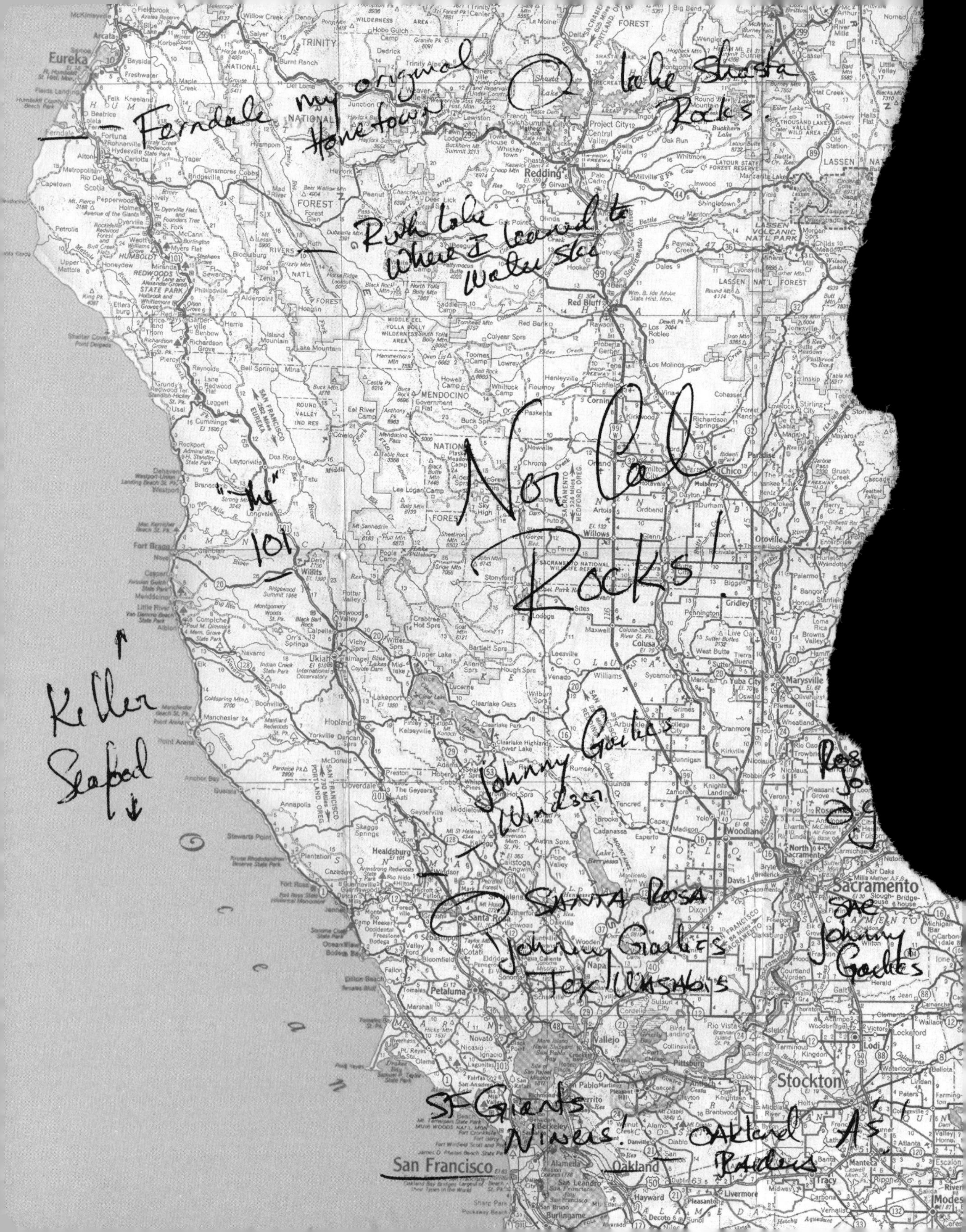

Ferndale my original
Hometown

① lake Shasta
Rocks.

Ruth Lake
Where I learned to
Water Ski

Nor Cal
Rocks!

"Me"
101

Killer
Seafood
↓

Johnny Garlies
Windsor

Ross

SANTA Rosa
Johnny Garlies
Tex Wasabis

See
Johnny
Garlies

SF Giants
Niners

Oakland A's
Raiders

the funky finds in flavortown

AMERICA'S CLASSIC JOINTS AND KILLER COMFORT FOOD

 GUY FIERI

WITH ANN VOLKWEIN

WILLIAM MORROW
An Imprint of HarperCollinsPublishers

NEW YORK TIMES BESTSELLERS BY GUY FIERI

Diners, Drive-ins and Dives: An All-American Road Trip . . . with Recipes!

More Diners, Drive-ins and Dives: A Drop-Top Culinary Cruise Through America's Finest and Funkiest Joints

Guy Fieri Food: Cookin' It, Livin' It, Lovin' It

PHOTOGRAPHY CREDITS: page 14, Pete Koroneos; 27, Jonathan Lakiote; 28–29, Edward Acker; 35, Roland Smith; 42–43, Katharine Kean, Alana Salcer, Evelyn Posada; 44, Walter Coker; 56–57, Julie Posner; 59 and 61, Joaquin Rodas; 63–65, Ginger Finnan; 67–69, Alice Keeney Wiggans; 73–77, Randi Anglin; 93–94, Devin Moeser; 95, Phillip Golding; 96–99, Stephen C. Ham; 116, Richard Fleischman; 145–147, Mike Spinelli; 176, Lorena Brown; 179, Carlos Guiaco; 184, 186, M. Leibert; 189, 191, 193, Ken Pagliaro; 194–197, Terri McCandless; 198, 203, Meghan Wilker; 214–216, Colin Kilpatrick; 233, 235, Nathan Dang; 241, Lucas Cochenet; 275, 277, Catherine Toth

PHOTOGRAPHS © COURTESY OF TELEVISION FOOD NETWORK, G.P.: pages 1, 8, 9, 11, 14, 37, 49, 51, 53, 61, 74, 82, 83, 85, 86, 91, 101, 103, 105, 109, 110, 151, 152–153, 156–157, 161, 163, 172–173, 183, 199, 208, 210–213, 218–221, 229, 245, 250, 253, 263, 267–268, 278, 283, 286–289

PHOTOGRAPHS COURTESY OF THE RESTAURANT: pages 16, 17, 18, 20, 50, 113, 121–125, 127–129, 139, 141–143, 165, 167, 169–171, 205, 223, 231, 239, 257, 259–261, 276, 290–291

ADDITIONAL LOCATION PHOTOGRAPHY COURTESY OF: Neil Martin, Anthony Rodriguez, Matt Giovinetti, and Jeff Asell.

HarperCollins books may be purchased for educational, business, or sales promotional use. For information please write: Special Markets Department, HarperCollins Publishers, 10 East 53rd Street, New York, NY 10022.

Designed by Kris Tobiassen
Foldout illustrated map by Joe Leonard

Library of Congress Cataloging-in-Publication Data has been applied for.

ISBN 978-0-06-224465-9

13 14 15 16 17 ID/RRD 10 9 8 7 6 5 4 3 2 1

TO ALL THE TRIPLE D FANS

This has been a phenomenal experience for the restaurants, the Krew, and me. But it would be nothing without you, the *crazy* fans, doing all you can to get out there and support these places and keeping the American spirit alive.

Guy!

CONTENTS

NORTHEAST AND MID-ATLANTIC

SOUTH

MIDWEST

WEST AND SOUTHWEST

HAWAII

CANADA

Introduction

As I sit down to write the kickoff to this third installment of what's become the *Diners, Drive Ins and Dives* series of books, I can't help but smile at what's become of this little-show-that-could. The Krew and I are braving the cold in Toronto, Canada (yes, that makes *DDD* an *international* show!), and while I'm writing about book three, I'm hitting some amazing joints that I already know you're going to dig in book four.

So far, the train to Flavortown has hit more than six hundred restaurants, celebrating what's great about the great American culinary landscape (and beyond), and as the reach of the show has grown, so has the *DDD* family, from the Krew to the fans to the owners and chefs. As I look back, it really feels like we've all grown together, and it truly has been a life-changing experience. I can think back to Season 1 and how little my then ten-year-old son, Hunter, was when he'd hitch a ride with me in the Camaro. Well, now I'm fighting him for the keys . . . he's driving! I remember specific days when great, lasting friendships were formed on the road with crew members like Chico and the Big Bunny, *DDD* legends like Gorilla, Panini Pete, Stretch, Hodad, Niko and

LIVE CAM: YA SEE, FIERI, YOU'RE IN MY TOWN, SO I GET TO DRIVE YOUR CAR!
IF I WAS IN NOR CAL, YOU COULD CRUISE MY VESPA!

TRYING A PIG EAR SANDWICH—IF I DON'T LIKE THIS, SHE MAY KICK MY BUTT.

Sikey, Reno . . . the list goes on and on. *DDD* has brought a lot of great people together in ways I never could have imagined.

And what makes it all the more fulfilling, real, and important is how you guys—the fans—have come along with us for the ride. You've watched the show grow. You've engaged in our culinary shenanigans. You've hit these funky joints, tried their food, and supported their great work. That's what makes the culinary world go 'round. Together we've created our own food culture. We've supported local businesses, and believe me, it's made a huge difference in many, many lives. We've done our part to preserve the great culinary traditions of many different kinds of folks and learned a lot along the way. And we've connected with each other in new ways through the great common denominator: food. I feel very fortunate that I get to meet all sorts of great people around the world who dig talkin' *DDD*—at my restaurants, on the street, on the air, and I've got to tell you, it makes all of the miles and long hours well worth it.

DDD is about celebrating the good in food. We don't review food. We root for it. I get asked over and over, "Is there anything you won't eat? Is there anything you don't like? Do you just automatically give everything a thumbs up?" Of course I don't love everything. Of course there are all sorts of things on any given menu that I wouldn't order. But that's not what we're all about. We're here to show you what you might want to eat out there—not what you shouldn't! Food is fun. Or at least we think it is.

So, as we continue on the road/ship/train to Flavortown in America and beyond, let's take a minute to enjoy the latest batch of greatest *DDD* hits, right here, right now, in *DDD3: The Funky Finds in Flavortown*. You're gonna dig our first native American restaurant, Tocabe: An American Indian Eatery, in Denver, and for one of our first international entries, check out Fresh Local Wild from Vancouver.

So, before we get to cookin', I've got to thank all of the ever-growing *DDD* family for comin' along for the ride. It's an honor to continue to be a part of your lives . . . to laugh together, to eat together, and to celebrate all that's great about food and the people who make it. Keep on cookin'.

Love, Peace & Taco Grease,

Guy!

The Krew

I appreciate all of the accolades that I get from the fans about *Triple D*, but I have to remind everybody to recognize the importance of a great offensive line to a quarterback, and that comes down to the Krew. They deserve a lot of credit. They arrive on location well before me and continue to work as I go on to the next location. The researchers, the drivers, the PAs, the audio, the directors of photography, producers, all of them deserve a big round of applause for a job well done. And as you'll see throughout the book, I've asked them for their insights into the funky joints in Flavortown. So be prepared, some of this may get weird.

Let me introduce the Krew:

KAT HIGGINS

Executive Producer
Started: Season 1

Kat doesn't have an official nickname. I like to call her "Mandu" as in Kathmandu, but she really is the Mama Bear, sometimes on the road with us, sometimes back at the nest (or den). I pick the cities, she starts research, we do the evaluation of the locations, and she solidifies the details, handles all the issues, keeps an eye on everything in the field, sets the tempo, and puts the show on the road. So maybe her nickname should be "Mama Bear" . . . but I know that ain't gonna stick, so we're still searching.

ANTHONY "CHICO" RODRIGUEZ

Director of Photography
Started: Pilot

Chico was the original director of photography and a founding member of the show. With his last name being Rodriguez, somehow the Freddy Prinze show came up in discussion and he got the name Chico and the Man. He's the proud father of two and lives in Minneapolis with his effervescent wife and their daughters, Ava and Vivian.

Chico: *Guy's manager, Reid, has recently called in a favor to see if there can be a change of time to add more hours in the day and days in the year, because he works 28/8 but somehow squeezes it into 24/7. Reid also travels around with Guy and is with us on DDD shoots. So Bunny and I have taken it upon ourselves, much to the head shaking (and laughing) of our producers, to build "mobile offices" for Reid. The man has to work, and well . . . Bunny and I want to create a great work environment for him.*

DAVID "BIG BUNNY" CANADA

Audio Tech
Started: Pilot

An original founding member of the show, David is an all-round utility player. He can fix it, build it, wire it, arrange it, cool it, heat it—you name it, "Big Bunny Can Do It." The reason he's called Big Bunny is that he's tall and when he puts the headphones up on his head they look like rabbit ears. He's also married to one of our favorite producers, Kate Gibson, who is now Kate Canada. They met on the show while filming at Mike's Chili Parlor in Seattle, Washington.

MIKE "FATHER TIME" MORRIS

Field Producer
Started: Season 1

You might recognize my ATO fraternity brother Mike from the movie *Maid in Manhattan* with Jennifer Lopez and Ralph Fiennes, in which he played a New York news reporter. Father Time always brings wisdom and jocularity to the set.

Father Time: *The owners of the places are so nice, but we're there for days, disrupting their routines and changing what they do while we're there. They have wireless microphones on and don't realize we can hear them thorough our headphones. Our sound guys alert us if there's any concern. So the owners probably wonder what's going on when after they've been back in the cooler talking to their help in private and say that they're exhausted or not used to being told what to do or whatever, and I somehow know to come talk to them and say, "Look, I know you're exhausted and not used to being told what to do."*
They must think we're mind readers. It helps to have insider information!

BRYNA "THE PIRATE" LEVIN

Field Producer
Started: Season 1

As I've mentioned before, Bryna likes big sunhats and she wears stripes all the time. The Pirate is probably one of the smartest people on the Krew. She's not only a producer but also a writer, does research for the show, and is a proud mother of two boys.

KATE "ASK KATE" GIBSON AKA "MRS. BUNNY"

Field Producer
Started: Seasons 2 to 5, then back for 13

Kate has never been officially given a name. After she married David we tried out Mrs. Bunny, but that didn't stick. She's been called Ask Kate because before you did anything you had to get her permission as a producer. She doesn't like the name, so we're taking suggestions. Kate is funny, opinionated, and hard-working— and that's what we love about her.

LIZ "ERD" POLLOCK

Field Producer
Started: Season 8

Liz is a fun-loving, always up for a good time, hard-working, overdedicated super producer. One night after a long shoot the name Liz just rolled into Liz-ERD, as in lizard—not a shining moment for name giving, but it stuck. (Plus, it's not like anyone really appreciates his or her nickname in the first place.)

MATT "BEAVER" GIOVINETTI

Director of Photography
Started: Season 1

Beaver is incredibly creative and always has an observation and a story to go along with it. I don't know exactly where the name came from . . . Beaver Cleaver, perhaps, the all-American good kid in the neighborhood. For example, as Chico tells it: "When Beaver first entered the TV industry, he thought it would be a good idea to do a demo reel, like anyone would do. But the unique Beaver spin was that he hosted it, mullet, Napoleon Dynamite glasses, and all. In the video Beaver explained that he prefers to shoot, direct, and edit all his own material, "but sometimes it just doesn't work out that way." Now, what didn't make the reel? Next time you see Matt, ask him about the Space Shuttle launch he shot . . . rather, ask him about the Shuttle launch that happened behind him while he was pointing at the wrong launch pad. Oh, Matt.

NEIL "BOY BAND" MARTIN

Associate Producer
Started: Season 3

For a full understanding of why he's called Boy Band, see page 113. When he first started with the Krew I didn't think he'd make it past day one, but he got better by day two, and now life wouldn't be the same without him on the Krew. If there's somebody who knows the rules of the road on *Triple D,* it's Boy Band. He's been there, done that.

JEFF "BUTTERBEAN" ASELL

Audio Tech
Started: Season 6

When we first met Jeff, there was a resemblance to the heavyweight boxer Butterbean—just because of the bald head, of course. Butterbean, just like Big Bunny, is an audio tactical warrior. If I need something done, fixed, whatever, they're on it—they're mercenaries. (And just for the record, everybody who has a copy of the first book, please go into it with your pen and correct this: it's not Assell, it's Asell.)

RYAN "DONNY" LARSON

Cameraman
Started: Season 11

Breaking into the Krew is a tough thing to do because we're a very tight-knit group. Ryan started as a PA following in the shadow of Neil, so that was not easy. But he made a name for himself, and why his nickname is Donny I do not know. He's since been promoted to cameraman.

JOSH "THE ICE MAN" BANE

Cameraman
Started: Season 13

Let's just say we call him The Ice Man because he keeps it so cool. (Who knows, there could be another reason for that name, but we don't want to get into that.) Josh had to break into the Krew and learn the ways, but he's so on point now.

KERRY "GILLIGAN" JOHNSON

Associate Producer
Started: Season 12

Not that there is always a clear understanding as to how a nickname came about, but this had something to do with the phrase "Hey, little buddy," from when the Skipper calls Gilligan . . . and then somebody gets a hat with the name Gilligan on it, and then it's all over, that's his nickname. But he's a student of the Neil "Boy Band" Martin school of PA—if I need it, Gilligan has already got it.

RON "FRAGGLE" GABALDON

Unit Manager
Started: Season 4

There was a series on HBO in the eighties called *Fraggle Rock*, and this guy is a character straight out of that show. He's got one of the most important jobs of anybody: taking care of my car. (About which there will be stories to follow—see page 25.)

TONY CARRERA

Production Assistant
Started: Season 13

Tony is the newest member of the Krew. He's the rookie and doing a good job. He doesn't have a lot to say, but he gets the job done. And there's a nickname to come . . . got any ideas?

RINO'S PLACE

HANDMADE, REAL-DEAL ITALIAN. PERIOD.

How do you begin to explain this place on the east side of Boston? It's a small, I mean small, little joint. Matter of fact, it's so small they had to open up the waiting area in the bar across the street just to handle their overflow after they were on *Triple D*. The food's outstanding, only to be eclipsed by the passion and generosity of Tony and his family.

★ TRACK IT DOWN ★

258 Saratoga Street
East Boston, MA 02128
617-567-7412
www.rinosplace.com

WITH MY HAIR, I SHOULDN'T BE AROUND FLAMES THAT BIG.

You know how much I love Italian—it's gotta be handmade, homemade, and the real deal. This place is all that. The chef, Tony Dicenso, is a second-generation owner who was born in Italy and came to the United States in 1985. He took over from his parents in 1994. As he says, "This is what I was made to do." He goes to the market two or three times a day to get the freshest produce, meats, and fish, makes things like his grandmother did, rolls the pasta out to order, uses nothing but the best, and serves it up in ridiculously large portions. I didn't know whether to hug him or kidnap him to California. You've got to come meet this cat.

KREW NOTES

Liz "Erd" Pollock: Food here, second to none. That aside, something felt strange at this shoot right off the bat. There was a lot of testosterone, I guess you'd say. Soon I realized the chef, the director of photography, and of course Guy were all Italian. Then I looked over and asked the audio tech if he was Italian too, and Guy said, "He's so Italian he has ricotta in his veins!" I'd like to say people normally listen to me on set, but I knew it was all over and I sat back, ate raviolis, and enjoyed the show.

Neil "Boy Band" Martin: For me, Rino's Place is one of the top three Italian places we've put on the show. Anytime someone tells me they're going to Boston, I tell them they must go and get the lobster ravioli, and if they have to wait in line to get in, they should wait. Tony is so meticulous about his product that he actually uses a teeny-tiny rolling pin to get the quarter ounce of meat out of the lobster legs.

LIVE CAM: A TEENY LOBSTER ROLLING PIN, PART OF TONY'S KEEBLER ELVES COOKING COLLECTION.

 ## RESTAURANT UPDATE

From the day after our episode of *DDD* aired, our business has grown tremendously! We've had customers from all over the world. Guy, along with the production company, told us to be prepared and ready. My initial thought was, *Really, how many people truly follow the show?* Well, let me tell you—still today, they haven't stopped coming. We recently opened up a lounge area where our customers waiting can enjoy a glass of wine, an ice-cold beer on tap, or even a light appetizer to hold them over. Our wait time can range anywhere from one to three hours, I kid you not. We couldn't be more grateful to Guy Fieri and the *DDD* crew.

—TONY AND ANNA DICENSO

RINO'S SPECIAL

ADAPTED FROM A RECIPE COURTESY OF TONY DICENSO, RINO'S PLACE

Serves 4

Four 4-ounce veal cutlets (scaloppini)

Four 4-ounce chicken cutlets

¼ cup all-purpose flour

½ cup plus 6 tablespoons olive oil

**12 shiitake mushrooms, cleaned and stems
    discarded, sliced**

3 ounces portobello mushrooms, finely diced

6 ounces oyster mushrooms, trimmed

3 tablespoons brandy

1 cup heavy cream

4 tablespoons unsalted butter

4 large shrimp, shelled and deveined

Salt and freshly ground black pepper

Chopped parsley leaves, for garnish

Pasta, for serving, optional

I STICK OUT LIKE A SORE THUMB!

LIVE CAM: EVERYONE'S EXCITED TO SEE IF THIS DUDE KNOWS WHAT HE ORDERED.

1. Preheat the oven to 225°F.

2. Pound the veal and chicken into ¼-inch-thick pieces between sheets of plastic wrap or waxed paper. Add the flour to a large shallow dish. Dredge the veal and chicken in the flour.

3. Heat ½ cup of the olive oil in a large sauté pan over medium heat. Working in batches, add the veal and chicken and brown on one side, then flip, cooking for a total of 5 to 6 minutes. Set aside in a warm oven.

4. In a medium sauté pan, heat 2 tablespoons of the remaining olive oil over medium heat. Add the shiitake mushrooms and cook until golden brown, about 5 minutes. Remove the shiitakes, set aside, and add another 2 tablespoons olive oil to the pan. Add the portobellos and cook for 3 minutes. Remove the portobellos, set aside, then add the remaining 2 tablespoons olive oil to the pan. Add the oyster mushrooms and cook for 7 minutes. Drain any excess oil from the pan and return the shiitakes and portobellos back to the pan. Remove the pan from the heat and pour the brandy into the pan. Using a long kitchen match, carefully ignite the brandy and burn off the alcohol. Return the pan to medium heat and stir in the cream and butter. Add the shrimp to the pan. Let cook and reduce for 4 minutes, or until shrimp are just cooked through then season with salt and pepper. You're ready to serve.

5. Arrange 1 piece of veal, 1 piece of chicken, and 1 shrimp on each plate. Top with some mushrooms and sauce and garnish with parsley. Serve over pasta if you like.

BROADWAY DINER

WHERE UNCLE GEORGE DRIVES THE BUS TO FLAVORTOWN

This is where the line "I'm driving the bus to Flavortown" was made famous. It was all because of this guy, Uncle George. Broadway Diner is one of those monster diners that everybody loves on *Triple D,* and the owner, George Kavourakis, is as full of life and flavor as the dishes he makes. Portions are huge, and the Broadway Festival seafood pasta . . . as I said on the show, if I were stuck on a deserted island and all we had to eat was seafood, I don't think I would get as much seafood as you get in that dish. And the goulash is goulicious. Watch out, everybody, 'cause George is going to be driving the bus to Flavortown.

You'll find homemade everything from everywhere in this place, and you'll feel like you're family. George runs the place with his daughter and nephew, and he does things his own way, like wrapping his salmon in ribbons of potato and serving it over spinach with a scampi sauce. He makes his own spice mixtures and cooks his pastas perfectly al dente. George came to the United States from Greece and started as a dishwasher more than forty years ago, and his commitment to the classic diner hasn't wavered. They're open twenty-four hours—I'd come here at four in the morning, and at five and six and seven. This is where to come when you're hungry.

> ★ TRACK IT DOWN ★
>
> **6501 Eastern Avenue
> Baltimore, MD 21224
> 410-631-5666
> www.broadwaydiner1.com**

KREW NOTES

Anthony "Chico" Rodriguez: Father Time's Big Race: We were in the middle of two big intersections in Baltimore, about to shoot the stand-up (Guy's opener) for the segment, and there happened to be *huge* orange construction drums in the background of where we wanted to shoot. So Mike (Father Time), being the ever-helpful producer that he is, offered to go move them. As he walked away, Guy gave me that sly smile, so I started rolling the camera. Father Time begins to move them and Guy yells, "Five feet to the left." So Mike struggles and rolls them to the left. Then Guy yells, "Nope, that's worse, go ten feet to the right," so Mike then struggles and rolls them to the right. Guy then yells, "No, try moving backward." So Mike moves them backward. Now this goes on for a good five minutes, while the camera is rolling and we're all laughing. Finally, Mike realizes what's going on and chases Guy all over, well, Baltimore.

JUST LIKE FATHER TIME—PLAYING IN TRAFFIC.

Mike "Father Time" Morris: Broadway Diner has a larger-than-life Greek chef, crankin' out huge platters of non-diner food in a classic diner in Baltimore. And yes, this is where Guy and Chico had me, the producer, out in front of the place moving parking cones around . . . just enjoying themselves at my expense. But after it was over I did chase Guy with an orange cone.

 ## RESTAURANT UPDATE

Since being on *Triple D* we've been fortunate to have visitors from all over the country stop in for a bite! Whether we're serving something that was featured on *Triple D*, one of our diner classics, or one of our new items, we're happy that people recognize the diner and George! It's amazing how far people will travel to try the Broadway Festival!

—PETE KAVOURAKIS

BROADWAY FESTIVAL (SEAFOOD PASTA)

ADAPTED FROM A RECIPE COURTESY OF CHEF GEORGE KAVOURAKIS, BROADWAY DINER

Serves 4

1 pound linguini

¼ cup olive oil

½ medium onion, diced

10 garlic cloves, sliced

One 28-ounce can crushed tomatoes

1 teaspoon salt

1 teaspoon ground black pepper

½ cup white wine

Two 5-ounce shell-on lobster tails, halved lengthwise

12 Manila clams, scrubbed

12 mussels, scrubbed and bearded

10 ounces large sea scallops

6 ounces calamari (tubes only), cut into rings

8 jumbo (U-12) shrimp, shelled and deveined

⅓ cup grated pecorino Romano cheese

¼ cup coarsely chopped fresh basil leaves

2 tablespoons chopped fresh oregano leaves

Extra-virgin olive oil, for garnishing, optional

UNCLE GEORGE IS SETTING FLAVORTOWN ON FIRE!

FATHER TIME IN HOT PURSUIT.

1. Bring a large pot of salted water to a boil. Add the linguini and cook according to the package directions for al dente, about 10 minutes. Drain and set aside.

2. To make the sauce, in a large skillet, heat the olive oil over medium heat and add the onion and garlic. Cook until softened but not browned, about 3 minutes. Add the crushed tomatoes and salt and pepper and simmer for 5 minutes. Next, add the white wine, lobster tails, clams, mussels, scallops, calamari, and shrimp. Cover and cook until the seafood is cooked through and opaque, 5 to 8 minutes. Remove and discard any shellfish that does not open. Add the cheese, basil, oregano, and cooked linguini. Toss until everything is coated with the sauce. Adjust the seasoning if needed and drizzle with extra-virgin olive oil, if using.

SIP & BITE RESTAURANT

COME FOR THE FOOD AND STAY FOR THE FLOOR SHOW

I'm not allowed to watch the rerun of *Sip & Bite* because I fall off my chair laughing. These guys are some of the funniest people I've met in my *Triple D* travels. The joint is legit, known to be the place to go by everybody and then some in Baltimore, and the crab cake is ridiculous. All the food is scratch made, and the spanakopita is an illegal boot-

★ TRACK IT DOWN ★

**2200 Boston Street
Baltimore, MD 21231
410-675-7077
www.sipandbite.com**

I'M *NOT TICKLISH* . . . BUT SOFIA STILL TRIED.

legged recipe. Yeah, you heard me, Sofia, bootlegged! You took it from your family, and I hope they're gettin' you back for it (*ha ha ha*). But really, what a fun place—you gotta check it out and make sure that the floor show is happening. Tony and Sofia Vasiliades are the Greek Lucy and Ricky show.

Sip & Bite is open 24/7, and it's been a landmark in this town since 1938. It started with Grampa Tony, then passed to his son George, then on to George's kid Tony. Sofia and Tony's families are from the "same little mountain" in Greece and together they serve up classic Greek dishes, family recipes like Sofia's grandmother's spanakopita, and a Maryland specialty or two, like their crab cakes full of lump crabmeat that still follow Tony's grandfather's recipe.

Priceless: "Hey, Sofia, smell the spatula, I think it smells like goat cheese . . . Gotcha!"

KREW NOTES

Liz "Erd" Pollock: Guy is always funny, period. But man, this day, I don't know if it was the tired sillies or too many Americanos, but the crew was on the floor as Guy did everything from having Sofia host the show to throwing food at her. He always has fun and makes everyone instantly at ease, but throwing food (at the chef, anyway) was a first and will go down as *DDD* history, at least for the crew.

Kerry "Gilligan" Johnson: Sofia was ready to take over the show—literally. And Michael Phelps frequents the restaurant.

TONY, SOFIA, AND YES, THAT'S MICHAEL PHELPS. EAT HERE AND WIN GOLD.

Ryan "Donny" Larson: This is where we celebrated Guy's manager, Reid's, birthday. We decorated the whole dining room with balloons and ribbons . . . and then we all pooled in and gave him twenty-eight cents.

 RESTAURANT UPDATE

When Guy came to visit our restaurant, it was a dream come true! After the airing of our episode on Food Network, we've had the pleasure of meeting so many wonderful fans of *Triple D*, many of whom have traveled great distances to stop by for a bite and a hello. We can't thank Guy, his crew, and his loyal fans enough for this great honor!

—TONY AND SOFIA VASILIADES

SOFIA'S SPANAKOPITA

ADAPTED FROM A RECIPE COURTESY OF SOFIA VASILIADES, SIP & BITE

Serves 12

⅔ cup extra-virgin olive oil

2 garlic cloves, minced

2 cups finely chopped leeks (white part only)

2 cups finely chopped shallots or onions

Three 10-ounce bags fresh spinach, roughly chopped

2 cups chopped scallions (white and green parts)

2½ cups cubed feta cheese

2 cups ricotta cheese

½ cup grated kefalotiri cheese (worth looking for, or substitute pecorino Romano)

2½ tablespoons finely chopped fresh dill

2 teaspoons finely chopped fresh mint

2 teaspoons ground black pepper

1½ teaspoons freshly grated nutmeg

4 large eggs, 2 whole, 2 beaten

1 cup olive oil, for brushing

1 box (16 ounces) phyllo dough

1. Preheat the oven to 350°F.

2. Heat the extra-virgin olive oil in large pot over medium heat. Add the garlic, leeks, and shallots and sauté until softened, about 5 minutes. Add the spinach and scallions and cover the pot for a few minutes until the spinach has wilted significantly. Uncover, reduce the heat to medium-low, and simmer to allow the liquid to evaporate (be sure not to let the spinach mixture burn). When most of the liquid has evaporated, about 15 minutes, transfer to a large bowl and let cool for 10 minutes.

3. In a separate large bowl, mix the feta, ricotta, and kefalotiri cheeses, the dill, mint, pepper, nutmeg, and 2 of the whole eggs. Gently fold the cheese mixture into the cooled spinach mixture.

4. Brush a 9 x 13-inch baking pan with some olive oil. Gently place 1 sheet of the phyllo in the bottom of the pan and brush with olive oil, making sure to coat well. Repeat this step 8 times. This creates a nice strong base for serving.

5. Pour in the spinach filling and spread it out evenly. Place 6 sheets of phyllo on top of the spinach, making sure to coat each layer of dough very well with olive oil. Also make sure to tuck in the edges of the phyllo around the filling all around the perimeter of the pan (to make it look pretty). Brush the top with the 2 beaten eggs (they give the spanakopita a beautiful brown color after baking). Score the pie in 12 square portion sizes. Bake for 1 hour, until the top is a deep golden brown, rotating halfway through the baking time.

COOK'S NOTE: Cover the phyllo dough with a slightly moist kitchen towel as you're working to keep it from drying out, and be sure to work quickly.

MOMENTS LATER, SOFIA TRIED TO HOTWIRE THE '68.

RINCON CRIOLLO

CUBAN FOOD MECCA

If you ask me to authenticate an Italian restaurant, I got you. Barbecue? I am totally down. Mexican? Been cooking it most of my life. But when it comes to Cuban . . . to make sure I was delivering you the real deal I had to call in one of my favorite chefs and one of the craziest people allowed on the planet: Chef Carl "The Cuban" Ruiz. Even before we visited the place, he knew about it. He told me it was as Cuban as Cuban gets, and coming from The Cuban, that's pretty darn Cuban. (That was a lot of "Cuban!")

★ TRACK IT DOWN ★

**40-09 Junction Boulevard
Corona, Queens, NY 11368
718-458-0236
www.rinconcriollo.wix.com**

When I say this place is authentic . . . the original restaurant was opened in Cuba in 1950, when current co-owner Rudy Acosta's grandfather started the business. All the recipes come from Rudy's great uncle, Rene Acosta, who still keeps an eye on the joint. The one condition Rene has is *Don't touch the recipes.* Judging by the made-to-order, killer arroz con pollo or the house favorite, ropa vieja, I'd say that's a fair deal. This isn't just a restaurant—it's a cultural experience.

MAX AND RUDY LIVIN' LARGE BEHIND THE BAR.

KREW NOTES

Bryna "The Pirate" Levin: It was my job to research locations for New York City, my hometown and the biggest food metropolis on the planet. It was challenging. I spoke to more than one hundred places and researched many more online before coming up with the eight places we would end up shooting. Guy's friend Carl Ruiz, a Cuban chef who frequently works with Guy, gave me the name of his favorite Cuban joint in Queens, Rincon Criollo. They passed the many layers of scrutiny a restaurant has to go through to make the cut. So of course Guy invited Carl out to cook a Cuban dish with him on the show with the owner. Carl comes to the set early and he's proud to be wearing a custom-made shirt, which is grand, but it's bright white and so is the owner's chef's jacket. I don't want two bright white shirts on my set—it wouldn't look good on camera and it would make the two of them look too much alike. So Carl goes a few doors down, where there's

IS THAT CARL "THE CUBAN" OR A LIDO DECK DANCER FROM THE LOVE BOAT?

a thrift store, and comes back with some shirts. He tries them on and they're all ridiculously large. He goes back for more, same bad results. Finally I go with him and we find something, it's blue, it fits, it's from Lands' End—something he would *never ever* wear under normal circumstances. So he's making his *DDD* debut and he's stuck in a secondhand purchase not of his own choosing. Aside from some minor muttering and a few veiled threats, he was a pretty good sport about it.

Then Guy, Carl, and the chef are making the first dish, and for some reason Guy asks Carl to dance and for even more unknowable reasons, Carl does. I find the whole thing more than silly and suggest that the "dance" shouldn't be in the finished piece. Well, not only did they use it in the segment, it's in the tease at the top of the show, it's in the year-end blooper reel, and it's in a webisode on the FN website. Shows how much I know, or maybe it just proves what a good dancer The Cuban is.

 ## RESTAURANT UPDATE

We've been getting a great number of fans of *Triple D* filling up our seats since the show aired. People from Washington, DC, Pittsburgh, even Canada have been coming, excited to try our delicious ropa vieja and arroz con pollo!

—RUDY ACOSTA

RINCON CRIOLLO'S ARROZ CON POLLO

ADAPTED FROM A RECIPE COURTESY OF RENE AND RUDY ACOSTA, RINCON CRIOLLO

Serves 4

About 6 tablespoons Spanish olive oil

1 whole chicken, cut into 6 pieces

1 Spanish onion, chopped (about 1½ cups)

1 green bell pepper, seeded and chopped (about 1 cup)

¾ to 1 cup Garlic Paste (recipe follows)

4 whole canned peeled tomatoes, crushed by hand

1½ cups white wine

1 bottle of beer, such as Budweiser

1 teaspoon dried oregano

1 teaspoon dried basil

1 teaspoon ground white pepper

1 teaspoon ground cumin

1 to 2 tablespoons chicken stock base

2 cups uncooked rice

About 2 tablespoons bijol (achiote or annatto powder)

Salt

1 cup green peas, for garnish

1 cup chopped roasted red bell pepper, for garnish

1. Preheat the oven to 350°F.

2. Heat the olive oil in a large Dutch oven (with a cover) over medium-high heat. Place the chicken pieces in the pot and cook for a few minutes on each side, just enough to brown the chicken, working in batches if necessary.

3. Place all the chicken pieces in the pot and add the onion, green bell pepper, garlic paste, and tomatoes. This is the sofrito. Cook this sofrito, stirring frequently, until the onions have softened, about 4 minutes, then add the wine. Pour in the beer (I always save myself a sip). Add the oregano, basil, white pepper, cumin, and chicken stock base.

4. Add the rice to the chicken and vegetables. Sprinkle in bijol until the rice turns a yellowish color. Season with salt. Bring to a simmer, reduce the heat to low, cover, and bake in the oven for about 40 minutes, until the rice and the chicken are cooked through. It's important that the rice is as risotto-like as possible; the rice should not be allowed to completely absorb all the juices in the pot.

5. Sprinkle the green peas and roasted red bell pepper on top to garnish.

GARLIC PASTE

Makes about 2½ cups

20 garlic cloves, peeled
2 cups vegetable oil

Place garlic cloves and oil in a blender. Puree until a paste forms. Store refrigerated in an airtight container for up to a week, or 2 months in the freezer.

COOK'S NOTE: Leftover paste can be used to make quick garlic bread, or it can be added to salad dressings, pasta sauces, or meat marinades.

JOHN'S OF 12TH STREET

OVER ONE HUNDRED YEARS OF HISTORY IN EVERY BADA-BING BITE

I don't know about you, but I'm a big fan of old-school mob movies. You know, *Goodfellas,* and in particular *The Godfather.* But coming from Cali, we don't have many hundred-year-old Italian restaurants like the kind you can find in a mob movie or in NYC's East Village, so when I got the lowdown on this joint where they're servin' up homemade pappardelle and veal meatballs—veal meatballs, are you kidding me?—it was time to step back in time.

Opened in 1908 by Umbrian immigrant John Pucciatti, this place comes by its old school the old-fashioned way. Since 1973, John's been run by Nicky Sitnycky (yes, that's his name—I thought it was a nickname!) in the front and Mikey "2 Names" Alpert in the back. The former owner, John's son Daniel, passed down to these former stockbrokers the original recipe book, and they didn't change an ingredient or method. Tradition is a beautiful thing. There's even a set of candles that have been burning since 1933, the year Prohibition ended.

★ TRACK IT DOWN ★

302 East 12th Street
New York, NY 10003
212-475-9531
www.johnsof12thstreet.com

KREW NOTES

Mike "Father Time" Morris: Doesn't get much more Italian than this place. You go here for your *Godfather* fix.

Kerry "Gilligan" Johnson: Gas up!

CAMARO-GATE

RON "FRAGGLE" GABALDON: Making a show like *DDD* is like being part of a well-oiled machine. What most folks forget is that the machine is made out of people. Let's not dwell on what a machine like that might look like, but for the most part it works. And some days the machine springs a gasket.

While shooting at John's in New York, Mario Batali dropped in to have some fun with us on the set. We put together a quick bit that had Mario drive off in the Camaro, leaving Guy with the tab. The weather was turning south that afternoon, giving us little time left to shoot outside before rain would make it impossible. The Camaro was ready with Mario in the driver's seat; they have a little exchange, and Mario drives off. Perfect on the first take! We all had a good laugh at the antics and waited for Mario to roll around the block so we could try it again. And we waited . . . Guy's phone rings and it's Mario. The Camaro stalled going around the corner. I took off at a sprint for the corner, going over what might have gone wrong with the '68. Was it the spark plugs? The fuel filter? Did it overheat? I'm not a mechanic, but part of my job is to keep up on the maintenance of the Camaro, and since it's a classic car, it requires a lot of fine-tuning and attention.

There was already a crowd gathered where the Camaro had come to a stop. Mario let me take over the car and walked back to the restaurant. I tried the engine to see if I could hear what the problem was, but a quick look down at the gauges was all I needed. *The Camaro was out of gas.* All the preparation, the organization that goes into each shoot, and the thing that trips me up is putting gas in the car. Fortunately, I didn't have much time to dwell on it, because that was when the rain started. I had maybe thirty seconds to get the roof up, and of course that would be a perfect time for the roof motor to quit. . . .

 RESTAURANT UPDATE

A lot of diners who saw the show remember the banter back and forth with Guy about measuring ingredients. So I tell them, "It's all about the one, two, 'tree,' right?" They say, "You're right!" They love that.

Just recently people drove three hours from Massachusetts just to dine at the restaurant and then drove three hours back home. Here's a conversation with Erin from Ohio while making a reservation:

Mike: When were you here last?

Erin: Never.

Mike: How did you hear about us?

Erin (a bit breathlessly): Guy tells me . . . *everything* . . .

—MIKE ALPERT

POLPETTE DI VITELLO (VEAL MEATBALLS)

ADAPTED FROM A RECIPE COURTESY OF MIKE ALPERT, JOHN'S OF 12TH STREET

Makes about 20 meatballs

½ loaf Italian bread, crust removed, roughly chopped (about 1½ cups)

¼ cup milk

2 large eggs

¼ cup grated pecorino Romano cheese

½ cup chopped scallions (white and green parts)

¼ cup Caramelized Onions (recipe follows)

2 tablespoons Worcestershire sauce

1 tablespoon dried basil

1 tablespoon dried oregano

6 garlic cloves, finely chopped

Salt and freshly ground black pepper

4 tablespoons unsalted butter, plus 2 tablespoons for serving

1 cup Marsala wine, plus a splash for serving

2 pounds ground veal

¼ to ½ cup breadcrumbs

½ cup marinara sauce for coating the cookie sheet, plus more for serving with the meatballs

2 tablespoons olive oil, for serving

Chopped freshly basil, for garnish

1. Preheat the oven to 350°F.

2. In a large bowl, combine the bread and milk. Squeeze the bread until the milk is absorbed and the bread dissolves. Add the eggs and mix together. Add the cheese, scallions, caramelized onions, Worcestershire sauce, basil, oregano, and garlic. Season with salt and pepper and mix together.

3. Melt the 4 tablespoons butter in the pan over medium-high heat, add the wine, and cook for 3 minutes to reduce. Cool.

4. Add the veal to the bowl with the bread mixture, then mix in the melted butter and wine mixture.

5. Gradually mix in the breadcrumbs until the mixture is loose but still able to hold its shape when rolled into a meatball.

6. Coat a baking sheet with marinara sauce. Roll individual meatballs (about 2 ounces or ¼ cup and 2 inches in diameter each) and place them on the sheet. Bake for 10 to 12 minutes, until golden brown.

7. In a large skillet over medium heat, combine the olive oil, 2 tablespoons butter, and a splash of Marsala wine. Heat the mixture, then add the meatballs until they are thoroughly brown, 8 to 10 minutes. Serve with marinara sauce and sprinkle fresh basil on top.

CARAMELIZED ONIONS

Makes ¼ cup

2 tablespoons olive oil or vegetable oil
1 cup chopped onions

Heat the oil in heavy skillet over medium heat. Add the onions and sauté. You want to hear some sizzle and see the onions just start to soften but not become brown. Lower the heat to the point where the oil is just barely sizzling and cook, uncovered, for 2 hours or more, until the onions are a deep caramelized brown. Stir about every 10 to 15 minutes. As the onions release their liquid, you may have to adjust heat to maintain some bubbling in the liquid. If necessary, add a little more oil.

COOK'S NOTE: Be patient and do not rush the process! Slow cooking ensures the best caramelization. You'll see some color change by the 1-hour mark. By the 2-hour mark the onions should be close to being their desired deep brown color.

CRAZY BURGER CAFÉ & JUICE BAR

WHERE BURGERS KNOW NO BOUNDS

★ TRACK IT DOWN ★

**144 Boon Street
Narragansett, RI 02882
401-783-1810
www.crazyburger.com**

You guys all know the tagline "slow down and take a look around," because the funky little joint with killer eats is right in front of you? Well, it's even happened to yours truly. My wife, Lori's, family is from Providence, Rhode Island, and every other summer we'd vacation down in Narragansett. Like anybody else, I'm always trying to get the inside scoop. I must have ridden by this place on my bike in the morning half a dozen times, but that early in the morning it was never open. Lo and behold, two years later I ended up back in Narragansett at Crazy Burger.

Owner Michael Maxon is crazy creative, to the tune of thirty-one different burgers, made with lots of sound effects, from wasabi mayo burgers with brie and onion rings to the phyllo-wrapped Luna Sea salmon burger with pistachio pesto—and it's not just burgers. Bottom line, this guy knows what he's doin'.

WHAT'S CRAZY—MICHAEL OR THE BURGERS? MOST SAY MICHAEL . . .

KREW NOTES

Matt "Beaver" Giovinetti: This was a crazy little place on the Rhode Island shore in the beautiful town of Narragansett with a very eclectic menu from chef/owner Michael Maxon. We shot here back in the days when we didn't close the restaurant, and it was crazy busy all day! I loved the juice bar at this place and the general manager, Casey Montanari, was amazing.

 RESTAURANT UPDATE

The show originally aired over three years ago, and it still causes a stir when it airs in repeats. Just today we had a gentleman from Kentucky who was in Rhode Island for a visit and came by as a result of seeing the show.

—MICHAEL MAXON

LUNA SEA BURGERS

ADAPTED FROM A RECIPE COURTESY OF MICHAEL MAXON, CRAZY BURGER CAFÉ & JUICE BAR

Serves 4

1 pound fresh salmon fillets, skin and bones removed, cut into small pieces

¾ cup Luna Sea Burger Pesto (recipe follows)

½ cup breadcrumbs, plus more if needed

½ teaspoon canola oil

4 sheets phyllo dough

Melted butter, for brushing

Aioli (garlic mayonnaise), for serving

1. Preheat the oven to 500°F.

2. Place the salmon in a food processor and pulse until finely chopped. Remove and place in a large bowl. Add ½ cup of the pesto and the breadcrumbs and stir until incorporated.

3. In a small sauté pan over medium heat, heat the canola oil and cook a small piece of the burger mixture to test for taste and consistency. If it's too moist, add more breadcrumbs.

4. Portion the burger mixture into four 6-ounce patties and arrange them on a baking sheet. Bake for 5 minutes. Remove from the oven and let cool slightly.

5. To wrap the burgers: Fold one sheet of phyllo dough in half, then not quite in half again, and brush with butter. Place the burger in the middle of the folded sheet. Fold the sides in, wrapping the burger completely. Brush the outside of the phyllo dough with butter. Flip the burger over so the seams are underneath the burger and then brush the top with butter. Repeat with the remaining phyllo and burgers.

6. Return the burgers to the 500°F oven for 3 more minutes. Remove from the oven, arrange on a serving platter, and serve with aioli.

LUNA SEA BURGER PESTO

Makes about 2 cups

3 cups lightly packed fresh basil leaves (about 2 ounces)

¼ cup lemon juice

¼ cup grated Parmesan cheese

2 cups toasted shelled pistachios

1 tablespoon roasted garlic

1½ teaspoons kosher salt

Pinch of freshly ground black pepper

1 tablespoon hot sauce

½ cup olive oil

Combine all the ingredients in a blender or food processor and puree. Store covered in the refrigerator.

SONNY'S FAMOUS STEAK HOGIES

HALF A CENTURY OF DOIN' IT RIGHT

Sonny's was a really interesting place. When you go you feel like you're walking into a cheese steak shop in Philly—lots of people moving fast, the smell of fresh baked bread in the air, and sandwiches you order by number.

Established in 1958, Sonny's Famous Steak Hogies is now run by Sonny's son John Nigro. They've got homemade sauce that's an old family

★ TRACK IT DOWN ★

1857 North 66th Avenue
Hollywood, FL 33024
954-989-0561
www.sonnysfamoussteakhogies.com

recipe and quality meats, but it's all in the fresh bread, some customers say. When we first met them they were baking thirty to fifty dozen rolls a day . . . bet they bake more now! For the cheese steaks, he cuts the rib-eye beef so thin there's only one side to it (I love that line). And man, they should make some folks in Philly nervous; this is the real deal. Now here's how you get to order one by number: "50" is like an "s" for sauce, and "o" for onions. A "9," you turn the number around and it's "p" for plain. So that would make a "95" a plain with sauce. You got that? Good. Me, I'll take a number 50 with green peppers and provolone, no . . . I'll take a number 90, make that a 95 . . . just give me all three. Second only to the cheese steak is the homemade meatball sub, or maybe the chicken parm. What's the family secret? John says, "Care about what you're doing and do it the right way."

KREW NOTES

Jeff "Butterbean" Asell: There is something about that fresh bread; I think it's a narcotic. Somebody needs to alert the FDA.

 RESTAURANT UPDATE

We're honored to be part of *Diners, Drive-Ins and Dives*. The customers have come from all over the country and are so friendly and excited to be here. The increase in business has been life-changing. Meeting and working with Guy was an unforgettable experience that I will treasure forever. The number one question we get is, "What is Guy really like?" All the employees reply that he was down to earth and a lot of fun. Thank you.

—JOHN NIGRO

I ATE SO MANY HOGIES THAT THEY'RE HOLDING ME UP.

SONNY'S STEAK HOGIE

ADAPTED FROM A RECIPE COURTESY OF JOHN NIGRO, SONNY'S FAMOUS STEAK HOGIES

Serves 4

⅓ cup blended canola/olive oil (60/40 ratio)

1 medium onion, sliced ¹⁄₁₆ inch thick (about 2 cups)

1¾ pounds rib-eye steak, sliced ¹⁄₁₆ inch thick

½ teaspoon salt, plus more if needed

4 tablespoons unsalted butter, melted

8 slices provolone cheese

Four 8-inch hoagie rolls (preferably homemade), cut horizontally to create a pocket

Topping suggestions: homemade tomato sauce, chopped bell peppers, or mushrooms

1. Preheat a large skillet over medium-high heat. Add the oil and stir in the onion. Place the steak on top of the onion, then add the salt and 1 tablespoon of the butter. Cover the skillet and cook for 2 minutes and 30 seconds, or until the meat is cooked on top and rare underneath. Using a fork and spatula, break up the steak and onions and mix together. Continue to cook for another minute, or until the meat is cooked through.

2. Add the remaining 3 tablespoons butter and the provolone to the skillet. Cover the skillet to melt the cheese. Taste and add salt if needed. Divide the steak mixture among the hoagie rolls and serve, with any toppings you like.

SEE THIS MAN, JOHN HIMSELF, FOR ONE OF THE BEST CHEESE STEAKS SOUTH OF PHILLY.

SOUTH

THE WHALE'S RIB RESTAURANT

FROM STONE CRABS TO OYSTERS, FRESH IS BEST

The Whale's Rib—I shoulda known when a joint is known for its "whale juice" that this was going to be a wild adventure. I showed up with a small case of laryngitis, so if you weren't watching the screen you might have thought Barry White was doing a cameo. (Tidbit: I had to do a voice-over for the opening because of my voice. First time ever . . . last time too. All cuz of the Super Bowl.) This was also where my bud "Brunch" showed up and enjoyed the restaurant so much he chose not to follow the TV eating etiquette and protocol of a few bites and finished off five different platters. Like I said, as soon as I saw whale juice I shoulda known to watch out for what was comin'.

Since owner Dale Stephenson opened almost thirty years ago, this place has been serving up super-fresh seafood a hundred yards from the beach. They've got the most distinctive tomato-topped oysters Rockefeller I'd ever encountered. As odd as it sounds, the acid of the tomato really does work in there. And that whale juice? Turns out it's a mayo-based sauce with mustard, vinegar, sugar, and pepper, and it goes with almost everything they serve, from the clams and linguine to the calamari salad, the rock shrimp or the whale fries. (No whale was harmed in the making of the sauce or fries.)

★ TRACK IT DOWN ★

2031 NE 2nd Street
Deerfield Beach, FL 33441
954-421-8880
www.whalesrib.com

KREW NOTES

Matt "Beaver" Giovinetti: Super nice people, and right down the street from where I lived before *DDD*. Guy actually interviewed my former boss, Henry Salgado.

Neil "Boy Band" Martin: Sometimes the crew misses out on a few important communications. When we were at the Whale's Rib, Guy invited a friend, nicknamed "Brunch," to come to the set, and I didn't know about it. I know most of Guy's friends, and for the most part, they know me. Arriving just as the police in Deerfield Beach were helping us wrangle the growing crowd, Brunch comes flying in and parks where we were holding spots for Guy, then gets out and confidently proceeds to allow himself onto the set. A nearby officer looks over to me to ask whether he is one of ours and all I could do was shrug my shoulders. This cop was ready to pounce and deal with the newcomer, but I figured

THIS IS MY BUDDY BRUNCH . . . HE ATE ALL FIVE OF THE DISHES BEFORE WE EVEN INTERVIEWED HIM.

I'd better look into the situation. So I asked a couple questions and right away knew things were good. Every now and again when I see Brunch I think about how funny Guy would have found it had he been in handcuffs when he arrived on set.

A HUGE CRAB IS PINCHING MY FINGER . . . OR I'M LOSING MY MIND. YOU PICK.

OYSTER ROCKS AT THE RIB

ADAPTED FROM A RECIPE COURTESY OF DALE STEPHENSON, WHALE'S RIB RESTAURANT

Serves 4 to 6

¾ cup drained and roughly chopped steamed spinach

¼ cup minced onion

1 cup grated Parmesan cheese

¼ teaspoon cayenne pepper

¼ teaspoon ground black pepper

3 tablespoons white wine

4 tablespoons unsalted butter, melted

Salt

2 dozen fresh raw oysters in the shell

3 Roma tomatoes, seeded and finely diced

6 large slices provolone cheese, quartered

Lemon wedges, for serving

Hot sauce, for serving

1. Preheat the oven to 400°F.

2. In a medium bowl, mix together the spinach, onion, Parmesan cheese, cayenne pepper, black pepper, wine, and melted butter. Season with salt. Shuck the oysters and leave them on the half shell. Top with a scant tablespoon of the spinach mixture and arrange them on a baking sheet. Bake for about 10 minutes until the spinach mixture browns on top. Remove from the oven and top each with some of the diced tomato and provolone cheese. Turn on the broiler. Place the oysters in the broiler and broil until the cheese melts and the cheese is browned and bubbly, 1 to 2 minutes.

3. Transfer the oysters to a serving platter and serve immediately with a wedge of lemon and a good hot sauce.

COOK'S NOTE: The hardest part of this recipe is to find fresh oysters and shuck them.

WE'RE GETTING PULLED OVER RIGHT NOW BECAUSE BEAVER ISN'T WEARING HIS SEAT BELT.

TAP TAP HAITIAN RESTAURANT

FOR THE BEST BITE ON THE BEACH, TAP THIS

This is another case of slowing down and taking a look around. That's all I had to do with Tap Tap. Been down to Miami a bunch of times for the South Beach Wine & Food Festival and driven right by the joint. I'd say, "Tap Tap, what is it—maybe a tapas restaurant? No, it's a dinner-dance joint, or maybe beers from around the world?" Finally went in and checked it out. Holy Haitian, the food is rockin'.

Owner Katharine Kean fell in love with the people and food of Haiti when she lived there as a filmmaker, so she opened Tap Tap more than fifteen years ago. She hired Haitian-raised Gary Sanon-Jules as a busboy; now he's running the place and serving up Haitian classics. From yellowtail to oxtail to conch, goat, fritters, and the house favorite, pork griyo—try it all and you'll want to move in along with me.

> ★ TRACK IT DOWN ★
>
> **819 5th Street**
> **Miami Beach, FL 33139**
> **305-672-2898**
> **www.taptaprestaurant.com**

KREW NOTES

Matt "Beaver" Giovinetti: Gary is the gentle giant, and such a phenomenal chef. I totally ripped off the watercress dipping sauce recipe and make it at home all the time. This is a *DDD* Krew favorite, and we always make a trip to Tap Tap whenever we're in South Beach. I can't begin to tell you how good the griyo is, and the malanga fritters, and the goat. Yes, try the goat!

Neil "Boy Band" Martin: We find ourselves in south Florida around my birthday quite a bit, so once again Guy, being the generous man he is, wanted to get me a special gift. He sent Ron ("Fraggle") in search of an overloaded tool belt, because when I'm on set, I'm notorious for having everything I need on me. Guy shouldn't have sent Ron, because Ron was going to impose his will on me (we never give our hotel key cards to him anymore if we leave something behind in our rooms, because he's constantly rearranging rooms as a practical joke). So Guy calls me over to his car, hands me a tool belt with a hammer, screwdrivers, markers, a rope with a dozen spring clamps, a wrench, and a small level, and says he wants me to wear it from now on. I wore it on set for a few months, until almost all the gear was absorbed by the production crew. Every time I wore the thing the spring clamps clanged against whatever I walked past.

YA SEE, GARY, I THINK I DESERVE THE GRIYO RECIPE . . .

GRIYO (FRIED MARINATED PORK CHUNKS)

ADAPTED FROM A RECIPE COURTESY OF GARY SANON-JULES, TAP TAP HAITIAN RESTAURANT

Serves 6 to 8

3 pounds boneless pork shoulder,
trimmed of fat

⅓ cup sour orange juice (or fresh lime juice),
rinds and pulp reserved

3 tablespoons salt

½ Scotch bonnet chile, chopped

10 garlic cloves, finely chopped (about ¼ cup)

½ cup chopped shallots

¼ cup olive oil

Canola oil, for deep-frying

¼ cup chopped fresh parsley

DISTRACT HER WHILE I MOVE IN ON THIS PLATE.

1. Massage the meat with the sour orange or lime rinds and pulp and 2 cups of very hot water. Drain. Cut the meat into 1½-inch cubes.

2. Marinate the meat in a large nonreactive bowl with the sour orange or lime juice, salt, chile, garlic, and shallots for at least 1 hour or overnight in the refrigerator.

OWNER KATHARINE CRUISING IN AN ACTUAL TAP TAP (LIKE A TAXI OR BUS) IN HAITI.

3. Heat the olive oil in a heavy pan (with a lid) over medium-high heat. Add the meat and the marinade. Lower the heat to medium-low and cook, covered, until the meat is tender, about 2 hours, adding extra water, if necessary.

4. Heat the canola oil to 350°F in a deep pot or fryer (the depth will vary according to the size of your fryer or pot; the meat should be submerged). Blot the meat dry very well with paper towels to prevent splatter. Fry the griyo until the meat is a deep reddish-brown color, 20 to 25 minutes. Watch closely toward the end to avoid overfrying. Drain on paper towels.

5. Transfer to a serving dish and pour the settled pan liquid from the bowl over the griyo. Garnish with the parsley.

CULHANE'S IRISH PUB

BRINGING ATTITUDE TO CLASSIC IRISH PUB GRUB

I say Florida, you most likely think seafood. If not seafood, then Cuban. If not Cuban, then what . . . Irish? It's not the first thing that comes to your mind, but it does to the four Culhane sisters. They opened up a real-deal Irish joint in a Florida strip mall, of all places. But don't let that strip mall appearance

DON'T LET THE SMILES FOOL YA . . . THEY MEAN BUSINESS!

★ TRACK IT DOWN ★

**967 Atlantic Boulevard
Atlantic Beach, FL 32233
904-249-9595
www.culhanesirishpub.com**

fool ya. You walk in the front door and you're transported to County Limerick, Ireland, where these girls were born and raised. And heed my warning, the Guinness Stew is funkin' unbelievable.

Mary Jane, Michelle, Lynda, and Aine hired longtime friend and head chef Olive Davis to serve up the food their grandmother and mother made. And the lady *really* cooks. Aside from the Guinness Stew, you've gotta try the Dinglefish Pie, hailing from a little fishing village eighty miles from where they grew up. It's got salmon, shrimp, and cod—holy boatload of seafood, captain. And don't overlook the lamb sliders. You'll need a bib and they may make you do a jig.

KREW NOTES

Jeff "Butterbean" Asell: Culhane's is prototypical *DDD*. It's in a strip mall, but it has authenticity that you'd never believe was behind the door. And it's the best little Irish joint I can think of.

Anthony "Chico" Rodriguez: Boy Band got his name from, well, his dramatic resemblance to many young musical hearthrobs. It happened to be his birthday during this shoot, so after we wrapped we blindfolded him. We sprayed his hair salt and pepper gray, made him put on a white tank top, a leather motorcycle jacket we rented, and some aviator sunglasses. From the picture, you'll not only realize how Boy Band got his name, but why "Ya Gotta Have Faith."

BOY BAND AS GEORGE MICHAEL . . . OR GEORGE MICHAEL AS BOY BAND?

Neil "Boy Band" Martin: I have great memories at Culhane's! We got to play host to a boy named Tommy who was going to be having heart surgery and wanted to visit our set and meet Guy. (Tommy's mom says he now has his new heart and is doing great!) And the guys treated me to something very special there the day of my birthday. I tend to grow what I like to call a "production beard" when I'm on the road. I shave before I hit the road, and then I just let it go. After a few days' growth, according to Anthony, I start to have this certain George Michael look going on. So Guy plotted with Ron and Anthony to go out and get a bunch of props, blindfold me, and dress me up. They undid the blindfold and showed me a mirror as someone in the bar began playing "Faith."

 RESTAURANT UPDATE

Since we were featured on *Triple D*, business has doubled, we see new faces every day from all over the USA, and we've have had international exposure, with shows airing in England and Ireland. We had to remodel and expand our kitchen to keep up with the volume. The Gift of Guy keeps on giving! We've engaged a real estate company to open restaurant number two, three, four, and grow. Our goal is to be the best Irish pub in America.

—THE CULHANE SISTERS

CULHANE'S GUINNESS BEEF STEW

ADAPTED FROM A RECIPE COURTESY OF CULHANE'S IRISH PUB

Serves 8 to 10

3 pounds cubed stew meat (we use beef tips)

1 tablespoon Culhane's Spice Blend RGP (recipe follows)

2 quarts stout beer, such as Guinness

¼ cup (½ stick) unsalted butter

2 cups diced yellow onions

2 cups sliced carrots

2 cups sliced cremini mushrooms

½ cup all-purpose flour

1 tablespoon salt

2 tablespoons granulated garlic

Demi Glace (recipe follows)

1 cup uncooked barley

Steamed diced Yukon gold potatoes (¾ cup per serving)

1. In a large covered container, marinate the beef in the spice blend seasoning and beer. Cover and refrigerate overnight to tenderize and "flavorize." Remove the beef from the marinade and set both aside.

2. In a braising pot or Dutch oven over medium heat, melt the butter and sweat the onions and carrots until the onions are translucent, about 10 minutes.

3. Meanwhile, in a separate pan over high heat, sear the marinated beef until browned on all sides. Set aside.

4. Add the mushrooms to the onions and sauté for 5 minutes. Stir in the flour, making a roux, and cook for 2 minutes, stirring. Add the reserved beer marinade, the salt, granulated garlic, 8 cups water, and the demi glace.

5. Bring to a simmer, then add the barley and beef. Return to a simmer, stirring constantly. Simmer the stew, uncovered, for 2 to 3 hours, until liquid is reduced by one-quarter, stirring occasionally. Serve with potatoes.

CULHANE'S SPICE BLEND RGP (ROASTED GARLIC PEPPER)

THIS RECIPE WILL MAKE EXTRA. YOU'LL BE SURE TO USE IT ON FRIES AND IN JUST ABOUT EVERYTHING YOU COOK UP!

Yield 2½ tablespoons

1 teaspoon onion powder

1 teaspoon garlic powder

1 teaspoon roasted granulated garlic (available at spicebarn.com)

1 teaspoon ground black pepper

½ teaspoon ground white pepper

1 teaspoon kosher salt

½ teaspoon ground allspice

½ teaspoon dry mustard (preferably Coleman's)

½ teaspoon dried basil

¼ teaspoon dried red pepper flakes

¼ teaspoon dried marjoram

In a bowl, combine all the ingredients. Store in an airtight container.

DEMI GLACE

Makes about 2 quarts

2 pounds veal marrow bones, sawed into 2-inch pieces (ask your butcher)

2 pounds beef marrow bones, sawed into 2-inch pieces (ask your butcher)

8 ounces tomato paste

2 cups chopped onions

1 cup chopped carrot

1 cup chopped celery

2 cups dry red wine

1 bouquet garni (1 sprig thyme, 1 sprig parsley, 1 bay leaf, 1 teaspoon peppercorns)

Salt

2 tablespoons olive oil

Freshly ground black pepper

1. Preheat the oven to 450°F.

2. Place the bones in a roasting pan and roast for 1 hour. Remove the bones from the oven and brush with half of the tomato paste.

THIS IS LIVING—GREAT TRIPLE D JOINT, AWESOME GIRLS FROM IRELAND . . .
AND MY FAVE LYNYRD SKYNYRD SHIRT!

LIVE CAM: I'D MET THIS CHARACTER IN THE PERSIAN GULF TWO YEARS EARLIER—
HIS NAME IS HOUSTON OYLER. NO KIDDING. AWESOME SAILOR!

3. In a medium bowl, combine 1 cup of the onions, ½ cup of the carrots, and ½ cup of the celery. Lay the vegetables over the bones and return to the oven to roast for 30 minutes. Remove from the oven and drain off any fat.

4. Place the roasting pan on the stove and deglaze the pan with 1 cup of the red wine, using a wooden spoon to scrape the bottom of the pan for browned particles.

5. Put the bones, vegetables, and liquid into a large stockpot. Add the bouquet garni and season with salt.

6. Add 4 gallons water. Bring the liquid to a boil, then reduce to a simmer. Simmer the stock for 4 hours, skimming regularly. Remove from the heat and strain through a China cap or fine-meshed strainer.

7. In a large stockpot over medium heat, heat the olive oil and sauté the remaining 1 cup onion, ½ cup carrot, and ½ cup celery until tender, about 15 minutes. Add the remaining tomato paste and brown for about 2 minutes. Deglaze with the remaining 1 cup red wine. Add the stock and simmer for about 1 hour over low heat. You will notice the stock turning into sauce consistency. Strain through a China cap or fine-meshed strainer. Season with salt and pepper.

VIRGIL'S CAFÉ

HOP ON OVER TO A SCRATCH-MADE PARADISE

I've tried some funky foods on *Triple D*: lamb's tongue, calf fries, chicken gizzards, lamb fries, escargot, turtle, you name it. But this was my first time on *Triple D* eating frog legs. Matthew Buschle, the chef and owner, is doing it all. You gotta hop on over (cheap frog one-liner) and check this one out.

★ TRACK IT DOWN ★

**710 Fairfield Avenue
Bellevue, KY 41073
859-491-3287
www.virgilscafe.com**

WOW, TRIPLE D FINDS IT ALL . . . AN INVISIBLE STAFF . . . AMAZING!

FROG LEG FACTORY.

Matt is dedicated to scratch-making food, from andouille to breakfast sausage to pastrami. And with that perfectly seasoned house-smoked andouille he does an etouffe that's rock star good. Matt lets himself go in all directions, from Creole to Cuban to, yes, lightly battered fried frog legs with pinot grigio mayo. If you like chicken wings, you'll love these.

KREW NOTES

Bryna "The Pirate" Levin: Virgil's was an interesting place for a lot of reasons. The chef, Matt Buschle, was very talented; he was also a self-proclaimed "fat man" who was worried about sweating on camera. To make sure he wouldn't bead up, Matt did not drink any liquids for twenty-four hours. When we wrapped, Matt broke his liquid fast with his favorite beverage: bourbon. We were all waiting for his body to go into toxic shock. This is also the first place we cooked frog legs on the show. They looked strange, and many of us hadn't tried them before, and I *can't* say they tasted like chicken.

 ## RESTAURANT UPDATE

Being on *DDD* has made a huge difference in the amount of people we normally wouldn't see. We've met people from all over the country, for that matter from all over the world.

—MATTHEW BUSCHLE

FROG LEGS WITH PINOT GRIGIO MAYO

ADAPTED FROM A RECIPE COURTESY OF MATTHEW BUSCHLE, VIRGIL'S CAFE

Serves 4

2 pounds (6 to 8) frog legs, split

1 cup buttermilk

3 cups all-purpose flour

1 tablespoon smoked paprika

2 tablespoons salt

1 tablespoon ground white pepper

Canola oil, for frying

Pinot Grigio Mayo (recipe follows), for serving

1. Place the frog legs in a large bowl and add the buttermilk. Cover the bowl and refrigerate overnight (at least a good 10 to 12 hours).

2. In a separate large bowl, combine the flour, paprika, salt, and white pepper. Dredge the frog legs in the flour mixture, coating them completely. Shake off the excess flour.

3. Heat enough oil to come halfway up the sides of a deep fryer or heavy-bottomed pot to 375°F.

4. Add the frog legs to the oil and fry until golden brown, 3 to 5 minutes. Transfer to a serving platter and serve with the mayo.

PINOT GRIGIO MAYO

About 2 cups

1 bottle pinot grigio
2 cups extra-heavy mayonnaise, such as Hellmann's
Salt and freshly ground black pepper

1. In a large sauté pan over high heat, bring the wine to a boil, then reduce the heat and simmer the wine for 35 to 45 minutes, until reduced to about 2 tablespoons and a syrupy consistency. Cool.

2. In a small bowl, combine 2 tablespoons of the reduced wine with the mayonnaise. Season with salt and pepper and refrigerate until needed.

YA GOTTA "HOP" ON OVER TO VIRGIL'S FOR SOME FROG LEGS. (SORRY, HAD TO DO IT—COULDN'T RESIST.)

SURREY'S CAFÉ AND JUICE BAR

NOT JUST PO-BOYS AND ÉTOUFFÉE

New Orleans is one of my favorite food towns ever. But, just so you know, it's not only about po-boys, jambalaya, and étouffée. Surrey's was exactly what we like to find on *Triple D*: a funky joint, out of the way, making real-deal food. They make their own granola, lox, and bagels, have a fruit juice bar with about twelve different types of fresh juice, and serve bananas Foster French toast—are you kidding me?

This place is the melting pot of the melting pots. It's eclectic and appealing, featuring whatever owner Greg Surrey likes. They make a local favorite, house-made boudin—then add it to a killer hash. And Chef Paul Artigues boils up those bagels from scratch while the lox is cured with salt, sugar, pepper, and dill. To the East Coast skeptics: He knocks them both out of the park.

★ TRACK IT DOWN ★

**1418 Magazine Street
New Orleans, LA 70130
504-524-3828**
www.surreyscafeandjuicebar.com

COOKIN', EATIN', AND LAUGHIN' . . . THE TRIPLE D MANTRA.

KREW NOTES

Matt "Beaver" Giovinetti: This is a super-funky juice bar and café in a beautiful New Orleans neighborhood. It was the first time we'd ever made bagels or lox on the show, and they rocked—and we all enjoyed the fresh juice every morning. I've visited this place twice since the show aired, and it's still crankin' healthy, fresh meals with something for everyone.

 RESTAURANT UPDATE

Stop by the original Surrey's Café or our new sister location, Surrey's Uptown at 4807 Magazine Street. People seem to like us, so we'll keep on opening. Let the juices flow!

—GREG SURREY

BANANAS FOSTER FRENCH TOAST

ADAPTED FROM A RECIPE COURTESY OF GREG SURREY, SURREY'S CAFÉ

Serves 4 to 6

Bananas Foster mixture

2 bananas

1 cup packed dark brown sugar

2 ounces cream cheese, softened

1½ teaspoons pure vanilla extract

French toast butter

2 large eggs

2 tablespoons sugar

1 teaspoon pure vanilla extract

1 cup half-and-half

Bananas Foster sauce

2 cups (4 sticks) unsalted butter

½ cup packed dark brown sugar

¼ cup rum

¼ cup heavy cream, at room temperature

1½ teaspoons pure vanilla extract

1 loaf French bread, cut into 4 pieces

1 banana, sliced

Canola oil

Powdered sugar, for garnish

A BADASS BAGEL BARN!

THE MONDAY BAGELS-N-LOX CLUB!

1. FOR THE BANANAS FOSTER MIXTURE: Thoroughly mix together the bananas, brown sugar, cream cheese, and vanilla in a bowl with a handheld blender until well combined and uniform.

2. FOR THE FRENCH TOAST BATTER: Whip the eggs and sugar with a whisk. Add the vanilla and whisk until the sugar has completely dissolved. Continue to whisk while adding the half-and-half.

3. FOR THE BANANAS FOSTER SAUCE: In a saucepan over medium heat, melt the butter. Add the brown sugar and cook for 5 minutes. Remove the pan from the heat and add the rum. Return the pan to the stove and cook over medium heat for 5 minutes more, to let the mixture thicken slightly. Add the cream and vanilla and whisk vigorously until the sauce is completely smooth. If it looks as if it's broken, briskly whisk until it comes together.

4. FOR ASSEMBLY: Cut each of the 4 quarters of the bread horizontally, leaving one long edge intact so the bread can hinge open. Add 1 tablespoon of the Foster mixture to each side. Let the mixture soak up for about 1 minute; repeat 3 more times. Place 8 thin slices of banana in each of the 4 "sandwiches" and slice each diagonally to make 8 triangular pieces in all. Pour the batter into a 9 x 13-inch baking dish and soak the 8 triangles for 10 minutes, turning once halfway through.

5. In a medium nonstick sauté pan, heat 1 tablespoon of canola oil over medium-high heat. Cook 2 triangles on all sides until golden brown. Continue to work in batches, wiping out the pan and adding new oil for each batch. Pour the warm bananas Foster rum sauce on a plate. Place the golden pieces of toast on top and garnish with powdered sugar.

MAHONY'S PO-BOY SHOP

DOING JUSTICE TO A CULINARY ICON

When you're in N'awlins (please don't call it New Orleans) and you have a po-boy, it's kinda like having pizza in New York City. When it's good it's really good, and when it's bad, well, it's still pretty good. But at Mahony's I gotta say these are great. So great I got my buddy Emeril to come down and eat a Peacemaker with me. I've been back a bunch of times since, and these folks continue to deliver.

As Emeril says, it's all about having good light and airy bread and high-quality ingredients. Chef and owner Benjamin Wicks delivers just that, in more than twenty-two creative ways. Keep an eye out for them at the New Orleans Fest—where they've won more than once.

★ TRACK IT DOWN ★

3454 Magazine Street
New Orleans, LA 70115
504-899-3374
www.mahonyspoboys.com

KREW NOTES

Anthony "Chico" Rodriguez: We happened to be shooting in New Orleans in late summer. It was hot and the air was humid and thick, which made kitchen shooting, well, on the warmer side. The kitchen in this otherworldly, *amazing* po-boy shop happened to be half of a screened porch—so it was essentially outside. To top it off, the incredible Emeril Lagasse was going to be on camera with us that day. We didn't want our chef, Guy, and Emeril looking like they just went swimming, so we had to come up with a way to cool the room. Enter Bunny. Now, imagine a movie where images of mathematical equations and drawings float by the screen as Bunny stares at the room, in the zone. Then, without a word, he goes to work. Between two fans, a rented portable AC, tarps, and duvatine cloth, somehow Bunny turned what would've felt like cooking in a hot tub to cooking in a cooler. We don't know how Bunny does the things he does to make our lives easier, but we're all glad he does.

BIG BUNNY IS ZEN MASTER OF ALL A/C.

 RESTAURANT UPDATE

Since the taping of the show we've been busier than ever. We have a line out the door almost every weekend and at lunch during the week. We've added a few new favorites to the menu since the taping of the show, so we now have an Italian sausage po-boy with broccoli rabe and provolone cheese, and it's delicious. Also, we've added our version of a club sandwich—grilled chicken thigh, bacon, and our famous root beer-glazed ham—and last but not least, a fried okra po-boy with homemade rémoulade sauce, yum!

—CHEF BENJAMIN WICKS AND STAFF

THIS IS THE PO-BOY MISSION CONTROL—A.K.A. ONE HOT KITCHEN.

THE PEACEMAKER

ADAPTED FROM A RECIPE COURTESY OF BENJAMIN WICKS, MAHONY'S PO-BOY SHOP

Serves 4

1 gallon peanut oil

2 cups all-purpose flour

4 cups cornmeal

4 cups oyster meat

Kosher salt

Four 6-inch loaves French bread

8 slices cheddar cheese

8 slices cooked bacon

Mayonnaise

Sliced pickles

Shredded lettuce

Sliced tomatoes

1. Heat the oil to 350°F in a large Dutch oven or deep fryer.

2. Mix together the flour and cornmeal. Toss half the oysters in the cornmeal and flour and move them around, coating each oyster completely in the mixture. Shake off the excess flour and cornmeal. Place the oysters into the hot oil and carefully move them around to prevent them from sticking together. Cook for 1 to 2 minutes, just until light golden brown. Drain and immediately season with salt. Repeat with the remaining oysters.

3. Place the oysters on one side of the French bread while they're still hot and add the sliced cheese and bacon. Spread the other half of the bread with mayonnaise and top with pickles, lettuce, and tomatoes.

NOW LISTEN HERE, GUIDO . . . I HEAR YOU'VE BEEN USING MY "BAM!" I EXPECT SOME ROYALTIES, YA HEAR!
(SIDENOTE: THANKS, EMERIL, FOR ALL YOUR SUPPORT—YOU ARE THE BEST!)

LOUIE AND THE REDHEAD LADY

THEY'RE NOT FANCY, THEY'RE FAMILY

Sometimes you get a feeling about a place before you even get there. My dad's name is Lewis James and my mom is a redhead, so it was just too coincidental that I'd be visiting a joint called Louie and the Redhead Lady. And what are they cookin'? Oh yeah, one of my favorites, grits. And on top of all that I swear Louie and I are related. What I recommend you do is jump in the car and come on down to Louie and the Redhead Lady and meet some relatives you never knew you had.

You'll find them twenty-five miles off the causeway from New Orleans. Get their "money" fried oysters with great crunch-ification, and their grits and veal grillade, which are a gravy-laden breakfast that eats like a dinner. And those fried green tomatoes, brother that's a symposium of flavor.

> ★ TRACK IT DOWN ★
>
> **1851 Florida Street**
> **Mandeville, LA 70448**
> **985-626-6044**
> **www.louieandtheredheadlady.com**

KREW NOTES

Bryna "The Pirate" Levin: This is a real family-run joint, with chef Louie, his wife, Ginger (a redhead), and their kids all pitching in. Guy and Louie had a real "bromance." Guy loved the food; Louie thought Guy was the greatest. Nobody has ever been more appreciative of being on the show than this bunch. To get to their place in Mandeville from New Orleans you have to take the world's longest bridge (literally; it's twenty-four miles), and after Katrina their business really suffered. Once the show aired they put up both a United States map and a world map and had any customers who said they were there because of our show put a pin in. They've since had to start on a second United States map, and the world map shows visitors from around the globe. Helping small family-run places survive is truly the greatest thing about working on this show, and nobody embodies that story better then this place.

 ## RESTAURANT UPDATE

Since our participation with Guy's *DD&D* experience, we've been joyfully moving 'n shaking with business and everlasting opportunity. On behalf of Chef Louie Finnan and his lovely Ginger, we extend our very humble appreciation for all you've done to encourage, include, and support all of our family here on Louisiana's Northshore. Most folks know the food is amazing in New Orleans (or the Southshore, as we call it), but it takes a diligent foodie to find the gems of the Northshore. For years we didn't have a sign—some folks thought we were an auto parts store.

After tasting our grits and grillades, Guy closed his eyes and it seemed like five minutes before he spoke. Guy gave us the courage

TRIPLE D WITNESS PROTECTION PHOTO.

to bottle Chef Louie's spices and sauces. Through the grace of Guy, we followed every single marketing idea he put on the plate. Guy (Guido) gave Chef Louie this nickname, The Godfather, and it suits him *soooo* well! A Food Network blogger told us we're all the buzz in Manhattan and came from New York put her pushpin on our map. We're definitely going to need a bigger map . . . and more shrimp!

Since the taping we're now blessed to have just opened a second location! Visit us in Hammond at 112 West Thomas Street, Hammond, Louisiana. Thanks again for including Louie and the Redhead Lady—"We're not fancy, we're family!"

—ANNE HILE

FRIED GREEN TOMATOES
WITH SHRIMP AND RÉMOULADE SAUCE

ADAPTED FROM A RECIPE COURTESY OF LOUIE FINNAN, LOUIE AND THE REDHEAD LADY

Serves 4

Fried tomatoes

3 cups vegetable oil

2 large eggs

1 cup whole milk

1¼ cups hot sauce, such as Louie's All Spiced Up Sauce

1 cup all-purpose flour

2 cups Italian breadcrumbs

1 tablespoon dry Italian dressing mix

2 green tomatoes, sliced ¼ inch thick

Shrimp

2 tablespoons dry crab boil seasoning, such as Zatarain's

1 onion, sliced

1 lemon, sliced

¼ cup hot sauce, such as Louie's All Spiced Up Sauce

8 large shrimp, shells on

Rémoulade sauce

½ cup mayonnaise (preferably Blue Plate)

1½ tablespoons Creole mustard, such as Zatarain's

1 scant tablespoon prepared horseradish

Juice of 1 lemon

1 teaspoon Worcestershire sauce

2 dashes of hot sauce, such as Louie's All Spiced Up Sauce

Shredded lettuce, for serving

Note: You can now order Louie's hot sauces at www.redheadladycollection.com.

RIGHT AFTER THIS PHOTO, LOUIE "THE GODFATHER" THREW ME IN THE BAYOU!

1. FOR THE TOMATOES: Preheat the oven to 200°F and heat the oil in a deep cast-iron or other skillet to 350°F. Beat the eggs, milk, and hot sauce in a shallow dish. Put the flour into another shallow dish. In a third shallow dish, combine the breadcrumbs and dry Italian dressing mix. Dip the tomato slices in the flour, then the egg wash, and then the breadcrumb mixture. (Hint: Use one hand for the egg wash and the other for the dry flour and breadcrumbs.) Transfer to the oil and fry until golden brown, 1 to 2 minutes. Drain on paper towels and keep warm in the oven until ready to serve.

2. FOR THE SHRIMP: Bring 4 cups water to a boil in a large saucepan and add the crab boil, onion, lemon, and hot sauce. Stir and add the shrimp. Boil until the shrimp turn pink, about 3 minutes. Drain, cool, and peel.

3. FOR THE RÉMOULADE SAUCE: Mix together the mayonnaise, mustard, horseradish, lemon juice, Worcestershire sauce, and hot sauce in a bowl.

4. TO SERVE: Line a plate with shredded lettuce. Add 2 slices fried green tomatoes. Top each tomato with 1 boiled shrimp. Fill a squeeze bottle with the remoulade sauce and drizzle decoratively.

THE GLASS ONION

FOUR-STAR FOOD FOR EVERYDAY PEOPLE

I've had great chicken all over the country, cooked just about every way I can imagine: fried, baked, barbecued, smoked. But when I found a joint that was confiting it and pan-frying it, I had to try it. This has a good shot at being the perfect poultry of Flavortown, especially with the red pepper relish. And if that wasn't enough, they do a brined, smoked pork loin po-boy that would rival those at some of my favorite po-boy shops in N.O. Chris Stewart and Sarah O'Kelley are fine dining veterans, bringing three- or four-star food to everyday people. They're inspired by local ingredients and their southern heritage, and let's just say it *all* works.

They've got a funky name, inspired by the Beatles' *White Album,* and some killer food. But I had a good feeling from the start. There's a jukebox in there, and it just so happened that when I walked in and went over to check it out, the first CD was Eric Lindell's, one of my favorite New Orleans musicians—who originally came from Northern California.

> ★ TRACK IT DOWN ★
>
> **1219 Savannah Highway**
> **Charleston, SC 29407**
> **843-225-1717**
> **www.ilovetheglassonion.com**

KREW NOTES

Bryna "The Pirate" Levin: This is one of my favorite locations. I loved the owners and the food they were making. Our shoot in Charleston was eye opening, the booming food scene there was amazing, and the Glass Onion is at the forefront of taking skills from fine dining and using them in an informal atmosphere at affordable prices. Sarah, partner and chef, was one of the first of several pastry chefs I've worked with recently who made me realize that the dessert/baking side can make just as profound and creative a contribution to a restaurant as the savory.

THAT SLY SMILE IS CUZ HE'S ONE OF THE CHICKEN MASTERS OF FLAVORTOWN.

Chris (also a chef and partner) is a man with some serious culinary credentials, and he mentioned to me, with some modest pride, that he could break down a chicken (cutting a whole chicken into eight usable pieces, eliminating the backbone) in under 1 minute. Not easy—time yourself. When Guy arrived, I repeated Chris's little brag, knowing Guy would challenge him to do it. Out comes a whole chicken and the watch. Chris is a little nervous, since he hadn't had to do that particular task in a long time. He worked fast, with Guy egging him on. Guy claimed it took him over two minutes, but he was just messing with him—he got it done in one minute fifteen, including cutting out the tenderloins for good measure. Go, Chris!

Kerry "Gilligan" Johnson: Curious if Guy used the same confit technique on his Thanksgiving turkey?

Jeff "Butterbean" Asell: I learned some power moves at the Onion that changed my own cooking forever!

 RESTAURANT UPDATE

Needless to say, an appearance on *DDD* certainly brings a boom to business. We gladly welcomed seeing nearly 60 percent more customers over the summer, when so many visitors make their way to Charleston. And we especially enjoyed hearing stories from folks who plan their trips around Guy's advice!

—CHRIS STEWART AND SARAH O'KELLEY

CRISPY CHICKEN LEG

ADAPTED FROM A RECIPE COURTESY OF CHRIS STEWART, THE GLASS ONION

We serve this with braised collard greens and grits or mashed potatoes (all those recipes are in our cookbook). And we garnish the chicken with Thunder Sauce, a sweet red pepper relish that we sell on our website.

Serves 6

6 whole chicken leg and thigh quarters
¼ cup kosher salt
¼ cup coarsely ground white pepper
12 fresh thyme sprigs
4 cups vegetable oil, rendered chicken fat, or lard, plus more for finishing
Salt and freshly ground black pepper

1. Place a chicken leg on a cutting board skin side down. Using a sharp knife, cut along the thigh bone of the chicken, away from the drum. Slide the knife along the bone, being careful not to cut a hole in the thigh. Remove the bone and chop off the tip of the drum. The chicken legs should be totally boneless except for the small bone in the drum.

2. In a small bowl, combine the salt, white pepper, and thyme. Liberally coat the chicken with the mixture. Lay the legs out flat, skin side up, and top the legs with the remaining mixture. Refrigerate, uncovered, for 3 hours. Remove the chicken from the fridge and rinse with cold water to remove all the thyme, salt, and pepper. The chicken will expel some liquid.

3. Preheat the oven to 325°F.

4. In a Dutch oven with a tightly fitting lid, shingle the chicken: The legs should be arranged in one flat layer, with each leg lying flat against the next, like roof shingles. Carefully cover the legs with the vegetable oil. You may need a little more or less, depending on the size of your container. Place the lid on the pot and put it into the oven. Cook for 3½ hours, or until the legs are a golden color. When the chicken is done, there will be small bubbles coming up from the bottom of the pot. Do not handle the chicken. Allow to cool completely before removing from the pot.

5. Increase the oven temperature to 400°F.

6. Carefully remove the chicken legs and pat them dry with paper towels. Heat an ovenproof sauté pan with 3 tablespoons of oil. Place the legs skin side down in the pan. Be sure to do this away from the heat to limit splattering. Put the sauté pan in the oven and bake for 10 minutes, never turning or flipping. Remove the pan and gently remove the chicken from the pan with a spatula. Serve immediately.

WHIPPED WITH A SWEET SMILE FROM SARAH.

MARTIN'S BAR-B-QUE JOINT

THIS *IS* THE HOUSE OF BARBECUE. GO WHOLE HOG OR GO HOME.

Sometimes you pull up to a place and you just know it's going to be good. Well, as I pulled up to Martin's my phone rang, and it was Kid Rock's manager telling me that Kid Rock wanted to talk about *Triple D*. (We rapped for about a half an hour and subsequently did the Kid Rock *Triple D* special.) Then I walked into the barbecue joint and met a sunburned fan who had been waiting for me all day. Next we got to chop some wood—I believe they had a Jack Daniel's–handled splitting maul—light a big smoker, and barbecue a whole hog. If they'd thrown in a little ice cold beer and some Hank Williams Junior, I might not have left—ever.

> ★ TRACK IT DOWN ★
>
> **7238 Nolensville Road**
> **Nolensville, TN 37135**
> **615-776-1856**
> **CB Channel #21**
> **www.martinsbbqjoint.com**

One time my buddy called and wanted to visit Martin's Bar-B-Que. I said I'd call and hook him up. It was about four in the afternoon. Pat Martin told me, "Sorry, partner, we done sold out." That's a real-deal BBQ joint. Cook what you got and sell it 'til it's gone. It's low and slow barbecue.

Pat's got a custom-made smoker for everything from ribs and chicken to brisket and turkey to a whole hog. And he even makes something called a redneck taco: pulled pork shoulder on a cornbread pancake with slaw and sweet Dixie sauce—totally ingenious.

PAT DOESN'T NEED TO HITCHHIKE TO FLAVORTOWN—
HE'S A LIFELONG RESIDENT!

KREW NOTES

Anthony "Chico" Rodriguez: People always wonder about what's the best part of the job. Is it the food, the travel, or making amazing television? The answer is: all of the above. But the single greatest thing is the people we meet. We have the opportunity to affect people's lives, which is really a gift to us. We had an incredible shoot with Pat and Martha Martin and cooked a whole hog, which is something you *must* do in your life. And if you do, go to Martin's—it's one of the best in the country. Several years after the shoot, I consider those guys my close friends and have visited them several times. Friendship—the best perk of the job.

Neil "Boy Band" Martin: Martin's Bar-B-Que is one of my favorite *Triple D* BBQ places. One of the things I remember about Martin's was a fan who arrived with his girlfriend around 8 a.m. When word got out that we were coming, he bleached his hair and showed up with high hopes of meeting Guy. The issue was that Guy wasn't scheduled to be there until 2 p.m. So this fan sat down on the sidewalk, ready to be first inside the restaurant when we opened the doors. When we told him he should probably leave and come back later, he insisted on staying put. While we did our B-roll shooting throughout the morning, he became more and more sunburned. The superfan finally got to meet Guy late that afternoon. He was one of the most dedicated people we've run into on the road.

NO, THAT'S NOT ME, IT'S A SUPERFAN, COMPLETE
WITH SUNBURN, WAITING OUTSIDE OF MARTIN'S TO
GET A PICTURE.

HOW TO COOK A WHOLE HOG

ADAPTED FROM A RECIPE COURTESY OF PAT MARTIN, MARTIN'S BAR-B-QUE JOINT

HOG SPECS

One whole dressed 165-pound hog

What does dressed mean? It means that all the internal organs have been removed. The skin must be left on the hog! This is *very, very, very* important. The head is also left on.

PIT SET-UP MATERIALS

100 standard cinder blocks

5 rods of ½-inch-thick re-bar, 60 inches long

4-foot level

Measuring tape

One 4½ x 3½-foot sheet of expanded metal or cattle fence

Mortar

One 6 x 5-foot sheet of roofing tin or sheet metal

BUILD THE PIT: The interior dimensions of the pit should be about 5 x 4 feet. It's like playing with LEGOs—just make some mortar and start stacking blocks on the ground. Leave an opening one cinder block wide in the second layer. When you get to the fourth row of blocks, lay your rods evenly down. Then lay the last row of blocks on top. The hole in the side is where you will feed the coals in under the hog. The sheet metal will be the lid, lying on the sides and the hog.

NOTE: If you want to get real kinky/permanent about this pit, then fill and pack it with sand as you build. This will cut fuel use by one third!

FUEL: Hickory. Other hardwoods such as oak are fine. Fruitwoods (apple, peach) or nuts (pecan) are fine as well. Do not use softwoods such as pine, or any other wood from the conifer family!

TOOLS: Short-handle flat shovel to shovel coals. Charcoal chimneys (to start the fire).

NOTE: Don't ever use lighter fluid—it's un-American. Amateurs, losers, and idiots use lighter fluid. If you've bought this book, you are inherently none of those three things, so let's make sure to teach others the correct way that real pitmasters start a fire. Lighter fluid makes your food taste like crap and is bad for the environment.

STARTING YOUR FIRE/BUILDING YOUR COALS

Ideally you want to use dry, seasoned wood. Start a huge fire—the kind that could probably get you a hefty fine—in a fire pit separate from your hog pit. You'll need to begin the fire at least six hours prior to beginning the hog to give yourself ample time to build up enough coals to begin cooking. Do not underestimate the amount of time needed to prepare your coals before you begin. Burn the wood down to a huge pile of coals. You'll need to continue feeding this fire to create coals until the hog is done.

PREP TOOLS NEEDED: Hatchet, 2-pound short-handle mallet, 8-inch chef's knife, paper towels

I'M NOT GIVING A CAPTION TO THIS . . . YOU JUST GO RIGHT AHEAD.

RUB PREP

This is a fantastic base recipe for a rub. These are the "core" ingredients you need to obtain a great "bark" or crust on your finished product. Use this as a base to start with and then add your own flavors to it—cayenne, nutmeg, whatever! Please note, though, that the ingredients need to be added in small amounts until you get it where you want it, 'cause once it's in it ain't coming out!

2½ cups brown sugar

2 cups kosher salt

2 cups garlic salt

2 cups granulated sugar

¾ cup paprika

⅓ cup lemon pepper

½ cup chili powder

¼ cup ground black pepper

MOP PREP

1¼ gallons apple cider vinegar

2½ cups crushed red pepper

7½ pounds (15 cups) granulated sugar

THIS IS LIKE CITY HALL IN FLAVORTOWN.

PROCESS

1. Lay the hog on its back. Place the tip of the hatchet under the neck where the top of the hog's spine is. Slowly tap the tip into the spine to get started. Begin "tapping" the hatchet with the mallet all the way down the spine. It is *very* important that you do not go too deep. The spine must not be split all the way in half in order to protect the hog as it cooks in the later hours of the process.

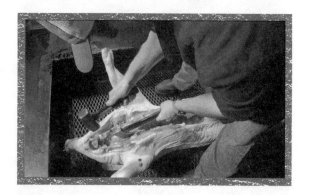

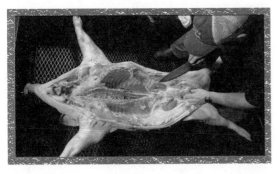

2. Using the chef's knife, cut away any organs and excess fat left inside the hog.

3. Sprinkle inside the hog liberally with all of the rub—apply it to all exposed meat. Do not apply to the skin.

4. Flip the hog over on the grate, face down, and spread the hog out flat.

5. Close the lid.

6. Begin putting coals from your firepit under the hog. Lay an initial uniform "bed" under the hog, then throw the coals under the hams and shoulders, being careful not to put much fire at all under the middle or belly of the hog. If you're sure you know what you're doing, then at this point I like to put a seasoned piece of wood on some of the coals for additional smoke, but you have to be *careful* against flare-ups, so manage your oxygen intake to the pit. Put the wood in the corner where it can't breathe air, so it can smolder. If you don't do this, don't worry—you're still gonna get *plenty* of smoke flavor.

7. Put your hand on the lid. If you can hold it there for 2 "Mississippis," you're pretty spot on. Any less and it's too hot, any more and it's too cool. If you want to get technical about it and use a thermometer, then manage your coals to a temp of 225°F to 250°F. No higher!

8. After about 6 hours, it's time to flip the hog. This will be a two-man job, so find a buddy. One of you gets on a shoulder leg and the other gets on a ham leg (from the same side, of course). Using paper towels to grab the legs (paper towels are awesome for getting a great grip on meat), count to three and flip the hog. You'll need to go in a motion of "up" and then over with it to ensure that the other two legs don't get caught on the grate and rip or tear the other half of the hog.

9. Using your mop, fill the rib cavities up. This is very important because this liquid is what's going to protect the belly meat—we call it the "middlin" meat—from overcooking while you're trying to get your shoulders and hams finished.

a. While you're at it, splash some around the rest of the hog for good measure. This really doesn't do a dang thing, but it makes you feel good about things and makes for good drama.

10. Now build your fire to where you can hold your hand on the lid for 3 seconds, or 200°F if you're using a thermometer.

a. At this point you're cooking what I call "clean." This means steady smoke, wispy blue smoke. *Not white smoke!* White smoke is heavy and choking, bitter and acrid. Blue smoke sweetens your meat—that is, BBQ.

11. Continue to cook until the meat is done. The total process should take you about 22 to 24 hours. A really good general rule of thumb is 1 hour per 8 pounds of meat. Your hams will be the last thing to finish—be careful not to over-cook your shoulders while getting your hams done. For the last couple of hours of cooking, you may only want to put coals under the hams.

a. When you think you're within an hour or so of it being done, quit putting coals under it. It's time to let it "glide." The heat in the blocks is your heat source now.

b. Note: Weather will play with the cook times. Humidity and cooler temps are a couple of things that can screw you up, but nothing screws with you more than wind! You can control a pit easier if it's 28°F and still than you can if it's 60°F with a 15 mph wind. Wind is tough on you! If it's windy, use an old quilt or movers' blanket or even a tarp to lay over the lid of the pit. Anything to keep the wind off of it!

12. When the meat is done, baste the heck out of it with the mop and let it sit for 30 minutes to 1 hour or so. You may need to crack the lid some to let additional heat out of it if you think it's still hot enough to continue the cooking process.

13. Pull it and serve it. The only thing that should be left when you're done is bones and skin. Don't get in there and start taking fat out of it. First of all, most of it has rendered out. Second, if you find yourself worrying about do-ing that, then you shouldn't be cooking a hog in the first place. Mix it all together and serve.

14. How to build a proper BBQ sandwich: On the bottom of a potato bun, layer 5 to 6 ounces of pulled whole hog. Next, layer ⅛ cup of slaw on top of the pulled pork. (*This is non-negotiable.*) Squirt some sauce on top of the slaw. Finish with the top of the potato bun.

MIDWEST

TRE KRONOR

REAL-DEAL SCANDINAVIAN FLAVORS IN . . . CHICAGO

Growing up as a kid in Ferndale, in Northern California, I was exposed to a large Scandinavian influence in the region. My family also hosted exchange students, one from Sweden and one from Norway. So, as you can imagine, I've had my fair share of Scandinavian food. I guess you could say I'm a little bit of an aficionado. I did eat the most ebelskivers of any of my friends in Ferndale at the Danish Hall one year, and just to establish my position on this, I am a proud owner of an ebelskiver pan. So I was so stoked to hear about Tre Kronor, because it had been a while since I'd gotten to enjoy some real-deal Swedish meatballs and ebelskivers.

This place is owned by a first- and second-generation Scandinavian couple, Larry Anderson and Patty Rasmussen, who are serving up rainbow trout with butter sauce, pickled herring (done ten different ways), gravlax, Swedish pancakes, and of course ebelskivers.

> ★ TRACK IT DOWN ★
>
> **3258 West Foster Avenue**
> **Chicago, IL 60625**
> **773-267-9888**
> **www.trekronorrestaurant.com**

KREW NOTES

Anthony "Chico" Rodriguez: The Ebelskiver Debacle We were in the middle of cooking with chef and co-owner Larry, having a great time, when Guy asked about ebelskivers. Larry said that his wife and co-owner, Patty, made amazing ebelskivers, so we called Patty into the kitchen. Guy was very excited at this point and talked to the camera about how they are made and the special pan that's used. Patty then offered to go make some, but forewarned that they take a while and it's a lot of work to cook them in these pans. Guy gave the green light, and while we moved on to cooking the dish for *DDD,* Guy kept talking to the camera about his excitement. Some time went by, then Patty opened the kitchen door announcing that they were done and was carrying a *huge* tray of warm, fresh, hot ebelskivers. Just as soon as we took notice of how delicious they looked, Butterbean turned and his arm caught the corner of the pan and *thhh-hwaaaatttttt*—that was the sound of the pan hitting the ground, as more than a dozen beautiful ebelskivers rolled along the kitchen floor. Patty had this look of shock and sadness, but it quickly turned into heavy laughter as Chico, Guy, Larry, and Boy Band were in full hysterics laughing! It was a great moment, and in the end, we had a fresh pan of delicious ebelskivers thirty minutes later, and Butterbean was happy.

Jeff "Butterbean" Asell: It's a really sad day when ebelskivers hit the floor. Sorry, Patty.

CHICO LOOKS SO SERIOUS, AND WHAT AM I DOING IN A LONG SLEEVE WHITE SHIRT?

SWEDISH MEATBALLS WITH PICKLED CUCUMBERS

ADAPTED FROM A RECIPE COURTESY OF LARRY ANDERSON, TRE KRONOR

Serves 8 (Makes about 72 meatballs)

½ cup (1 stick) unsalted butter

1 large onion, finely chopped

¾ cup heavy cream

¾ cup water

1 tablespoon salt

1 teaspoon ground black pepper

¼ teaspoon ground nutmeg

¾ cup plain breadcrumbs

1½ pounds ground beef

1½ pounds ground pork (or more beef)

2 large eggs

3 tablespoons vegetable oil

Pickled Cucumbers (recipe follows)

Brown gravy and lingonberries, for serving

1. In a large sauté pan over medium heat, melt the butter. Add the onion and sauté until browned, 15 to 20 minutes, stirring regularly. Set aside.

2. In a medium bowl, whisk together the cream, water, salt, pepper, and nutmeg. Add the breadcrumbs and stir to moisten. In a large bowl, with your hands, thoroughly mix the meat with the eggs. Add the sautéed onions to the meat mixture and combine. Add the moist breadcrumb mixture and thoroughly mix again. Refrigerate for 30 minutes to allow the ingredients to set up.

3. Preheat the oven to 350°F.

4. Form 1-inch meatballs (about 1 ounce each) and set them on a baking sheet. Refrigerate the meatballs for 15 minutes to firm up (they'll be easier to work with). Working in batches, in a sauté pan over medium-high heat, heat the oil and cook the meatballs until evenly browned and cooked through, 5 to 7 minutes. Transfer the browned meatballs to a baking sheet in the oven as you go to keep them warm.

5. Serve the meatballs with pickled cucumbers, brown gravy, and lingonberries.

PICKLED CUCUMBERS

Makes about 4 ½ cups

2 cups white wine vinegar
2 cups sugar
¼ cup chopped fresh dill
¼ cup chopped fresh parsley
6 medium cucumbers, thinly sliced

In a large (1 gallon) bowl or storage container, whisk together the vinegar and sugar and ½ cup water until the sugar is dissolved. Whisk in the dill and parsley. Place the cucumbers in the pickling solution, cover, and refrigerate for about 4 hours or overnight, stirring once.

TASTE OF PERU

WHERE TO GO FOR PERUVIAN, PERIOD

Chicago always delivers the killer food. Cemitas Puebla, Paradise Pup, Irazu . . . the list goes on and on and on. But I gotta tell ya, one of my all-time faves (and my first cultural experience in Peruvian food) was discovered at Taste of Peru.

★ TRACK IT DOWN ★

6545 North Clark Street
Chicago, IL 60626
773-381-4540
www.tasteofperu.com

Owner and chef Cesar Izquierdo learned all his authentic recipes from his mother. He's got tamales wrapped in banana leaves (not corn husks) with a vinegar-onion giddyup—some of the best masa I've ever had (and I am body by tamale). From paella to ceviche, as Cesar says, Peruvian food is still revealing itself to the world. And the lomo saltado (rib eye) is fantastic. I don't care—if you live within two hundred miles, you should walk here. And when you go in, make sure that Cesar is there. Easy to spot, he's probably the tallest Peruvian dude you'll ever meet. Ask him to show you the spinning top on a string . . .

THIS FLAME IS HUGE—CESAR IS SO TALL THAT HE MAKES IT LOOK SMALL.

LIVE CAM: HERE I SHOW CESAR HOW THE SAUTÉ PAN IS LIKE A TENNIS RACKET.

KREW NOTES

Matt "Beaver" Giovinetti: Cesar is a prince, and the food is prepared with love you can taste. This was the first time we'd done a Peruvian place on the show, and we all got hooked. We ate anticuchos (cow heart), and this is where I learned that seasoning the masa is the only way to make tamales. Guy's standup included a shout-out to Maria Carrera. Cesar and his wife gave Guy a traditional Peruvian toy called a trompo, or spinning top.

 ## RESTAURANT UPDATE

Since the show aired we continue to be very busy. Chicagoans who were not aware of us drop in, and we get people coming here from all over the country. Often the phone rings with someone who's downtown on business asking for directions to make our restaurant their dinner destination.

Sadly, I lost my younger brother, and our restaurant manager, to cancer earlier this year at the young age of fifty-three. Augusto's memory is with us every day, and we are forever grateful to *Diners, Drive-ins and Dives* that he was able to share this exciting time in our lives and our business.

—CESAR IZQUIERDO

LOMO SALTADO

ADAPTED FROM A RECIPE COURTESY OF CESAR IZQUIERDO, TASTE OF PERU

Serves 6

1½ pounds sirloin steak

2 tablespoons minced garlic

2 teaspoons soy sauce

Salt and freshly ground black pepper

3 tablespoons vegetable oil

2 medium onions, sliced (about 1 pound)

2 medium tomatoes, sliced into ¼-inch-thick half moons

¼ cup white vinegar

¼ cup beer

French Fries (recipe follows)

2 tablespoons chopped fresh parsley

Cooked white rice, for serving

1. Slice the steak against the grain into 1½ x 2 x ¼-inch slices. Rub the meat with the garlic, soy sauce, and pinches of salt and pepper.

2. Heat a cast-iron pan or wok over high heat with half the oil. Add half the meat and pan-fry until browned, turning once, about 5 minutes total. Remove the meat, reserve, and repeat with the rest of the oil and meat.

3. Add the onions and toss repeatedly, cooking until soft and slightly caramelized, 5 to 7 minutes, then add the tomatoes and vinegar. When the tomatoes are slightly softened, 2 to 3 minutes, add the beer and quickly toss to combine.

4. Gently mix in the French fries and steak to heat through.

5. Garnish with chopped parsley and serve with white rice.

FRENCH FRIES

2 large russet potatoes (about 1¼ pounds), the bigger the better
Canola oil, for deep frying
Salt and freshly ground black pepper

1. Wash and peel the potatoes, then cut them into medium fry shapes.

2. In a deep pot, filled with oil 3 to 4 inches deep, heat the oil until it bubbles (about 300°F). Add the potatoes and fry, in batches if necessary, until they become tan, 5 to 10 minutes. Drain on paper towels.

3. Increase the temperature of the oil to 350°F. Once the oil comes up to temperature, fry the fries for a second time, until lightly golden brown and crispy, 5 to 10 minutes.

4. Drain on paper towels and season with salt and pepper.

SO WHERE'S THE TRIPLE D POSTER GOING TO GO, CESAR?

IRAZU

I AM FREAKIN' FOR SOME COSTA RICAN

I tell you guys all the time, Chicago has some bomb food, and this just takes it another step. Costa Rican–born Miriam Cerdas-Salazar came up with the eclectic menu twenty years ago, and now her son Henry is running the joint. The three key ingredients to Costa Rican food, according to Henry: vegetables, meat, and chicharron. Most people's idea of chicharron is just fried pork skin. Well, not at Irazu. No, here it's pork belly, so you get meat and fried skin and the bean mayo (they make their own sandwich spread out of cooked-down black beans and caramelized onions) on French bread. Chef Omar Cadena also serves up the popular "pepito" steak sandwich—a family recipe with an authentic homemade black bean paste.

Plus my favorite—which you didn't see on the show 'cause I talked too long and I wouldn't shut up in my excitement about it—was the oatmeal milk shake. OMG-oatmeal. That's reason enough just to go in. A poor man's milk shake. And here's a little gift—see the recipe on page 91 (this is why you bought the book). You know that you gotta try the oatmeal milk shake.

★ TRACK IT DOWN ★

1865 N. Milwaukee Avenue
Chicago, IL 60647
773-252-5687
www.irazuchicago.com

LIVE CAM: MIRIAM CERDAS BROUGHT ON THE TRUE FLAVORS.

KREW NOTES

Matt "Beaver" Giovinetti: This place has the most incredible seafood paella I have ever seen on the show.

 RESTAURANT UPDATE

Thanks to *Triple D*, our customer base has been greatly expanded, and visitors to Chicago now have Irazu on their destination list. The increased volume has allowed us to insulate our patio during the colder months and offer year-round "outdoor" seating.

—HENRY CERDAS

Nice Business Plug!

OATMEAL SHAKE HEADACHE . . . AHHHH!

CHIFRIJO

ADAPTED FROM A RECIPE COURTESY OF MIRIAM CERDAS-SALAZAR, IRAZU

RECIPE PRONOUNCED *CHEE-FREE-HO*

Serves 4

Pico de gallo

1 large red tomato, chopped

1 medium white onion, chopped

¼ cup chopped fresh cilantro leaves

1 jalapeño, minced (optional)

Juice of 5 limes or lemons

½ teaspoon salt

Chicharron

4 cups vegetable oil

1 pound slab whole pork belly with skin still
on, or 1 pound slab unsalted, uncured raw
whole bacon, cut into 1-inch pieces

8 to 10 garlic cloves, crushed

2 tablespoons salt

Black beans

½ pound black beans, washed and rinsed

2 whole garlic cloves, plus 1 clove, minced

2 tablespoons vegetable oil

1 small yellow onion, finely chopped

1 teaspoon salt

1 teaspoon ground cumin

1 teaspoon ground black pepper

1 tablespoon Salsa Lizano (a Costa Rican
condiment, available online at
amigofoods.com)

IT'S RIGHT HERE—IRAZU!

White rice

1 tablespoon vegetable oil

1 garlic clove, minced

¼ cup finely chopped yellow onion

1 cup uncooked white rice (medium or long grain)

½ teaspoon salt

1 Hass avocado, quartered

Salsa Lizano, for serving

Tortilla chips, for serving

1. **FOR THE PICO DE GALLO:** In a large bowl, combine the tomato, onion, cilantro, and jalapeño, if using. Add the lime or lemon juice (there should be enough juice that it's just underneath the tomato, onion, and cilantro mixture). Add the salt. Mix well, cover, and let sit in the refrigerator for at least 30 minutes.

2. **FOR THE CHICHARRON:** Heat 1 cup of the oil in a medium saucepan over medium heat. When the oil is hot, add the pork (you should be able to hear the sizzling fry song). Cook the pork for 20 minutes, stirring very often, until it is brown and crispy. Add the garlic and salt continue to stir until pork has a lovely golden brown color, another 20 minutes.

3. Remove the pork from the heat and set aside to cool fully, 1 to 2 hours. (The first steps of the chicharron cooking process can be done the day before.) Cut the pork into small dice.

4. Add the remaining 3 cups oil to a medium saucepan over medium-high heat. When the oil is very hot, flash-fry the diced chicharron until it has a deep rich brown color and a crunchy texture, about 60 seconds. Set aside on paper towels to drain.

5. **FOR THE BLACK BEANS:** In a medium saucepan, combine 5 cups water, the black beans, and the 2 whole garlic cloves. Bring the mixture to a boil over medium-high heat, then reduce the heat and simmer for 8 to 10 minutes.

6. Meanwhile, in a medium sauté pan or skillet over medium heat, add the oil, minced garlic, and onion. Cook, stirring occasionally, until the onions are golden, 5 to 8 minutes.

7. Add the sautéed onions and garlic, the salt, cumin, black pepper, and Salsa Lizano to the beans and bring to a boil, then reduce the heat to a simmer. Give one more stir, cover, and cook until the beans are tender, about 1 hour.

8. FOR THE RICE: In a medium saucepan over medium-low heat, combine the oil, garlic, and onion. Sauté until the onion is translucent, about 5 minutes. Add the rice, salt, and 1½ cups water. Bring the rice to a boil, then lower the heat to a simmer, cover, and cook for 35 minutes, or until the rice is fully cooked and fluffy.

9. TO ASSEMBLE: Add a spoonful of black bean liquid to each of 4 bowls. In each bowl, put 3 heaping tablespoons of rice, 4 tablespoons of black beans, and 4 tablespoons of the diced chicharron. Top with 2 to 3 tablespoons of pico de gallo. Cut each avocado quarter into thin slices and fan them on top. Generously drizzle with Salsa Lizano and serve with tortilla chips and an ice cold beverage.

MY STAINLESS-STEEL DRUMMING WILL MAKE ANYONE DANCE.

1. **Rainbow Drive-In,** Honolulu, Hawaii
2. **Fresh Local Wild,** Vancouver, British Columbia
   Tomahawk Restaurant, North Vancouver, British Columbia
   The Red Wagon Café, Vancouver, British Columbia
   Meat & Bread, Vancouver, British Columbia
3. **Otto's Sausage Kitchen,** Portland, Oregon
   Bunk Sandwiches, Portland, Oregon
   Pok Pok, Portland, Oregon
4. **Bar Gernika,** Boise, Idaho
   West Side Drive In, Boise, Idaho
5. **Schellville Grill,** Sonoma, California
   Café Citti, Kenwood, California
   La Texanita, Santa Rosa, California
   Catelli's, Geyserville, California
6. **Jamie's Broadway Grille,** Sacramento, California
   Café Rolle, Sacramento, California
7. **Pier 23 Café,** San Francisco, California
   Rocco's Café, San Francisco, California
   Bubba's Fine Diner, San Anselmo, California
   Sol Food, San Rafael, California
8. **Aldo's Harbor Restaurant,** Santa Cruz, California
9. **Mac's Fish and Chip Shop,** Santa Barbara, California
10. **North End Caffe,** Manhattan Beach, California
    Fab Hot Dogs, Reseda, California
    Mambo's, Glendale, California
    Mama Cozza's, Anaheim, California
    Paul's Coffee Shop, Fountain Valley, California
11. **Tioli's Crazee Burger,** San Diego, California
12. **Forte European Tapas Bar & Bistro,** Las Vegas, Nevada
    The Coffee Cup, Boulder City, Nevada
13. **Roberto's Authentic Mexican Food,** Anthem, Arizona
14. **Standard Diner,** Albuquerque, New Mexico
15. **Lauer-Krauts,** Brighton, Colorado
    Tocabe: An American Indian Eatery, Denver, Colorado
16. **Noble Pig Sandwiches,** Austin, Texas
17. **Cattlemen's Steakhouse,** Oklahoma City, Oklahoma

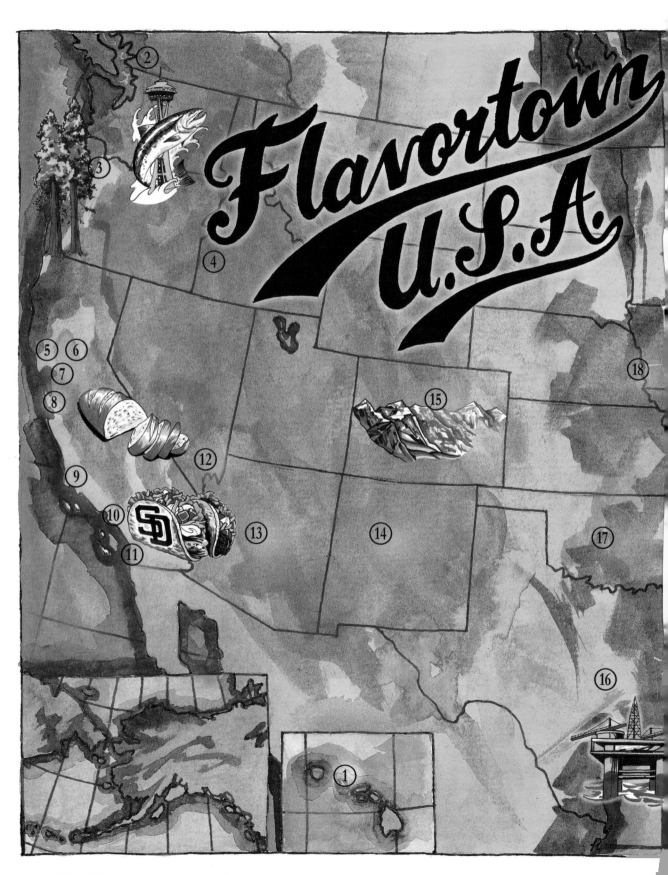

Flavortown U.S.A.

SHE'S SO HAPPY TO BE HERE—TRUST ME, YOU WILL BE, TOO!

AVENA (OATMEAL) SHAKE

ADAPTED FROM A RECIPE COURTESY OF MIRIAM CERDAS-SALAZAR, IRAZU

Serves 2

2 cups almond milk

¼ cup uncooked rolled oats

⅛ teaspoon ground cinnamon

⅛ teaspoon pure vanilla extract

2 tablespoons raw honey or maple syrup

2 cups ice cubes

Combine all the ingredients in a blender and blend until smooth. Pura vida!

BIG & LITTLE'S

GOURMET FAST FOOD DONE RIGHT

Ever walk into a place and say, "Are these guys for real?" They started as a tiny, funky little joint with monster portions, but that's not the surprising thing. The question is, how can they really be scratch-making all this killer food for those prices? They've got a pork po-boy with a maple glaze . . . I'm sorry, did I say maple glaze? It's maple mayonnaise, but don't tell the boys I said that. This thing is big enough to feed my son Ryder's entire soccer team. Then there's a fish and chips that's the size of a whale tail, and just when you think you've got some idea of what's going on in this joint, they serve you up foie gras and fries. These guys are big on imagination and little on reality, and that's what makes them so cool, 'cause there's no way you can get this quality of food for those prices.

Gary Strauss (Big) and Tony D'Alessandro (Little) opened in 2009, putting it all on the line, and people showed up for the outrageous food. They're rockin' it, and I hear they grew into bigger digs since the show aired. You can't beat that with a stick.

> ★ TRACK IT DOWN ★
>
> **860 North Orleans Street**
> **Chicago, IL 60610**
> **312-943-0000**
> **www.bigandlittleschicago.com**

KREW NOTES

Jeff "Butterbean" Asell: The rental cars in Chicago must have an autopilot, because I always end up back at B&L's.

RESTAURANT UPDATE

When we first opened, we started with 600 square feet. That was enough for eight stools. After the show aired we moved across the street to a larger location with about 1,500 square feet and about 55 to 60 seats. Four months after that move, we rented the space next door and expanded to about 3,000 square feet by tearing down a wall. Now we seat about 100, plus about another 40 seats outside in the summer. That's 140 people on a nice day, and we fill it! We now do private parties due to a high demand from customers. The menu has more than tripled, and still continues to grow. Our staff has more than doubled. Every day we get new customers from outside the States because of *DDD*. We still have our regulars from day one who come almost every day. And "Little" has cooked every order and never, ever missed a day. We work sixteen hours a day and love every moment.

—GARY STRAUSS (BIG) AND TONY D'ALESSANDRO (LITTLE)

NEW BIG & LITTLE'S DELIVERY VEHICLE.

FOIE GRAS AND FRIES

ADAPTED FROM A RECIPE COURTESY OF GARY STRAUSS AND TONY D'ALESSANDRO, BIG & LITTLE'S

Serves 1 to 2

1 pound russet potatoes

About 8 cups peanut oil (make sure you fill the pot only half full)

Salt and freshly ground black pepper

9 ounces foie gras (about a half a lobe)

1. Cut the potatoes into ¼-inch strips or to a french fry size of your liking. Soak them in cold water for about 10 minutes. Drain and dry.

2. Heat a deep pot with the peanut oil over medium heat to 350°F. (A candy thermometer works well.) Fry the potatoes until golden, about 7 minutes. Remove them to paper towels to drain and let rest for 5 minutes. Fry a second time, until golden brown, 6 to 10 minutes. Place the fries in a wide bowl and season with salt and pepper.

HE'S GONNA GET RUN OVER . . . PS, NICE BILLBOARD!

3. Cut the foie gras into three ½-inch-thick lobes, about 3 ounces each. Use a knife to score an X or a tic-tac-toe into the lobes for presentation (don't cut all the way through). Sprinkle with salt and pepper. Heat a large skillet over a high heat for 7 to 10 minutes, until you see smoke. Place all three pieces in skillet and sear each side for about a minute for medium rare, longer if you desire medium (about 2 minutes each side).

4. Place the cooked lobes over the fries. There will be a pool of foie gras fat that rendered in the pan. *It's like gold.* Pour it over the lobes and fries together.

BIG AND LITTLE—CAN YOU TELL WHY? (SEE, THEIR POSE IS THE SAME AS THE LOGO . . . FOR REAL!)

3 SISTERS CAFÉ

A HAVEN FOR ALL, FROM VEGANS TO MEAT-EATERS

★ TRACK IT DOWN ★

**6360 Guilford Avenue
Indianapolis, IN 46220
317-257-5556
www.3sisterscafein.com**

Like I said when I first got to this place, it's a made-for-TV movie. Waitress meets line cook, they fall in love, buy a restaurant . . . oh yeah, here comes the spin, it's a vegetarian place, and now they're going to serve meat. Moira Sommers and her partner, Alex Munroe, dove in and never looked back. They cater to everybody with this menu, from vegan chili to barbecued chicken with bacon—and a juicy au jus pork and kale sandwich. (My mouth just went in to full Niagara.)

That's just the precursor to this place. If that wasn't enough for you, this is all going on in a house from the late 1800s, and to top it all off there's the dessert . . . this ain't your grandmother's cheesecake. Alex, please send me one. It's a full orchestra of flavor.

MOIRA AND ALEX WITH THEIR KICKASS PIE.

A FUNKY OLD HOUSE OF GOOD FOOD.

KREW NOTES

Mike "Father Time" Morris: In Native American culture, the three sisters are corn, beans, and squash. I'm from Indiana, and this place is in the heart of Indianapolis, Broad Ripple, one of the hippest areas of the city and such a cool place to go for a meal. It's in an old house with multiple dining rooms, and the nicest people run it—real Hoosier hospitality.

Bryna "The Pirate" Levin: Alex Munroe and his wife, Moira Sommers, got married late in life, and they both brought kids to the marriage. The restaurant feels like you're in someone's home. The Goat Cheese Pie recipe came about by chance when Alex went to make a blueberry cream cheese pie, and saw he was out of cream cheese but had goat cheese. He also put in finely chopped fresh basil. Sounds like it wouldn't work, but it's an amazing combination. The tart goat cheese changes the dish into something wholly original and startlingly delicious.

BLUEBERRY GOAT CHEESE PIE

ADAPTED FROM A RECIPE COURTESY OF ALEX MUNROE AND MOIRA SOMMERS, 3 SISTERS CAFÉ

Makes 1 pie

Crust

2 cups all-purpose flour

½ cup (1 stick) cold margarine, cubed

1 tablespoon sugar

Pinch of salt

Cold water

Filling

½ cup soft goat cheese

½ cup heavy cream

1 large egg

½ cup light brown sugar

¼ cup all-purpose flour

Pinch of salt

1 tablespoon finely chopped fresh basil

5 cups fresh blueberries

Topping

1 cup sliced almonds

½ cup sugar

⅓ cup margarine, melted

I SPRAY PAINTED THE DDD LOGO IN THE DINING ROOM—AWESOME!

1. FOR THE CRUST: Combine the flour, margarine, sugar, and salt in a large bowl. Work with your fingers gathering and crumbling until you have a crumbly mixture about the size of peas.

2. In 2-tablespoon amounts (about ½ cup total), slowly add cold water, gently incorporating by hand. As soon as the dough comes together in a ball, wrap in plastic wrap and chill for 30 minutes.

3. FOR THE FILLING: Mix together the goat cheese, heavy cream, egg, brown sugar, flour, salt, and basil in a bowl. Add the blueberries and combine; the texture will be like a thick cake batter.

4. FOR THE TOPPING: Mix together the almonds, sugar, and margarine in a bowl and set aside.

5. Preheat the oven to 350°F. Roll out the dough on a floured surface to ⅛-inch thickness and place into a 10-inch pie pan. Trim and crimp the edges and prick the bottom of the crust with a fork. Par-bake the crust for 15 minutes, or until firm. Let cool slightly. Pour the filling into the crust and sprinkle the topping over the top. Bake for 35 to 40 minutes, until slightly bubbling and the crust is browned, rotating the pie halfway through. Let the pie cool for 30 minutes on a wire rack before serving so the filling can firm up.

ZYDECO'S

THE CAJUN CULINARY EMBASSY OF INDIANA

You can find a lot of good Cajun style food around the country, but having a Cajun or Creole New Orleans experience isn't just about the food, it's about the people, energy, and environment. Don't get me wrong, making your own boudin and tasso, and throwing your own Mardi Gras party doesn't hurt either. That's why I'll tell you, one of the real-deal New Orleans experiences you'll ever get is at Zydeco's . . . in Mooresville, Indiana.

★ TRACK IT DOWN ★

**11 East Main Street
Mooresville, IN 46158
317-834-3900
www.zydecos.net**

They've got blackened catfish with crawfish tails, jambalaya, étouffée, po-boys, fresh seafood flown in from Louisiana—you name it. Co-owner Carter Hutchinson was born in New Orleans and grew up along the Gulf Coast. When he moved north to marry his wife, Deb, they opened this joint and started cooking his favorite dishes from childhood. When you cross over the threshold, you're in Louisiana . . . And you better bring your "A" game.

KREW NOTES

Ryan "Donny" Larson: Once you're inside, Guy's got it right—you really are in *New Orleans*!

LIVE CAM: SHOWING MY MAD NINJA SKILLS . . . I THINK!?

NOPE, NOT BOURBON STREET—IT'S THE DINING ROOM AT ZYDECO'S.

ZYDECO'S BBQ SHRIMP

ADAPTED FROM A RECIPE COURTESY OF CARTER HUTCHINSON, ZYDECO'S

Serves 4 to 6

2 cups (4 sticks) unsalted butter

½ cup chopped green onions

¼ cup Worcestershire sauce

1 tablespoon liquid crab boil, such as Zatarain's

1 tablespoon cayenne pepper

1 tablespoon red pepper flakes

1 tablespoon kosher salt

1 tablespoon cracked black pepper

1 tablespoon dried thyme

6 garlic cloves, chopped

2 bay leaves

Hot sauce, such as Tabasco

1 lemon

12 jumbo (U-12) shrimp, with heads and shells on

Crusty bread, for serving

Melt the butter in a large saucepan over medium heat. Add the green onions, Worcestershire sauce, crab boil, cayenne, red pepper flakes, salt, black pepper, thyme, garlic, bay leaves, and 5 or 6 shakes of hot sauce. Cut the lemon in half, squeeze in the juice, and drop the lemon halves into the pan. Bring to a boil, but don't let the mixture smoke. Add the shrimp in flat rows on top. Cook until pink, about 2 minutes per side. Pour the shrimp and liquid onto a plate and serve with crusty bread.

COOK'S NOTE: The top of the shrimp head should *not* have a red spot; the shrimp should be completely gray, and the fresher the better. You want to cook this dish with the head and shell on the shrimp. It's good to let the mixture soak for a bit, but don't overcook, or the shrimp will have a rubbery texture.

DEB LETTING THE GUESTS KNOW THAT THEY'D BETTER FINISH THEIR MEALS OR SHE'LL TAKE THE BEADS BACK.

UNION WOODSHOP

A KID ROCK PICK THAT TAKES THE WHOLE HOG

I shoulda known that Kid Rock wouldn't have invited me up to check this out if it wasn't the real deal. This place does it all, starting with the whole hog: They break it down, grind it into sausage patties, make their own sausage links, cure their own bacon, and make their own ice cream down in the funky basement kitchen that has more smoke than a rave club—from the meat to the cheese, they do it all.

★ TRACK IT DOWN ★

**18 South Main Street
Clarkston, MI 48346
248-625-5660
www.unionwoodshop.com**

Chef Aaron Cozadd makes the ice cream in sixty seconds with liquid nitrogen (freaky!). That's right, at negative 325°F—watch your toes. Then he serves it in a maple-bourbon-vanilla sundae with house-smoked Spanish peanuts. Shut the front door, son of Tatum O'Neal, that's dynamite. (The smoked peanuts are what makes it.)

Then, on the final leg of the Kid Rock culinary cruise, we ended up at the brewery where Kid Rock made Badass Beer. Now if you're going to call it Badass beer it better be badass, and all I can tell you is the name fits the bill. Just like his music, the dude delivers. Not one to stray far from his roots or waver on his stance to do good for the city of Detroit, when Kid Rock's Badass producer unexpectedly closed shop in 2012, Rock knew what to do: build a world-class brewery in the heart of the city staffed by Detroiters and supporting Detroit. Opening Summer 2013. Badass Beer: Troubled Has Been Brewed.

SIDENOTE: Rumor has it that there may have been ten cases of Badass longnecks loaded into the '68 and hauled back to California. Now, we all know that's illegal, but tell me you didn't love *Smokey and the Bandit*. Does somebody smell a remake?

KREW NOTES

Liz "Erd" Pollock: Bourbon in liquid nitrogen ice cream, piles of smoked meats busting out of a bun, Kid Rock and Guy Fieri? Come on, this is one shoot I can't believe I was paid for. These two guys together make a great thing even better, and I just sat back and enjoyed.

Jeff "Butterbean" Asell: Okay, I am an Iowan. To love a sandwich made of three kinds of pork is in my DNA.

Neil "Boy Band" Martin: Homemade ice cream is always awesome, but making it with liquid nitrogen is like working with the mad scientist in Flavortown!

 RESTAURANT UPDATE

We had a blast making the show, and it has had a huge impact on business. On a side note, we just opened up our new joint, Vinsetta Garage. It's in *the* classic car garage that has been servicing stock and custom rides since 1919 on historic Woodward Avenue. We honored the space and created a menu to complement it.

—AARON COZADD

KID ROCK SHOWING ME THE "TRIPLE D HUNCH."

MAPLE BOURBON SUNDAE

ADAPTED FROM A RECIPE COURTESY OF AARON COZADD, UNION WOODSHOP

Serves 4

Vanilla ice cream

1 quart half-and-half

1 cup minus 1½ tablespoons sugar

½ vanilla bean

3 large egg yolks

Liquid nitrogen, optional

Maple bourbon sauce

1 cup pure maple syrup

⅛ teaspoon salt

¼ vanilla bean, split

½ cup (1 stick) cold unsalted butter, cubed

1 tablespoon bourbon

Smoked peanuts

One 12-ounce container Spanish peanuts

1 cup soaked hickory wood chips

NOTE: For the best, smoothest results, the chef recommends using the liquid nitrogen method for freezing if you can secure some from a local gas company.

TIPS FOR SAFE HANDLING: 1) Wear dry gloves to protect your hands from the (very) cold bowl and long pants in case it spills. 2) Make sure the nitrogen has boiled completely off your food before serving or eating. 3) Handle the dewar containing the liquid nitrogen carefully, and never use it in an unventilated space. If it punctures, leave the room and open windows, as the resulting lack of oxygen can cause asphyxiation.

1. FOR THE ICE CREAM: Place the half-and-half and sugar a medium saucepan. Split and scrape the seeds from the vanilla bean. Add the bean and seeds to the pan. Bring the mixture just to a simmer over medium heat, stirring occasionally, about 10 minutes. Remove from the heat.

2. In a medium bowl, whisk the egg yolks until they lighten in color. Temper the cream mixture into the eggs by gradually adding small amounts, until about a third of the cream mixture has been added. Pour in the remainder, return the entire mixture to the saucepan, and place over low heat. Continue to cook, stirring frequently, until the mixture thickens slightly and coats the back of a spoon and reaches 185°F. Pour the mixture through a fine-meshed strainer into a container and place the mixture in the refrigerator uncovered. Once it is cool enough not to form condensation on the lid, 15 to 20 minutes, cover and store for at least 4 hours in the refrigerator, until the temperature reaches 40°F or below.

3. IF YOU DON'T HAVE LIQUID NITROGEN: Pour into an ice cream maker and process according to the manufacturer's directions.

If you can secure some liquid nitrogen: Place the ice cream into the mixing bowl of the ice cream maker. Attach the paddle attachment. With the mixer set to the slowest speed, slowly pour a steady inch-wide stream of liquid nitrogen directly from the dewar into the bowl. Pour for about 5 seconds, then listen for 10 to 15 seconds. If there is little or no change in sound, continue to run the mixer and add liquid nitrogen in 5-second pours. When the sound changes to a deeper, almost chunky rhythm, stop the mixer, clear the "fog," scrape down the sides of the bowl, and check the texture. After one or two more additions of nitrogen, the mixture should reach the consistency of soft-serve ice cream. Pour into a freezer container and store in the freezer for 8 to 12 hours before serving.

4. FOR THE MAPLE BOURBON SAUCE: Place the maple syrup, salt, and vanilla bean in a small saucepan. Bring to a boil, then turn the heat to medium-low, and simmer for 10 minutes.

5. Remove the pan from the stove. While whisking, add the cold butter a few pats at a time. When the butter is completely incorporated, add the bourbon. Set aside.

6. FOR THE SMOKED PEANUTS: Prepare a stovetop smoker according to the manufacturer's instructions using the hickory wood. Place the peanuts in the smoker. Close the lid and smoke for 30 minutes over low heat. Check about every 10 minutes to stir and make sure the nuts don't burn. The nuts will be turn reddish orange in color.

7. FOR SERVING: Spoon 2 scoops ice cream in a bowl per serving. Drizzle with maple bourbon sauce and garnish with smoked peanuts.

CASPER'S & RUNYON'S NOOK

ALL-AMERICAN STUFFED BURGERS WITH MORE THAN SEVENTY YEARS OF HISTORY

Everybody told me about this place in St. Paul where they stuff the burger, so you know I had to head to the Nook. Now comes the tough part: backing it up. Were they as good as people said, or just local legend? In a cramped space and cooking in a closet-size kitchen, the boys did well. These good buddies have a lot of energy. Fast forward three years and the Nook burned down. But then everyone wondered: Will the rebuilt restaurant have the same appeal? So we rolled back into town to find that the boys have built a nice, new, big kitchen, and they now have a Triple B Burger (which I think they meant to call the *Triple D* Burger, but we'll let it go).

Mike Runyon and Ted Casper started running this joint when they were only twenty years old. The original place opened in 1938, so there was a lot of history to uphold. To get some seasoned advice, they turned to one of the former owners, Mickey Braunsen, who owned the place from 1967 to 1997. They make everything the way Mickey did, with fresh beef, fresh buns, and fresh-cut fries. And yes, they stuff their burgers with cheese. It's a cheese explosion—and the bun is fantastic; they're making them fresh daily right down the street.

> ★ TRACK IT DOWN ★
>
> **492 Hamline Avenue South**
> **St. Paul, MN 55116**
> **651-698-4347**
> **www.crnook.com**

KREW NOTES

Kat Higgins: This joint is has a special place in my heart. One of my first assignments on *DDD* in mid-2007 was to find a burger dive in the Twin Cities area, which just so happens to be my hometown. I took this assignment to heart and visited the Nook one night for a Juicy Lucy (St. Paul's iconic stuffed burger) and realized that a dude from my elementary school was one of the owners.

Liz "Erd" Pollock: People always ask me, what's Guy like? Well, here's a perfect example. He returns to shoot another round of *DDD* in Minnesota. The schedule is *tight* and *hectic* for him per usual, but he insists on fitting in an on-camera visit to the Nook to congratulate them on rebuilding after the fire that could have ended the Nook forever. Never question it—Guy cares about every location we shoot at, sincerely and deeply.

Ryan "Donny" Larson: I've had many different burgers on the road shooting camera for *DDD*. As a native of Minneapolis, I can tell you in my opinion, the Nook has the best burger in the whole country. Period.

LIVE CAM: MIKE AND TED ENJOY WATCHING ME STUFF MY FACE WITH THEIR STUFFED BURGER.

TRIPLE B BURGER (BOURBON BACON BURGER)

ADAPTED FROM A RECIPE COURTESY OF CASPER'S & RUNYON'S NOOK

Serves 6

2 pounds USDA choice Angus ground chuck

Salt, pepper, and garlic salt

12 slices thick-cut smokehouse bacon, cooked until crispy

6 thick slices smoked cheddar cheese

6 fresh bakery buns, toasted and buttered

Sweet Bourbon Sauce (recipe follows)

LIVE CAM: TED AND MIKE WITH FORMER OWNER AND MENTOR MICKEY BRAUNSEN.

1. Preheat a grill or a griddle over medium-high heat.

2. Make six ⅓-pound burger patties. Lightly season the patties with salt, pepper, and garlic salt.

3. Grill the patties to medium, 2 to 3 minutes per side. Add 2 strips of bacon to each patty. Melt a thick slice of smoked cheddar over each bacon burger.

4. Place the burgers between the buns, drizzling a generous amount of bourbon sauce on each burger.

SWEET BOURBON SAUCE

Makes 3 to 4 cups

Dry mixture
¼ cup cornstarch
¼ cup powdered sugar
⅛ teaspoon cayenne pepper
⅛ teaspoon salt
⅛ teaspoon ground black pepper

Wet mixture
¾ cup bourbon
2 tablespoons soy sauce
2 tablespoons Worcestershire sauce
2 tablespoons pure maple syrup
⅓ cup sesame oil
2½ tablespoons balsamic vinegar
1 teaspoon Dijon mustard
1 teaspoon minced garlic
1 teaspoon minced onion
1½ teaspoons Tabasco sauce
½ cup packed brown sugar
½ cup granulated sugar

1. In a bowl, mix together all the dry mixture ingredients.

2. In a large sauté pan over low heat, combine all the wet ingredients with 1 cup water. Bring to a simmer and slowly add the dry mixture to the wet, whisking vigorously as you go. When the mixture is well combined, cook for 1 minute more and turn off the heat.

MIDWEST

NYE'S POLONAISE ROOM

POLKA, PRIME RIB, AND PIEROGIES . . .

Some of the Krew members who helped develop *DDD*, the dudes from Match/Cut Productions, are Minneapolis residents. So whenever we'd go into town for meetings or to shoot some episodes of *Triple D*, one way or another, at some time or another, we'd end up at Nye's—to lay witness to the world's most dangerous polka band. (RIP Ruth Adams.) And we were usually there so late at night that we didn't get a chance to try the food. But I was told time and time again how off the hook the pierogis were, or that I had to try the prime rib. Finally we ate there on a break from shooting across the street at Kramarczuk's, and that's when I knew right away that one day *Triple D* would pay Nye's a visit.

Al Nye opened the place in 1950, and it's been a local favorite ever since. Tony Jacob is the current owner and chef Pauly Fohrenkamm is the current pierogi meister, serving up classic Nye's. You can eat this midwestern bar staple in the piano bar listening to songs that grandma used to sing. And that prime rib? It's done right. Nye's is a guaranteed good time.

> ★ TRACK IT DOWN ★
>
> **112 East Hennepin Avenue**
> **Minneapolis, MN 55414**
> **612-379-2021**
> **www.nyespolonaise.com**

NOW THAT DUDE IS ROCKIN' A KEWL GOATEE. (DUDE IS ON THE RIGHT . . .)

KREW NOTES

Neil "Boy Band" Martin: Nye's is special to me for many reasons. My grandmother frequented it when she was in her thirties, and she got very excited when I told her we were going to put it on the show. It was also where my father met Guy for the first time. I introduced the two of them, and my dad left some very heartfelt words with Guy, thanking him for all the opportunities this show has allowed me. To thank us for introducing him to Nye's, Guy asked the whole *Diners* crew to be part of the show! The episode includes us polka dancing and Matt singing at the piano bar. We had our crew wrap party at Nye's and later learned that's when Jeff proposed to his girlfriend. Last, I keep track of all my locations and remember a lot of milestones. Nye's was my two hundredth *Triple D* location.

Kat Higgins: The owner dressed up like Guy for Halloween! It's a special place, and like Neil, it was my two hundredth location since I'd started on the show.

Matt "Beaver" Giovinetti: I'm known on the crew as the karaoke singer. Guy gave me a chance to *shine* in a cameo appearance at this treasured karaoke venue. Funny thing is that we had to use a song that was in the public domain, and the only one Mike the piano player and I could agree on was "Shine On, Harvest Moon." I wanted to rock the house with my old standby, "Copacabana."

 RESTAURANT UPDATE

We still see the *Triple D* crew, and we've sold more of our already popular prime rib and pierogies than ever before!

—TONY JACOB

POTATO AND CHEESE PAN-FRIED PIEROGI

ADAPTED FROM A RECIPE COURTESY OF PAULY FOHRENKAMM, NYE'S POLONAISE ROOM

Serves 8 to 10 (Makes 48 pierogis)

Mashed potato filling

1 pound unpeeled red potatoes

Kosher salt

4 tablespoons unsalted butter

¼ cup cream cheese

3 tablespoons sour cream

½ tablespoon granulated garlic

¼ teaspoon onion powder

¼ teaspoon ground black pepper

¼ teaspoon ground white pepper

8 ounces soft European farmer's cheese

Milk, to thin, if needed

Pierogi dough

2 pounds all-purpose flour

½ tablespoon olive oil

1 large egg

½ teaspoon kosher salt

1¾ cups warm water (110°F)

Nonstick cooking spray

To serve

½ cup olive oil

1 medium sautéed julienned yellow onion

Sour cream

2 tablespoons unsalted butter, preferably clarified butter, melted

1 teaspoon chopped fresh parsley

1. FOR THE MASHED POTATO FILLING: Boil the potatoes in a large saucepan filled with water and 2 tablespoons salt. When the potatoes are soft, 20 to 25 minutes, drain off the water and place the potatoes in a mixer bowl with the dough hook or paddle attachment. Add the butter right away so it will start to melt. Add the cream cheese, sour cream, granulated garlic, onion powder, and black and white pepper and mix on medium speed until smooth and free of all lumps. Add the farmer's cheese and mix on high speed for a couple minutes, until a little fluffy. Loosen with milk if it's too thick and dense to create a slightly fluffy consistency. Season with salt. Remove from mixer and reserve, covered, in the refrigerator.

2. FOR THE PIEROGI DOUGH: In the bowl of a stand mixer fitted with a dough hook, combine the flour, olive oil, egg, salt, and 1¼ cups of the warm water. Start the mixer on low speed for a minute, then switch to high for another couple of minutes, until the dough pulls away from the bowl. Turn the mixer speed down to medium and slowly add the remaining ½ cup warm water. When the water is absorbed, return the mixer to high speed and beat the dough for 10 minutes until smooth and firm.

3. Remove from the bowl. Cut the dough into 4 pieces. Form into balls, spray with nonstick cooking spray, wrap in plastic wrap, and let rest in a warm area for 20 minutes.

4. Spray the counter or a large cutting board with nonstick cooking spray and roll one of the balls of dough to a consistent thickness of between ⅛ and ¼ inch. Spray the dough with nonstick cooking spray. (If it gets too thin, that's okay, as you can gather the dough and roll out again.) Using a 3-inch circle cutter, press down hard and give a slight twist to completely separate the dough circle from the rest of the dough. Repeat to cut more circles with the rest of the dough balls, using the scraps as you go. Just gather and re-roll.

5. Flip the circle cut-outs to the other side; they are ready to be stuffed.

6. Line a baking sheet with parchment paper and spray with nonstick cooking spray (so the delicate dough doesn't stick). Place about 1 teaspoon of the potato and cheese filling in the center of each piece of dough. (Use a bamboo skewer or large toothpick to remove the filling from the spoon to keep your hands clean.) Pick up each pierogi with two hands and fold the dough over the filling. Slightly pull out both sides at the base of the fold, then continue to pull, then pinch, and form and seal as you continue around the half moon. Doublecheck for any areas that aren't smooth or completely sealed. Repeat to make the rest of the pierogies, placing them on the prepared baking sheet as you go.

7. In a large saucepan, bring 12 cups water and 1 tablespoon kosher salt to a rapid boil. One by one, drop in the pierogis. Par-boil them until they float, about 5 minutes. Place them back on the baking sheet to let cool.

8. TO SERVE: Cover the bottom of a sauté pan with the olive oil and place over medium-high heat. Add the pierogis and pan-fry, working in batches; they should sizzle once they hit the oil. After a minute or so, flip them, looking for a golden brown color. Plate with the sautéed onions and a side of sour cream for dipping. Drizzle with butter and sprinkle with parsley.

PIZZERIA LOLA

THE PIZZA PRINCESS SERVES UP OFF-THE-HOOK PIES

I've been hypnotized by pizza—sucked into the vortex of the high-temperature oven, mesmerized by the culinary wizardry of Ann, the pizza princess, and duped by the doctor of extreme ingestion, my brother from another mother, Andrew Zimmern. Now, just so you understand, this is just my weak attempt at creating sorry excuses as to why and how I ended up eating a pizza with a raw egg on top. OMG, what was I thinking? It goes against everything I've ever said! And you want to know another sad fact? It was actually really good.

They've got a copper-covered, French-made Le Panyol pizza oven here, and chef Ann Kim knows what she's doing with it, serving up all sorts of creative nine-inch pies. It all starts with her forty-eight-hour dough, and she prepares house-made fennel sausage using heirloom pork and serves it on a pepperoni pizza. But she also does a pizza with homemade kimchi and house-made Korean sausage with Serrano peppers, scallions, sesame oil, and soy chili glaze. Of all the joints we've tried, this place is right up there.

> ★ TRACK IT DOWN ★
>
> **5557 Xerxes Avenue South**
> **Minneapolis, MN 55410**
> **612-424-8338**
> **www.pizzerialola.com**

MY KRYPTONITE.

THIS DUDE IS CRAZY (THE GUY ON THE LEFT, NOT IN THE MIDDLE).

KREW NOTES

Kerry "Gilligan" Johnson: Only Andrew could get Guy to eat eggs!

Jeff "Butterbean" Asell: When Guy flicked a wad of dough onto my bald dome here, I was strangely OK with it. On the *DDD* crew it's just a matter of time before some food gets thrown. We've become quite weary of watching if a little smirk crosses Guy's face, because most often something will be traveling across the room at a high velocity in the very near future. Father Time takes the brunt of this, as he's slow moving and an easy target. Neil had a long period where he couldn't be hit, much like Neo in *The Matrix,* and I remember some accurate fire when he hit my hand, the only exposed target, through a dishwasher at twenty feet. Guy has mad accuracy. At Pizzeria Lola, some poolish (dough starter) was thrown at Josh and splatted onto his forearm. This stuff has the consistency of fluffy marshmallow, with a heavy yeasty smell. Next thing I know the glop of poolish ends up on my bald forehead. Everybody cackled, while I tried to scrape the mess off my face. It looked as if there might have been a loose pigeon in the joint.

 RESTAURANT UPDATE

Since being a part of the *DDD* experience, we've welcomed folks from Alaska to Bali to our little neighborhood spot. We've opened our doors and changed from being just a dinner and weekend hot spot to being open for lunch seven days a week. We're also opening another local pizzeria called Hello Pizza, featuring classic East Coast–style pizzas and slices.

—ANN KIM

PIZZERIA LOLA'S SUNNY-SIDE PIZZA

ADAPTED FROM A RECIPE COURTESY OF ANN KIM, PIZZERIA LOLA

The pizzas at the restaurant are baked in a wood-fired oven at temperatures upward of 900°F. This dough recipe has been adjusted for the home cook to bake successfully out of a conventional oven.

Serves 2

One 9-ounce dough ball (recipe follows)

Semolina flour or cornmeal

3 tablespoons heavy cream

4 tablespoons grated pecorino Romano cheese

½ cup thinly sliced leeks (white and light green parts only)

10 to 12 paper-thin slices of guanciale (or substitute diced pancetta or bacon)

2 tablespoons extra-virgin olive oil

4 large eggs

Freshly ground black pepper

1. Place a baking stone on the middle shelf of the oven and preheat the oven to 500°F (or as hot as the oven can be set) for at least 1 hour.

2. Push out the pizza dough by hand or with a rolling pin until you reach the desired shape for your crust, about 10 to 12 inches if round. Set the rolled dough on a pizza peel dusted with semolina or cornmeal. Spread the cream over the surface of the dough with a spoon or pastry brush, leaving a ¼ inch border. Sprinkle a layer of pecorino, leeks, and guanciale over the pizza. Finish with a drizzle of olive oil.

3. Carefully slide the pizza from the peel directly onto the hot baking stone. Meanwhile, crack 2 eggs into a small ramekin bowl and set aside. After about 3 minutes, when the pizza has set, slowly pull out the middle rack until you have enough room to gently pour the 2 cracked eggs on top of the pizza. Carefully push the rack back to its original position and cook until the egg whites and yolk have set to a sunny-side up consistency. It should take 6 to 8 minutes total bake time, depending on the oven.

4. Remove the finished pizza from the oven and slice through the yolks; the yolks should be runny. Top the pizza with black pepper and serve.

PIZZA DOUGH

Makes about two 9-ounce dough balls

12 ounces (3 cups) bread flour, plus more for dusting
½ ounce instant yeast (2 packets, or 4½ teaspoons)
1 cup cold water
1½ teaspoons sea salt
Olive oil, for greasing the bowl

1. In the bowl of a standing mixer with a dough hook, combine the flour and yeast. Add the water and salt and mix on low speed for 1 to 2 minutes, until combined. Let the dough rest for 15 minutes, then mix again on medium-low speed for 2 minutes, or until the dough no longer sticks to the side of the bowl. The dough should still be tacky to the touch, but not so wet and sticky that it does not hold its shape. If the dough is too dry, slowly add water 1 tablespoon at a time. If it is too wet, gradually mix in flour by the tablespoon until you reach the desired consistency. Do not overmix the dough.

2. Transfer the dough to a well-floured counter and begin to gently roll it into a ball. Place the ball in a large bowl that has been brushed with olive oil, coating the entire ball in oil. Cover the bowl in plastic wrap and let sit at room temperature for 30 minutes. Immediately place the bowl in the refrigerator and let it rest overnight.

3. The next day, remove the dough 1 to 2 hours before you plan on making pizzas. Transfer the dough to a floured counter and divide into 4 equal pieces with a knife or pastry blade. Gently round each piece into dough balls and brush with olive oil. Loosely cover the dough balls with plastic wrap until you are ready to make pizzas. You can keep the extra pizza dough balls in the refrigerator for up to 4 days or freeze them wrapped in wax paper and placed in a freezer bag for up to 2 months.

SMACK SHACK AT THE 1029 BAR

A GOURMET FOOD TRUCK PULLED UP TO A DIVE BAR

Smack Shack has one of the coolest bars and the best people to hang with that I've ever met. Most of the customers come from the greater Minneapolis area, and some of that bunch are the hard-working krew of *Triple D*. The Krew has a track record of taking me to some of the coolest places with the greatest food, and when I was told I was going to go to a Bar 1029 (real catchy name) and eat out of a funky little lunch truck

★ TRACK IT DOWN ★

1029 Marshall Street Northeast
Minneapolis, MN 55413
612-379-4322
the1029bar.com/smack-shack.html

called the Smack Shack, I was game. But did I expect it to go the way it did? No way! The food was outrageous, and I didn't win one time out of a hundred on those damn pull-tabs (see page 124)! (For the uninitiated, they're like a paper version of a slot machine.)

Smack Shack started out as a lobster truck, then chef Josh Thoma joined forces with buddy Troy Olson, owner of the 1029 Bar. They've got some killer lobster mac and cheese and lobster rolls, but Chef Josh's got turf as well as surf. Check out their outrageous low and slow cooked lamb sandwich with saffron and lemon aioli and harissa with fennel seed slaw—served with an au jus. It's the sandwich of sandwiches.

YOU WILL HAVE THE SAME LOOK AFTER EATING CHEF JOSH'S FOOD!

KREW NOTES

Liz "Erd" Pollock: This is what it is all about: A true dive cleverly hiding an *amazing* chef, with me being one of his biggest fans. I worried a bit when Guy was coming—would he love the food as much as I do? I held my breath as he took his first bite . . . then bites . . . then, smiling, Guy said it was one of the best lamb sandwiches he's ever had. Whoo-hoo! Props to Smack Shack. You do not mess around.

Matt "Beaver" Giovinetti: The 1029 Bar is a total neighborhood dive bar with a friendly, diverse crowd, stiff drinks, pull tabs, and karaoke. Ever since chef Josh Thoma and the Smack Shack rolled into the tiny little kitchen, the food has been off da hook. It's a small menu, exceptionally executed, and absolutely the best lobster rolls you'll ever have. Chef Josh Thoma was a champ, and he and Guy had amazing chemistry on camera. Because I want to open my own *DDD*-style joint one day, I volunteer time in the kitchen with chef Josh and his crew to learn the ropes. The Smack Shack and the 1029 Bar are about as DDD as *DDD* gets.

 ## RESTAURANT UPDATE

Things I never knew before *DDD*:

- It's really hard to cook with your left hand: Shooting requires many different angles that make you have to face the camera and occasionally flip, whisk, or add an ingredient with your "off" hand.

- You really get to know the crew on a personal level. I was so much more relaxed shooting with them after a short amount of time. They're all so easy to talk to that you forget about the camera/lights/sound gear and just talk to them like friends.

- Guy is the show: From the first moment *DDD* contacts you, know this. He does everything from choosing the dishes for your episode to setting up shots in the kitchen. He also made me laugh so much during our shoot that my face hurt by the end of the day.

—JOSH THOMA

ROASTED LEG OF LAMB SANDWICH

ADAPTED FROM A RECIPE COURTESY OF JOSH THOMA, SMACK SHACK

Note: As this recipe makes quite a healthy amount, the lamb could be served as a dinner entrée, with the sandwiches made from the leftovers the next day.

Makes 8 sandwiches

¼ cup canola oil

¼ cup chopped fresh rosemary

¼ cup chopped fresh thyme

1 garlic head, peeled and chopped

Kosher salt and freshly-cracked black pepper

1 rolled and tied boneless leg of lamb (about 7 pounds)

1 baguette, split horizontally

Harissa (recipe follows)

Saffron Aioli (recipe follows)

Fennel Seed Slaw (recipe follows)

1. Combine the canola oil, rosemary, thyme, garlic, and some salt and pepper and rub all over the leg of lamb. Wrap and refrigerate overnight.

2. Preheat the oven to 225°F. Roast the lamb in a roasting pan until the internal temperature has reached 135°F (for medium rare), 3 hours and 30 minutes to 4 hours and 30 minutes. Let rest for 20 minutes.

3. Toast the baguette. Slice the lamb and place it on the baguette along with some harissa, saffron aioli, and fennel seed slaw. Cut into 8 portions and serve.

HARISSA

Makes about 4 cups

2½ pounds red Fresno chiles or other hot red chiles, roughly chopped

3 tomatoes, roughly chopped

2 carrots, roughly chopped

2 celery ribs, roughly chopped

3 garlic heads, unpeeled, halved horizontally

¾ cup vegetable oil

1 bunch fresh parsley

2 tablespoons fresh thyme leaves

1 scant teaspoon kosher salt

½ cup tomato paste

1. Preheat the oven to 375°F.

2. Combine the chiles, tomatoes, carrots, celery, garlic, vegetable oil, parsley, thyme, and salt in a large braising pan. Roast for 1 hour, stirring every 10 to 15 minutes. Mix in the tomato paste and 2 cups water and stir. Continue cooking, stirring, until the vegetables are very tender, 3 more hours. Remove from the oven and cool. Pass through a food mill or mesh strainer to remove the garlic skins. The harissa may be divided into ½ cup portions and frozen on a cookie sheet.

MY SPRAY-PAINTED FACE ON A COP CAR DOOR—WOW!

SAFFRON AIOLI

Makes about 2½ cups

2 garlic cloves

1 tablespoon salt

2 large egg yolks

¼ cup Harissa (see above)

¼ cup lemon juice

⅛ cup saffron tea (mix ⅛ teaspoon saffron threads with ¼ cup boiling water,
     steep for 15 minutes, and strain)

2 cups canola oil

Combine the garlic and salt in a food processor and process to form a paste. Add the egg yolks, harissa, lemon juice, and saffron tea and combine. Slowly add the canola oil with the machine running until the oil is emulsified.

COOK'S NOTE: Food Network Kitchens suggest caution in consuming raw and lightly cooked eggs due to the risk of salmonella or other food-borne illness. To reduce this risk, we recommend you use only fresh, properly refrigerated, clean, grade A or AA eggs with intact shells, and avoid contact between the yolks or whites and the shell. For recipes that call for eggs that are raw or under-cooked when the dish is served, use shell eggs that have been treated by pasteurization or another approved method to destroy salmonella.

SMACK SHACK PULL-TAB ATTACK.

FENNEL SEED SLAW

Makes 4 heaping cups

1 tablespoon fennel seeds

½ cup mayonnaise or aioli

½ cabbage head, shredded

½ yellow onion, thinly sliced

¼ cup flat-leaf parsley leaves

3 tablespoons red wine vinegar

1 teaspoon sugar

Kosher salt

1. Toast the fennel seeds in a dry skillet over medium-low heat until fragrant, 3 to 4 minutes, stirring often.

2. Combine the fennel seeds, mayo, cabbage, onion, parsley, vinegar, and sugar. Season with salt. Refrigerate for 15 minutes before serving to meld the flavors.

ALWAYS A PARTY AT 1029. THIS IS MONDAY AT 9:15 A.M. . . .

GRINDER'S PIZZA

COME FOR THE FOOD . . . AND THE ART, AND THE GOOD TIMES

An old auto parts store turned restaurant, run by a transplanted East Coast sculptor. Check your attitude at the door, says owner Stretch, and this place and the food are both off the hook. His pizzas range from classic to chili-tater-tot, his cheese steaks are better than the ones he grew up eating in the Philly area, and his hot wings will put you down for the count. As Stretch says, art, like food and music, crosses all cultural boundaries. So he's got a gallery, a sculpture garden out back, and a music venue. But that's not all—there's the Hungarian Delight on Mondays, when George Detsios, a retired restaurateur and friend of Stretch's shows up to cook up his chicken paprikash. Mark your calendars.

> ★ TRACK IT DOWN ★
>
> 417 East 18th Street
> Kansas City, MO 64108
> 816-472-5454
> www.grinderspizza.com

When I met Stretch it was clear that he was larger than life. I was told he was an artist (I was raised in a really big art community) and a restaurant owner. It's hard to be one, but both? Really hard—a real wow. My doubts were quickly put to rest. Grinders has an open space with an outdoor theater for concerts, and Stretch has a monster warehouse, literally jaw-dropping, featuring his incredible artwork. Standing there talking to him I couldn't help but think, how can you be this good? After we shot the show, I was leaving to go to the American Royale. The name of my competition BBQ team is Motley Cue, so Stretch took my logo, which is tattooed on my arm, and cut it out of metal—then brought it down to my team. We became instant buddies. Then he came out to my birthday with a watermelon catapult . . . that began the crazy life of Stretch and Guy.

When we prepared to do the Guy Fieri Road Show, I asked him if he could construct a twenty-five-gallon margarita machine. He says "I got it" after three minutes, then called me about a month later with the solution. He had a glass milk tube coming from the bottom and two industrial-size garbage disposals, and he built the whole margarita machine on wheels with a foot pedal activator. That thing has been onstage for two Road Shows and has been used at South Beach Wine & Food Festival.

The story of Stretch continued when I started going to military bases to entertain the troops. Stretch, Gorilla, Sarah from Blue Moon, and Panini Pete now call themselves The Mess Lords and travel all over the world doing live cooking shows for the troops.

Stretch loves his friends, enjoys life, makes great food, and is an incredible artist—and you can now catch his new show, *Eating the Enemy*, on Animal Planet. P.S. Now, Stretch, this better make up for your not being in the first two books. Ha ha ha.

★ RESTAURANT UPDATE

Since *DDD* aired, our biz has gone through the roof and Guy and I have become friends. The Grinders Krew rose to the occasion to handle the new flow of customers from around the world. From ocean to ocean to the Far East, Grinders' reputation has been thriving, so we've opened Grinders West at 415 East 18th Street and in spring 2013 will open Grinders Roadhouse. It's been a great ride that I'd do over and over again. Thanks, Guy Ferrari.

—STRETCH

That's funny G.

BENGAL TIGER PIZZA

ADAPTED FROM A RECIPE COURTESY OF STRETCH, GRINDER'S PIZZA

Makes one 18-inch pizza

One 16-ounce pizza dough ball from your local grocery or pizzeria

Pesto (recipe follows)

All-purpose flour, for dusting

About 1 cup shredded mozzarella cheese

About 1 cup shredded provolone cheese

2 cups cooked tandoori chicken

5 ounces fresh crabmeat, picked over for shells

One 4-inch piece heart of palm, thinly sliced

¼ cup finely chopped fresh cilantro leaves

1. Preheat the oven to 500°F. Place a pizza stone on the middle oven rack. Let the dough come to room temperature, about 15 minutes. (Meanwhile, you can make the pesto.)

2. On well-floured surface, roll and stretch the dough into an 18- to 20-inch round. You may need to allow the dough to rest for another 5 minutes after rolling the first time and then roll again to reach that diameter.

3. Place the dough on a well-floured pizza peel and spread with ¼ cup pesto. Top with the cheeses, chicken, crabmeat, and heart of palm.

4. Slide the pizza from the peel to the stone and bake for 8 to 10 minutes, until the crust is golden brown and the cheese is golden. Top the pizza with the cilantro and serve.

PESTO

Makes about 1 cup

Leaves of 1 bunch fresh basil (about 5 ounces)

¼ cup fresh cilantro leaves

2 garlic cloves

Salt and freshly ground black pepper to taste

¾ cup olive oil

Combine all the ingredients in a blender and blend until well combined. Keep any leftovers in the refrigerator for up to 3 days.

STRETCH AND THE PRINCE OF PAPRIKASH.

GEORGE DETSIOS'S CHICKEN PAPRIKASH

ADAPTED FROM A RECIPE COURTESY OF STRETCH, GRINDER'S PIZZA

Serves 6 to 8

½ cup olive oil

3 quarts sliced yellow onion (about 5 large onions or 10 or so medium onions—yeah, it's a lot of onions)

1 cup peeled garlic cloves

1 cup paprika

2 cups tomato juice

4½ pounds bone-in chicken pieces (see Note)

2½ tablespoons salt

Egg noodles or spaetzle, for serving

1. In a Dutch oven over medium heat, heat the olive oil. Add the onions and garlic and cook until very soft and translucent, about 20 minutes.

2. Add the paprika and stir together. Add the tomato juice, chicken, and salt. Cover, bring to a boil, then reduce the heat and simmer for 45 minutes, or until the chicken is tender, stirring occasionally to prevent scorching. Serve with noodles or spaetzle.

COOK'S NOTE: This recipe can be made with skin-off chicken to make it less fatty.

TWENTY-FIVE GALLONS OF FUN.

THE FLAVORTOWN FOUNTAIN OF YOUTH.

BIG MAMA'S KITCHEN AND CATERING

SOUL FOOD IN OMAHA—IT'S ALL RIGHT EAR, RIGHT NOW

At Big Mama's Kitchen it's all right ear, right now . . . or it coulda been the left ear. What a crazy place with true Southern specialties, and then some. Collard greens, sweet potatoes, oven-fried chicken, and then a spicy little wonder called the Afro Burger. People say you can taste the love in the food when Patricia Barron (Big Mama) cooks. She's bringing everybody to the family table. It's the kind of food she grew up on, but what about that Afro Burger? She picked up that idea during a church mission to Africa. It's spicy, a little sweet, and made with Angus beef.

But one of the most talked about bites, seen across the world, is the floppy wonder (can you "ear" what I'm sayin'?): the pig ear sandwich. I thought I was gonna die, but I gotta tell ya, it wasn't as bad as you might think. Next time you're in Omaha, stop by and say hi to Big Mama.

> ★ TRACK IT DOWN ★
>
> **Big Mama's**
> **3223 North 45th Street**
> **Omaha, NE 68104**
> — and —
> **Big Mama's Sandwich Shop**
> **2416 Lake Street**
> **Omaha, NE 68111**
> **402-455-6262**
> **www.bigmamaskitchen.com**

KREW NOTES

Neil "Boy Band" Martin: Big Mama's kitchen was quite the find for *Triple D.* Soul food found in the middle of the Midwest, and since that's where I'm from, I was ready. It was my first time experiencing soul food on the show, and there we were, standing in an old cafeteria in the middle of Omaha. One of the featured dishes at Big Mama's was the pig ear sandwich. I am usually open to trying new things, but this kinda freaked me out (we had to pull the hairs out of the ear before boiling it in a slow cooker for service).

Tasting the ear wasn't the worst thing. We sometimes like to play "hide the meat" with members of the crew in their gear bags. In between scenes, someone managed to walk away with one of the raw ears and crammed it into the bottom of Matt's backpack. We continued shooting, and seven hours later we wrapped for the night and noticed a very distinct odor coming from our gear. Matt went on a mission to find the putrid scent, and upon opening the zipper of his bag was blasted by the smell of lukewarm pig ear, which is similar to week-old gym socks. Fortunately for us, the smell lasted for weeks.

RESTAURANT UPDATE

We can't begin to tell you what your show has done for our restaurant. When Guy came in 2008 we'd only been open a few months, and very few people had heard of us. Big Mama and her staff have put their heart, soul, and most of Big Mama's retirement money into this restaurant. Being on the show has brought customers from not only Omaha and the surrounding communities but from all over the world: Canada, Australia, the United Kingdom, and many other countries.

We're now in our fifth year, and we sell our cornbread mix, relishes, and jams in about eight local grocery stores and in the restaurant. We have merchandise customers can buy with the Big Mama's logo, including T-shirts and aprons. We're so honored to have been on the show. You have no idea how many lives have been changed.

So much has happened since Guy came and filmed. Big Mama lost her mother in 2008, her youngest daughter in 2009, and her beloved husband in 2011. But through all of the loss and hardship she never stopped working and never closed the restaurant—we just kept going because we knew we had a unique, great-tasting product. (Not to mention that Big Mama loves to cook and feed people.) It took her some time getting used to people asking to take her picture—she's somewhat of a celebrity.

We're opening up Big Mama's Sandwich Shop at 2416 Lake Street, in a building that's being repurposed by a local artist community here in Omaha. We're also in negotiations to move the restaurant to a new location. The old building is unique but very hard to find, and we didn't get any foot traffic. We've always known that if we were more centrally located we'd get more business.

—GLADYS HARRISON, GENERAL MANAGER

PIG EAR SANDWICHES WITH PICKLED ONIONS

ADAPTED FROM A RECIPE COURTESY OF GRANDMOTHER LILLIE GLEASON
AND PATRICIA BARRON CHEF/OWNER, BIG MAMA'S KITCHEN

Makes 4 sandwiches

4 fresh pig ears, washed and trimmed

1 tablespoon kosher salt

1 tablespoon No-Salt Seasoning

1 tablespoon lemon pepper

1 teaspoon minced garlic

1 cup apple cider vinegar

4 hamburger buns

Pickled Onions (recipe follows)

Yellow mustard

1. Trim any hairs from the ears and wash them thoroughly. Place in a slow cooker. Add the seasonings, garlic, and vinegar. Fill the slow cooker with water. Cook on high for 7 to 9 hours—do not undercook the ears. They'll be tender when ready. Remove the ears from the slow cooker and set aside on a towel to drain.

2. Serve on a toasted bun with as many pickled onions and as much yellow mustard as you like.

GUY ASIDE

The pig ear sandwich has a unique texture. If you prefer a crispy pig ear, follow these steps: After slow cooking, remove from the slow cooker and drain on a dry cloth. Heat oil for frying in a large Dutch oven to 350°F. Dredge in flour, egg, and panko breadcrumbs and fry the ears for about 10 minutes, flipping after 5 minutes, until golden brown.

PICKLED ONIONS

Makes 1 quart

1 cup red wine vinegar

2 tablespoons sugar

1 teaspoon mustard seeds

1 teaspoon kosher salt

1 medium red onion, thinly sliced

2 dashes of ground allspice

Special equipment: 1-quart mason jar

In a large saucepan, combine the vinegar, sugar, mustard seeds, and salt. Bring to a boil over low heat, stirring until the sugar and salt are dissolved. Cool the mixture for 10 minutes. Add the onion and allspice. Pour into the mason jar, let cool, and refrigerate overnight before using.

THAT WOULD BE A PIG'S EAR! A MOMENT I'LL NEVER FORGET.

MELT BAR AND GRILLED

HOME OF THE PARMAGEDDON

To say that a grilled cheese is just a grilled cheese would be like telling Fab Hot Dog that a hot dog is just a hot dog, or telling Panini Pete that a beignet is just fried dough. At Melt, oh, there's bread and there's cheese but what this crazy chef puts in between may blow your mind—hence, the Parmageddon. There's pierogi, kraut, and sharp cheddar, and then it goes into the meltification machine—it's outta bounds and so much more than a grilled cheese sandwich. Chef Matt Fish wanted to put what you get at a four-star restaurant into a form that everybody is used to. He does grilled cheese more than thirty ways. His Tokyo tuna melt sandwich uses sushi-grade tuna with a killer wasabi ginger dressing. Or how about peanut butter banana cream cheese? Or jalapeño popper grilled cheese?

Sidenote: You know the old saying, "If Mama ain't happy, ain't nobody happy?" Well, I got one right behind that: "When Aunt Polly ain't happy, ain't nobody happy." And when Aunt Polly says you gotta go to Melt, you go to Melt.

> ★ TRACK IT DOWN ★
>
> **14718 Detroit Avenue**
> **Lakewood, OH 44107**
> **216-226-3699**
> **www.meltbarandgrilled.com**

AUNT POLLY WAS HAPPY, SO WE WERE ALL HAPPY.

KREW NOTES

Matt "Beaver" Giovinetti: Grilled cheese goes super-gourmet! Chef Matt is doing things with grilled cheese that most people never dream of. Guy's Aunt Polly joined the shoot, and we love Aunt Polly—that fiery redhead!

Neil "Boy Band" Martin: Guy really keeps his crew on their toes; it's something he's known for. If someone isn't paying attention, they're likely to get whacked by whatever piece of food is nearby. Usually Mike Morris is the target of the food brigade, but I've had a fair share of raw ingredients thrown my way. In Cleveland Guy was determined to get me. At our first location, he tossed a berry at me, but I saw it coming and ducked to avoid it. At the second location, he tried to be sneaky with a piece of raw dough, and once again I ducked and he missed.

Melt Bar and Grilled was the third location of the shoot pod. I take a lot of photos while on set, and at some point the setting on my camera slipped into automatic and the flash accidentally went off right in the middle of the bite of the Parmageddon he was taking. I instantly knew I was in trouble, and I immediately turned around to adjust my camera settings. Out of the corner of my eye, I could feel Guy staring through me, and I could see him raise his arm to throw. I knew it was coming, and it wasn't just a piece of raw meat, it was the entire sandwich he had in his hand. I ducked again and saw the sandwich explode against the wall in front of me. He'd missed again, and he lost it! He was laughing so hard, no longer mad at me for busting the bite he was taking. It was a great laugh for all of us.

Guy has since changed his technique with me, and now I'm blasted with more raw meat and dough products than I'd like to admit. The moral of the story is, if you are on set, pay attention and don't screw anything up, or something will be thrown at you. Guy has a scope of some sort that gives him amazing accuracy.

THE PARMAGEDDON

ADAPTED FROM A RECIPE COURTESY OF MATT FISH. MELT BAR AND GRILLED

Makes 1 sandwich

1 tablespoon vegetable oil

2 potato-cheddar pierogi (we get them freshly made locally—worth looking for)

Three ¼-inch-thick onion slices, grilled until tender

1 cup shredded Napa cabbage

1 teaspoon Kraut Spice Mix (recipe follows)

¼ cup vodka

¼ cup apple cider vinegar

2 slices artisanal bread, cut 1-inch thick

2 tablespoons unsalted butter

2 slices (4 ounces total) cheddar cheese

1. Heat a sauté pan over high heat for 30 seconds. Add the vegetable oil and heat for 30 seconds. Add the pierogi to the pan, ribbon side up. Cook for about 30 seconds, until browned. Flip the pierogi and brown the opposite side. Flip the pierogi again and add the onions, cabbage, and kraut spice. Cook for 20 seconds. Remove from the heat and add the vodka and vinegar. Return to the heat and cook to reduce until nearly all the liquid is gone, about 4 minutes.

2. Preheat the oven to 350°F.

3. Prep the bread slices by coating each side of each slice with a thin layer of butter. Place the slices of bread on a flat-top grill or sauté pan over medium-high heat. Brown the bread until the butter on top begins to melt. The color should be an even shade of medium toasted brown. Flip the bread and brown the opposite side to medium toasted brown, about 2 minutes.

4. Flip the bread back over and choose which sides have the better, more even browning. Remove the bread with tongs and place open-face on a small baking sheet, with the more evenly browned sides facedown.

5. Add the cheese slices to the bread, one on each side. Place the pierogi evenly on one slice of the bread. Place the kraut and onion mixture evenly on the other slice of the bread.

6. Place the bread in the oven and bake for 3 minutes, or until the cheese is completely melted.

7. Remove the baking sheet from the oven and close the sandwich. To cut in half, make one straight diagonal cut across the sandwich.

KRAUT SPICE MIX

Makes about 1¼ cups

2 tablespoons kosher salt

2 tablespoons ground black pepper

¼ cup celery seeds

1 tablespoon ground coriander

¼ cup caraway seeds

1½ teaspoons chili powder

½ cup light brown sugar

Place all the ingredients in a medium bowl and blend with a whisk until well combined. Store in a lidded jar.

THE PARMAGEDDON

2 POTATO & CHEESE PIEROGI
FRESH NAPA VODKA KRAUT
GRILLED ONIONS
SHARP CHEDDAR

ONLY AT
MELT bar & grilled
CLEVELAND, OH
meltbarandgrilled.com
ON THE MENU
everyday

MOMOCHO

HOME OF MOD MEX

Warning: Eric Williams, the owner and chef at Momocho, is culinary crazy. Where's a dude from Erie, Pennsylvania, get off funk-ifying traditional Mexican fare? He's serving six different guacamoles—and one of them contains smoked trout and bacon—and twelve different types of taquitos, with one called the Machaca that's made with brisket rubbed in coffee. The list goes on and on.

I like to check out Mexican food all over the country, and one thing I've learned on *Triple D* is there is good Mexican food, and there is great Mexican food. Chef Williams is doing what he calls Mod Mex to introduce Cleveland to new flavors. I'd say he succeeds—there are about nineteen things going on in my mouth, and that's just from the guacamole. This guy's out of control—and I like it. Brother, come open one in Cali, *please*. Momocho really means crazy ridiculous in Spanish—P.S. come wearing the stretch pants and muumuu, you're gonna need 'em.

> ★ TRACK IT DOWN ★
>
> **1835 Fulton Road**
> **Cleveland, OH 44113**
> **216-694-2122**
> **www.momocho.com**

KREW NOTES

Bryna "The Pirate" Levin: Eric Williams does amazingly creative Mexican with a serious chef's culinary flair. His creative takes on Mexican flavors and ingredients floored us all, including Guy. There was a dish that we weren't cooking on the show, Pork Carnitas, that's a Guy favorite, and Eric wanted him to try it. Guy called it "crazy good" and immediately came up with a new name for it. He enthused that he was flying down the highway to Flavortown for some "Thunder Pork," and he couldn't stop saying the name, giving it an announcer's volume and flair. He tried to convince Eric to change the name from Carnitas to Thunder Pork on the menu. Not sure Eric took him up on it, but it's what we called it from then on.

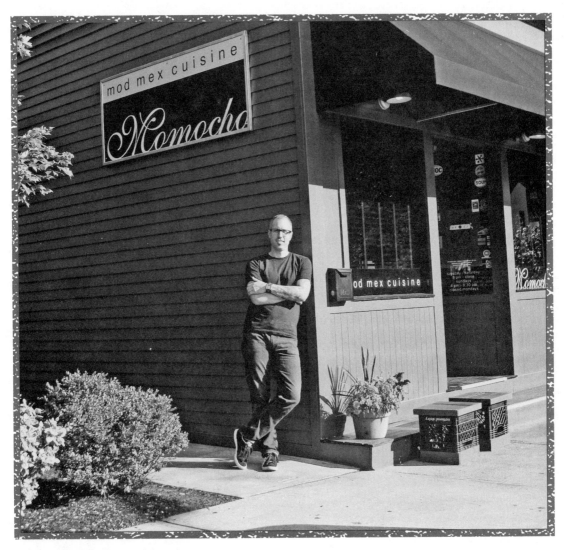

THE MADMAN OF MOD MEX!

 RESTAURANT UPDATE

DDD fans are coming from Texas, New York, Florida, and even Canada to visit Cleveland's Momocho Mod Mex restaurant, and the overwhelming question is, "What did Guy eat?" The Machaca Taquito is now the most popular dish at Momocho, and total sales have increased nearly 40 percent annually since the show aired in March 2010. Viva Momocho!

—ERIC WILLIAMS

BRAISED BEEF BRISKET (MACHACA)

ADAPTED FROM A RECIPE COURTESY OF ERIC WILLIAMS, MOMOCHO

Makes 5 cups shredded beef, about 6 servings

Rub mix

2 tablespoons ground coffee (preferably Guatemalan bean)

¼ cup ancho chile powder

¼ cup kosher salt

One 3½-pound-piece beef brisket (do not trim the fat)

1 cup dry red wine or burgundy wine

¾ cup tomato juice

2 tablespoons lime juice

½ cup red wine vinegar

1 tablespoon ground coffee (preferably Guatemalan bean)

2 tablespoons ancho chile powder

2 tablespoons kosher salt

½ cup chopped garlic

½ tablespoon ground black pepper

½ tablespoon ground cinnamon

2 dried bay leaves

1 large Spanish onion, cut into quarters

For serving: corn or flour tortillas, sautéed peppers and onions, salsa verde, and guacamole

1. Preheat the oven to 300°F.

2. To make the rub mix, combine the ground coffee, ancho powder, and salt. Season the brisket with the rub mix.

3. Preheat a grill or sauté pan over high heat and grill-sear the brisket on both sides for 5 to 7 minutes total to brown and caramelize the outside.

4. Cut the brisket into 4 equal-size pieces and place them in a large braising pan or Dutch oven. Add the remaining ingredients and enough water to cover the brisket. Cover the pan with the lid and roast in the oven for 3 ½ to 4 ½ hours, until the brisket is fork tender and falls apart easily.

5. Discard the onion and bay leaves and remove the brisket from the liquid. Reserve the liquid to serve or reheat. Pull or shred the brisket by hand or with kitchen tongs.

6. Serve with corn or flour tortillas, sautéed peppers and onions, and sides of salsa verde and guacamole.

I TRIED TO TRADE HIM STRAIGHT ACROSS—THE '68 FOR THE KILLER LOW-RIDER BIKE—BUT IT WAS A NO-GO!

ROBERTO'S AUTHENTIC MEXICAN FOOD

A FAMILY AFFAIR, FROM GAS STATION TO ANTHEM

Update: This just in—Gotta give you the lowdown on the showdown. This was the first time we shot a *Triple D* joint in a gas station. The menu and the food—I couldn't believe it was coming out of a gas station. As we were putting this book together we did some checking and found out there were some not so favorable comments on the Web for this place, which made no sense—it couldn't be the same spot. Turns out we were right, they've moved on from the gas station and are over in Anthem, Arizona.

Using family recipes from owners Maria Estrada and Roger Amaya, this is home cooking from scratch, from carne asada to tamales and al pastor. For years Roger and Maria lured people away from the pumps with the aromas wafting from their flat top, with great success. But now I hear they've got the space to match the great food out in Anthem. And get this, Maria and Roger

★ TRACK IT DOWN ★

39510 North Daisy Mountain Drive,
Suite 170
Anthem, AZ 85086
623-465-1515
www.robertosaz.com

used to be married—but they're still best friends, their whole family lives near each other, and they run the place as an extended family business. Trust me, the love and respect comes out in the food too.

KREW NOTES

Bryna "The Pirate" Levin: Sometimes Guy likes to challenge himself to try new things, which is a lot easier to do in advance, on paper, before you get into the kitchen. Well, here we made menudo, a soup with beef stomach (tripe) and cow's hooves. Tripe has what most would consider a "difficult" texture. I can't eat it at all—in fact, the sight of it makes me close my eyes. Guy got through the cooking of it, but he really, really, *really* didn't want to taste it. But the cameras were rolling and we were all watching . . . so he did, quickly and in small quantities, immediately followed by a couple of fresh tortillas. All I can say is he was very glad to leave the back kitchen and go up front for some carne asada and al pastor tacos off the grill.

 RESTAURANT UPDATE

Living closer to home and providing more services prompted Roberto's to relocate in May 5, 2009, from the gas station to the heart of Anthem, Arizona. Now we offer fountain drinks, beer, and Maria's homemade margaritas. Plus, as you come in, you can see our open kitchen. We're very grateful to *Diners, Drive-ins and Dives* for having included us in their production.

—ROGER AMAYA

A FLAVORTOWN FLAT TOP.

AL PASTOR

ADAPTED FROM A RECIPE COURTESY OF ROGER AMAYA, ROBERTO'S AUTHENTIC MEXICAN FOOD

We're very proud of our al pastor. The recipe is still being served in our family restaurant in Chihuahua, Mexico, in the same simple manner it's been made since the early 1950s. The traditional way to serve this is with 6-inch soft corn tortillas. They taste much better if you warm your tortillas in the pan before you cook your meat. We love to use just a light topping of pico de gallo, because you really want to taste the flavor of your homemade al pastor.

Serves 4 to 6

3 pounds boneless pork butt

1 tablespoon salt

½ tablespoon granulated garlic

Pinch of ground cumin

1 cup mild chile powder, such as New Mexico chile powder

½ cup white vinegar

2 whole bay leaves

One 8-ounce can medium pineapple chunks, with juices

Fourteen 6-inch corn tortillas

Pico de gallo, for serving

1. Keeping the pork bundled together, cut it into ¼-inch-thick slices, then cut the slices into ¼-inch cubes.

2. In a blender, combine the salt, granulated garlic, cumin, chile powder, vinegar, and bay leaves. Press the liquefy button and blend until the mixture has turned into a paste, about 1 minute.

3. Place the pineapple and juice in a sauté pan over medium heat and cook until the juice reduces to half, about 8 minutes. Let cool.

4. Heat a 12-inch sauté pan over medium heat. Stir in the diced pork, spice mixture, and pineapple and juice and cook for 40 minutes. The marinade and pineapple will break down the proteins, and the tender meat will become very juicy. The meat mixture will transform from a red paste to more of an orange color.

POLICE OFFICERS KNOW GOOD FOOD!

POSING WITH RAW PORK . . . ONLY IN A TRIPLE D BOOK.

JAMIE'S BROADWAY GRILLE

KILLER FOOD, GREAT PEOPLE . . . AND NO SIGN

I lived in Sacramento while attending American River College for a year and thought I had a pretty good awareness of the places to eat. But when I was in the area opening Tex Wasabi's, I headed over to the TV station and wondered how I'd never come across a restaurant across the street from the station called Jamie's. Oh . . . because they *don't have a sign out front*! If you go to the back parking lot facing the freeway you'll see one, but in front it looks like the Moose lodge. Maybe they keep it that way because the place is already packed—and even more packed now. I go back there and have to wait for a table.

This kind of looks like a dive bar from the outside but the prime rib is literally smokin' out back, all is homemade, and all is fresh. Owner Jamie Bunnell started as a soda jerk and fifteen years later opened a place of his own. He learned how to cook through the school of hard knocks. Forget burgers and fries, at his joint he's knocking out Kobe chuck roast and garlic steak sandwiches made with marinated filet mignon. I have nothing to say . . . it's beautiful. What's his secret? Jamie says, "You put some good food in their tummies, throw two cocktails down their throats, and they start to like ya." Crazy how that happens—that's how I got all my buddies.

★ TRACK IT DOWN ★

427 Broadway
Sacramento, CA 95818
916-442-4044
www.jamiesbroadwaygrille.com

KREW NOTES

Neil "Boy Band" Martin: I love Jamie's Broadway Grille! This place is the definition of the show, because it's the kind of place Guy always talks about. Jamie's is a hidden gem. Guy made a big deal about the fact that there wasn't a sign out front, so he found an old unused banner inside and painted a sign for them, then stapled it to the front of the building.

We shot there around Halloween in 2008—that was the year I dressed up as Guy for Halloween, and I had some of my family come visit us on set. I hadn't seen them in a few years, so they must have been curious as to what was going on that compelled me to go full blond as part of my costume that year.

One of the funniest moments in the history of *Triple D* happened here as Guy left us alone for about twenty minutes to make an impromptu visit to the TV show *Sacramento and Company,* which has their studio directly across the street. (See *More Diners, Drive Ins and Dives* for my full account of the story—the video is searchable on the Internet.)

MY TWIN, BOY BAND.

GARLIC STEAK SANDWICHES

ADAPTED FROM A RECIPE COURTESY OF JAMIE BUNNELL, JAMIE'S BROADWAY GRILLE

Makes 12 sandwiches

Garlic marinade

2 cups peeled garlic cloves

About 1 cup extra-virgin olive oil (just enough to cover the garlic cloves)

1 tablespoon kosher salt

1 tablespoon freshly ground black pepper

Steaks

3-pound center-cut filet mignon roast or châteaubriand, cut into 12 steaks, about ½-inch-thick each

Garlic bread

12 bolillo rolls or small French rolls (about 5 x 3 inches)

12 garlic cloves, peeled and minced

1 cup (2 sticks) unsalted butter

Salt and freshly ground black pepper

Optional garnishes

Mayonnaise

Sautéed Vidalia onions or shallots

Cheese: blue, fontina, Swiss, or Monterey Jack

Mushrooms: white button, criemini, chanterelle, or porcini, sliced and sautéed with butter and white wine or vermouth

1. Preheat the oven to 350°F.

2. To make the garlic marinade, place the garlic cloves in a 1-quart ovenproof dish and add enough olive oil to cover. Top with the salt and pepper. Cover with aluminum foil and roast the garlic for 45 to 60 minutes, until it is soft and light brown. Let cool and puree in a food processor or blender; transfer to a container, cover, refrigerate until cold.

YA SEE, GUY . . . LONG BLOND IS WAY BETTER.

3. Place the steaks in a resealable plastic bag and cover with the marinade. Place the bag in a bowl and refrigerate for at least 2 hours or up to overnight.

4. Let the steaks to come to room temperature and discard any extra garlic marinade.

5. Heat a cast-iron or other heavy-bottomed skillet over high heat, or set up a grill over a hot fire. Add the steaks and sear for about 2 minutes on each side, until they are browned and almost charred. (Don't look away!)

6. Cut the rolls or baguette in half.

7. Combine the garlic and butter in a saucepan and cook over medium heat for 5 to 10 minutes, until the garlic is very soft and lightly browned (but not burned). Season with salt and pepper.

8. Heat a large sauté pan or grill over medium heat. Dip the cut surface of the rolls or baguette in the garlic butter and toast in the pan or grill, butter side down, until lightly browned but still soft.

9. Assemble the sandwiches with the steak and whatever garnishes you desire. We like to serve them with homemade fries, potato salad, or a simple tossed green salad.

CAFÉ ROLLE

A TICKET TO LYON, VIA NOCAL

As an exchange student, you gain an appreciation for culture and food. And this place was a full-on flashback to my student days in Chantilly, France. This dude has got the vive la France attitude and passion. What you see on TV is how French the dude is. I can come here and really get my French food fix.

William Rolle grew up in Lyon, where his parents ran the equivalent of a French deli, just like this one. He makes it

> ★ TRACK IT DOWN ★
>
> **5357 H Street**
> **Sacramento, CA 95819**
> **916-455-9140**
> **www.caferolle.com**

THAT'S HOW I ⌃ ROLL.
Café

WILLIAM AT HIS PARENTS' PLACE IN LYON.

all just like his parents did, at a decent price. Fast food the French way means topping salad with quiche Lorraine and always having chicken pâté on the menu. When people ask William what pâté is, he replies, "French meatloaf." That's some meatloaf. He also smokes salmon over hickory, more than sixty pounds a week, just like his dad did. And he serves lentil salad with roasted prawns and a Dijon vinaigrette, croque monsieur with brie on baguettes, and a big side of personality. *I like how he Rolles.* (Couldn't resist.)

Special Note: This is also the location where I got the call from the publisher that the first Triple D book was a number one *New York Times* bestseller.

KREW NOTES

Bryna "The Pirate" Levin: The owner of this tiny French café in Sacramento was the most charming expat Frenchman we've ever shot with. He had a cartoon accent and loved to exclaim and gesticulate in a manner I consider very French. He had a quirky habit: Whenever he stepped into the walk-in refrigerator, a place where he normally had complete privacy, chef William would immediately begin to sing and whistle a French tune, loudly and with great dramatic flair. Well, on this day he was wearing a mike, and it became a running joke to listen to his song every time he had to get something out of the walk-in. The unfortunate thing is that we couldn't include it in the piece, as it was completely charming.

 RESTAURANT UPDATE

Lot of fans have been showing up from England, Canada, and all over the States after the show. Thank you!

—WILLIAM ROLLE

CAFÉ ROLLE CHICKEN GOAT CHEESE PÂTÉ

ADAPTED FROM A RECIPE COURTESY OF WILLIAM ROLLE, CAFÉ ROLLE

Serves 4

¼ cup half-and-half

3 large eggs, whisked

2 ounces sourdough bread, ripped into ½-inch chunks

1 pound boneless, skinless chicken breast

1 teaspoon salt

2 teaspoons ground black pepper

2 teaspoons herbes de Provence

4 ounces soft goat cheese

2 teaspoons minced fresh parsley

Green salad, French baguette, and Dijon mustard, for serving

Special equipment: meat grinder

1. Preheat the oven to 350°F. Line a 9 x 5-inch loaf pan with 2 strips of parchment paper, leaving an overhang of 1 inch on all sides.

2. In a bowl, whisk together the half-and-half and eggs, then soak the sourdough bread in the mixture.

3. Season the chicken breast with the salt, pepper, and herbes de Provence. Place on a nonstick baking sheet and bake in the oven for 15 minutes. (Note: The chicken will *not* be cooked through, but that is correct.) Set aside to cool for 5 minutes.

4. Combine the bread and egg mixture, cooled chicken, goat cheese, and parsley in a meat grinder or food processor. Grind or process until blended all together. If using a food processor, mix in the parsley after all has been combined.

5. Place the chicken mixture in the prepared loaf pan.

6. Bake the pâté for about 40 minutes, until the temperature in the middle reaches 160°F on a meat thermometer.

7. Set the loaf pan on a rack on the countertop to cool completely, then refrigerate for 2 hours to firm up.

8. Slice the pâté and serve it with a green salad, French baguette, and Dijon mustard.

FOOD GADGET ENVY.

BUBBA'S FINE DINER

A SUPER-PREMIUM DINER

Like I've told you, rule 206 of the *Triple D* code: You can never judge a menu by the joint's name. This "super premium diner," as some guests call it, is knockin' out traditional diner food with classically trained flair. Just as I said on the show, the ahi pot stickers are out of bounds!

Even the basic stuff here, from breakfast to sandwiches, has something special. Try the Crème Brûlée French Toast or the crisp Soft-Shell Crab BLTs with Thai Basil Aioli and Heirloom Tomatoes. They've even got traditional Italian brass dies to make their dough . . . yep, this is not your average diner, it's "super premium."

★ TRACK IT DOWN ★

**566 San Anselmo Avenue
San Anselmo, CA 94960
415-459-6862
www.bubbasfinediner.com**

NEVER JUDGE A JOINT BY ITS NAME—LET'S GO SEE IF THEY SELL SHRIMP. (GET IT? BUBBA GUMP'S . . . HA HA.)

DEEP CULINARY MOMENT!

KREW NOTES

Mike "Father Time" Morris: A classic soda shop straight out of the *Archie* comics. This is where I had to leave the show for a while, to take a job in New York City, and Guy and I took a walk in this small Cali town. I was sad to leave my friends and the show. Thankfully, I was able to come back and join everyone some months later.

 RESTAURANT UPDATE

Bubba's Fine Diner has been cooking up and reinventing the diner classics in Marin for more than twenty-eight years, and now there's a new chef at the helm of this San Anselmo institution. Rene Cage has stepped into the kitchen, bringing with him new favorites like Six-Hour Smoked Barbecue Ribs and Crispy Oven-Fried Chicken. The menu has expanded, edging toward more southern flavors, and the vibe of Bubba's is now a little more "comfortable kitchen" than retro 50s. But the old favorites remain—Ahi Tuna Potstickers, Soft-Shell Crab BLTs, Crème Brûlée French Toast—and the old style of cooking does too. All the food's still made here, still made fresh, and still made from scratch.

—JOHN SARRAN

AHI TUNA POTSTICKERS

ADAPTED FROM A RECIPE COURTESY OF JOHN SARRAN, BUBBA'S FINE DINER

Makes 40 potstickers

½ pound sushi grade ahi tuna

2½ tablespoons minced fresh ginger

½ bunch green onions (white and light green parts), minced

1 large egg white

1 tablespoon sherry

1 tablespoon soy sauce

40 wonton wrappers (see Cook's Note)

Nonstick cooking spray

Soy dipping sauce

¼ cup soy sauce

¼ cup rice wine vinegar

1. To make the filling, place the tuna on a cutting board. Remove the skin, if any, finely chop the fish, and place it in a large bowl. Add the ginger, green onions, egg white, sherry, and soy sauce. Toss to combine, cover, and refrigerate for about 30 minutes.

2. To assemble the potstickers, have a cup of water, the filling, and the wonton wrappers handy. Lay a few wrappers out flat on a countertop. Place about 1 teaspoon of filling into the center of a wrapper. Dip your finger in the water (or use a wet brush) and run your wet finger (or wet brush) along 2 connected edges of the wrapper to create a moist strip. Fold the wrapper over on the diagonal. The 2 moist sides will bond to their dry counterparts to make a nice little triangular pocket. Remember that the water acts like glue. Thus, if wet edges are folded to the dry edges, all is well; otherwise your potstickers will come open. (If you get pulled away in the process of assembling, cover the wrappers with a kitchen towel to keep them moist until you get back.)

3. To give the folded-over wrappers that traditional pleated potsticker look, after you moisten the sides with water, fold them over into 3 or 4 small pleats, then seal the moist pleated edge to the dry side of the potsticker as usual.

4. Put the assembled potstickers on a parchment-lined baking sheet as you finish them, making sure they do not touch each other. If they are left touching, they will stick together, which is bad news because when you go to separate them, you'll have potstickers with holes. This is less of a problem if you use traditional potsticker wrappers, as they are thicker.

5. When all the potstickers are assembled, you can cook them immediately or freeze them for future cooking. We freeze them by the hundreds at the Diner, placing them in airtight containers suited for freezer storage.

6. To cook the potstickers, heat a griddle, wok, or sauté pan over medium-high heat. When hot, cover the bottom with nonstick cooking spray. Put the potstickers in the pan and cover with a tight-fitting lid (or, if you're working on a griddle, use a pan to cover the potstickers).

7. Lift the lid, toss in about ¼ cup water, and quickly close the lid. Let the potstickers steam for about 4 minutes. If you really need to satisfy your curiosity and take a peek, just be sure to add more water. The result should be potstickers with a crispy golden brown bottom and a soft pasta top.

8. To make the soy dipping sauce, combine the soy sauce and rice wine vinegar.

9. We serve them at the Diner on a bed of garlic-sautéed spinach with the soy dipping sauce. (Chopsticks are provided.) I also recommend them with any good commercial spicy chili oil.

COOK'S NOTE: Most markets will carry wonton wrappers, or you could use egg roll skins if you prefer. Some stores even carry potsticker skins. Any trip to a well-stocked Asian market will make the task of obtaining the wrappers easy. We make our own here at Bubba's Fine Diner, but that's another story.

The number of completed potstickers will depend on the size of the wrappers, which in turn will determine the amount of filling you put inside. We use medium wonton skins at Bubba's, and we end up with about 40 potstickers. You might want to enlist some help if you're making a lot of these, as the task goes much more quickly with more hands. Not hard to do, but time-consuming.

SOL FOOD

REAL DEAL PUERTO RICAN IN MARIN

....

You guys are always looking to me for recommendations for the funky joints, the killer food, the funny story, and the interesting characters. Well, what about me? Don't you think I'm looking for that too? So it's great when family and friends come to me with the real-deal places. For this one I gotta give props, all my love, and thanks to my little sister, Morgan. She showed up with a bottle of vinegar hot sauce, but not just a regular bottle—kinda like a funky old Coke bottle with a pepper floating in the vinegar and a wine cork jammed in the top. She said it came from a place called Sol Food. I said, "Soul? Like collard greens and fried chicken?" And she

---

★ TRACK IT DOWN ★
....

**811 4th Street
San Rafael, CA 94901
415-451-4765
www.solfoodrestaurant.com**

FINALLY A REAL PRO ON THE CAMERA . . . TOO BAD THE ROOKIE IS
DOING THE TASTING. HA HA.

LIVE CAM: COOKING WITH SOL.

TO MORGAN, WITH LOVE

The food at Sol was outrageous and the experience with my mom, Hunter, Jules, and Morgan was unforgettable, as it was the last time I had Morgan on *Triple D*. Rest in Peace, Bips, namaste. Love, your brother.

said, "No, sol like the sun." Chef and owner Sol Hernandez's father was born in Puerto Rico, and she discovered it for herself when she spent nine months there at the age of twenty. She brought her passion for her heritage here, to Northern California. Her picadillo is the bomb, and she makes everything from tostones to mofongo to all kinds of fresh sandwiches—she's got everyone covered. As Sol herself says, coming to her place is the cheapest vacation you'll ever have.

KREW NOTES

Anthony "Chico" Rodriguez: Because I'm Puerto Rican, Guy decided to turn the tables and have me taste some of the food, so he turned the camera on me. I have to say, it was incredible, and the only downside is that it's not down the block from my house.

PICADILLO

ADAPTED FROM A RECIPE COURTESY OF SOL HERNANDEZ, SOL FOOD

Serves 4 to 6

2 tablespoons canola or vegetable oil

½ pound ground beef

⅓ cup recaito (cilantro-based seasoning sauce, Goya carries it)

2 garlic cloves, minced

1 teaspoon salt, or to taste

¼ teaspoon freshly ground black pepper

¾ cup tomato sauce

1 tablespoon dried oregano

½ cup small Spanish olives stuffed with pimento

Sautéed sweet plantains or rice and beans, for serving

Heat the oil in a medium heavy sauté pan or skillet over medium-high heat. Add the ground beef and cook, stirring, for 3 to 5 minutes, until the beef is mostly brown with a few areas of pink. Add the recaito and stir. Lower the heat to medium and add the garlic, salt, and pepper. Stir in the tomato sauce, oregano, and olives and simmer for 10 minutes. Serve with plantains or with rice and beans on the side.

COOK'S NOTE: This recipe may seem a bit salty for some palates, but when paired with the sweet plantains it balances well. If you don't serve it with plantains, you may want to adjust the amount of salt.

THAT BEAUTIFUL REDHEAD BEHIND ME IS MY WONDERFUL LITTLE SISTER, MORGAN.

WOW, TIME FLIES—THAT'S HUNTER TO THE LEFT, THEN MORGAN'S SON, JULES, WITH MORGAN HOLDING COURT. SO MISSED!

ROCCO'S CAFÉ

COME FOR KILLER ITALIAN AND THE DOUBLE D SHOW

In San Fran there are a lot of Italian restaurants owned by a lot of characters. One of my favorites is Rocco's. The food is legit, but it's more than just that. Owner Don Dial (Double D) and his team really give you an experience. I send people in there all the time and he treats them like family.

Rocco was Double D's grandfather, who ran his own joint for thirty years. Don's going on twenty years himself, and he's keeping some of Grandpa's favorite recipes alive. From the deeply flavored beef Bolognese over polenta to lemony chicken piccata, he's doing it all from scratch. The clams over linguine is a Rocco's fan favorite, and I just had to "borrow" the recipe to make some fans of my own (you can too). This guy is a high-energy machine. Go and check out the Double D show.

★ TRACK IT DOWN ★

1131 Folsom Street
San Francisco, CA 94103
415-554-0522
www.roccoscafe.com

THE KULINARY DRIVE-BY

So I'm walking out of Rocco's and a black van drives by, creeping slowly like the Scooby-Doo wagon, but blacked out. Two dudes with dark sunglasses appear; I freeze. Then they look over at me and say, "Hey, you, Guido!" I look over at them with my heart racing. One of my camera guys is ready to jump on me, 'cause it looks like a full-blown drive-by. All of a sudden one dude says, "Hey, it's me, it's Gorilla." My buddy Gorilla was just going on a vegetable run for his restaurant, Gorilla Barbeque in Pacifica.

Whew!!

KREW NOTES

Neil "Boy Band" Martin: We travel so much for this show that life is bound to happen to us at some point. One thing I'll always remember about Rocco's is that the day before we were to fly out to San Francisco, Matt pulled a muscle in his back and we had to find a replacement camera operator on twelve hours' notice. This was the third year of us doing the show, and the first time something like this had happened. Until this time, only Anthony and Matt had ever shot the show and we were worried about how a new shooter would be and how it would affect the look of the show. So Matt still came out and directed Tony (who we've since become friends with) while sitting in a chair and looking at a giant monitor he had to share with our producer. It was mainly funny to us, because Matt was all drugged up on Midol and we gave him a good deal of grief about his choice of narcotics. I guess it works *great* as a muscle relaxant!

 ## RESTAURANT UPDATE

Being on *Diners, Drive-ins and Dives* certainly helped our business in many ways, and it's very evident each time our episode, "All Over the Map," repeats. It's an amazing show with an amazing following, and I'm grateful that our story, and now recipes, are able to be shared with the rest of the country.

—DON "DOUBLE D" DIAL

IS DOUBLE D ABOUT TO PULL OUT A RABBIT?

Good one.

LINGUINE WITH CLAMS IN WHITE SAUCE

ADAPTED FROM A RECIPE COURTESY OF DON DIAL, ROCCO'S CAFÉ

Serves 4 to 6

2 tablespoons chopped garlic

1 tablespoon olive oil

6 whole fresh clams (preferably Manila)

One 10-ounce can whole baby clams, juice and all (important—not frozen; you need the juice)

¼ cup white wine

Pinch of chopped fresh flat-leaf parsley

1 cup half-and-half

1 teaspoon unsalted butter

1 pound cooked linguine

Add the garlic and olive oil to a sauté pan over high heat. Add the 6 whole fresh clams and the can of whole baby clams, including the juice, the white wine, parsley, half-and-half, and butter and cook, reducing the sauce until slightly thickened, about 10 minutes. Serve over the linguine.

COOK'S NOTE: When boiling water for your pasta, make sure there's plenty of salt in the water. The pasta will then have flavor—no adding of salt to the finished dish needed.

THIS IS OLD SKOOL KULINARY GANGSTA!

DOUBLE D WAS ROWING US ASHORE IN FLAVORTOWN. THE ONLY
WAY TO SHUT THAT MOUTH IS WITH LINGUINE AND CLAMS.

FAB HOT DOGS

LET THE WEENIE WIZARD GO WILD ON YOUR DOGS

When a dude is having hot dogs shipped in from New Jersey, you know they gotta be legit. But he's not letting the wiener do all the work—he's bustin' out some killer sauces, condiments, and accoutrements that would make you think you're in the heart of New York City.

In the world of regional culinary turf wars, Joe Fabrocini has broken a few rules. He's a New Jersey transplant who opened up a hot dog joint outside of Los Angeles. How's he doin'? Deep-fried, wrapped in bacon, and dressed with fresh-made relishes and sauces, these dogs have it going on. He's got the Teriyaki Slaw Dog, the Polish Kansas City Dog, the Texas Burrito Dog, the LA Street Dog . . . and the Bald Eagle Sauce is unreal. With every dog made to order, it's nonstop flavor—fetch this.

★ TRACK IT DOWN ★

**19417 Victory Boulevard
Reseda, CA 91335
818-344-4336
www.fabhotdogs.com**

 RESTAURANT UPDATE

Since taping the show we'ved moved to a bigger location, and we love seeing *DDD* fans that come from all over the country, signing their *DDD* scrapbooks, and taking pictures with them. Thanks, Guy!

—JOE FABROCINI

YA GOTTA DIG A SIGN THAT HAS "RIPPERS" ON IT.

JUST SMILE, HONEY . . . GUY AND THE CAMERA TEAM WILL LEAVE SOON . . . I HOPE . . .

THE RIPPER

ADAPTED FROM A RECIPE COURTESY OF JOE FABROCINI, FAB HOT DOGS

Bald Eagle Relish is traditionally served at Fab's on a hot dog known as the Ripper. It's a dog that's specially made for deep-frying, and it's called the Ripper because the skin rips when you fry it. This dog is native of New Jersey, and a version is also served at Rutt's Hut in Clifton, New Jersey. This beef and pork dog also contains semolina and soy protein, which cooks out of the interior of the dog when it's fried and leaves the inside light and fluffy. It's not available in the retail market, but you may substitute any dog you like. A grilled dog is preferred.

Bald Eagle Relish (recipe follows)

Grilled hot dogs, for serving

Steamed buns, for serving (place them on a wire rack over gently simmering water for a few minutes just before serving)

Make the Bald Eagle Relish the day before you'd like to serve the hot dogs. Serve the relish with grilled dogs on steamed hot dog buns.

FLAVORTOWN MUG SHOTS . . . I THINK I KNOW SOME OF THOSE PEOPLE.

BALD EAGLE RELISH

Serves 24 (1 quart)

4 cups diced shredded cabbage

1 cup diced yellow onion

¼ cup grated carrot

1 tablespoon minced garlic

3 cups dill pickle relish

½ cup chile powder

4 tablespoons ground black pepper

4 tablespoons paprika

2 tablespoons celery salt

3 tablespoons packed brown sugar

¼ cup apple cider vinegar

3 cups brown deli mustard

In a medium bowl, combine all the ingredients except the mustard. Mix in the mustard bit by bit until the ingredients are well coated but not runny. Refrigerate and serve the next day. Store, covered, in the refrigerator for up to 3 weeks.

STARTIN' OFF WITH JUST SIX, HUH? MUST BE HIS FIRST TIME!

LA TEXANITA

SECRET'S OUT—CHECK OUT ONE OF MY HOMETOWN FAVORITES

I've heard from just about everybody, "You took our favorite restaurant, featured it on *Triple D*, and now it's so hard to get in there!" Well, if it makes you feel any better, I've done it to my myself. One of my favorite places in my hometown is La Texanita—it's packed, and understandably so.

Owner Alma Mendez takes care of my family and friends with some of the best Mexican food around. She makes it all from scratch using family recipes. From handmade tortillas to the deceptively simple carne asada tacos, it's just so good. Best taco truck–style tacos you'll ever have, with good reason—she started out with a taco truck. But the posole . . . I gotta say, I even dig the hoof.

P.S.: Alma, the only thing I want from this is to have the posole be available *every day*! (It's so killer.)

★ TRACK IT DOWN ★

**1667 Sebastopol Road
Santa Rosa, CA 95407
707-527-7331
www.latexanita.com**

KREW NOTES

Mike "Father Time" Morris: This is a little family-run joint in Guy's hometown, Santa Rosa, where hardly a word of English is spoken, and where the

IT'S A DISNEY MOVIE . . . LA TEXANITA TACO TWINS.

LIVE CAM: DAD, YOU SURE YOU WANT TO GIVE UP OUR SECRET?

locals go for outstanding Mexican food. The owner had her hair cut just like Guy's (by Guy's hair designer Rel Salon) and she looked just like Guy during the shoot.

Ryan "Donny" Larson: I've only visited here as a patron. I stop in every time I'm in the NoCal area. It's one of my top five favorite Mexican restaurants.

Matt "Beaver" Giovinetti: This place is as authentic Mexican as you can get. It's close to where Guy lives, and he and his Krew eat there all the time. Guy could not believe how simple the steak taco recipe is—he kept expecting more ingredients or a long marinade or something more than onions, steak, lime juice, salt, and pepper, grilled and caramelized to perfection. So good!

RESTAURANT UPDATE

We continue to do what we do best. Although we're busier than ever, we've changed very little in recent years. Customers return many times to enjoy the consistently delicious food and the great feelings about the place. It's simple , but we continue to do our best. Fresh, authentic Mexican family food with plenty of variety and happily served as if you were a guest in a home. There's no need to change the recipe for the best handmade tortillas, so we don't. One little secret—we've added a wonderful new dish. It's Cochinita Pibil, a deeply marinated pork roasted in banana leaves, served with pickled red onions and habanero chiles. You'll like it with rice and beans or in a taco!

—ALMA MENDEZ

POSOLE DE LA TEXANITA

ADAPTED FROM A RECIPE COURTESY OF ALMA MENDEZ, LA TEXANITA

There are several cuts of fresh pork used in this traditional holiday or weekend dish. You may need to visit a Latin or Mexican butcher if you want the most authentic flavors, as you'll need the butcher to cut the pieces with bones as well. This is an important heritage dish that is served on special occasions, and a large family or small crowd usually consumes the entire pot of posole. Thus, the number of servings for this recipe is rather large. Posole is served in big individual bowls and is accompanied by flavor-boosting garnishes that are arranged on large platters on the table. The corn tortilla tostadas are served whole, then you break them into pieces as you eat.

Serves 10

3 pounds pork butt, cut into 3- to 4-inch chunks

1½ pounds pork backbone, cut into 3-inch pieces with bones (Spanish = *espinazo*)

1½ pounds unsmoked pork hock, cross-cut with bones (Spanish = *chamorro*)

2 pig's feet (about 1½ pounds), each cut into 4 pieces (lengthwise, then crosswise; ask the butcher to do this)

1 whole garlic head (unpeeled is fine)

1 medium white onion, cut in half

1 tablespoon salt

1 gallon water

2 tablespoons chicken consomme powder (such as Knorr Swiss)

About ¾ cup Guajillo Chile Sauce (recipe follows)

Two 14-ounce cans whole hominy, drained and rinsed

Traditional garnishes for serving: crisp corn tostada shells, chopped white onion, lime wedges, sliced radishes, shredded cabbage

Garnishes popular in the United States: cilantro, cubed avocado, grated cheese, homemade Salsa de Chile de Árbol (recipe follows)

1. Wash all the meat thoroughly and cut into uniform 3-inch chunks if necessary. Place the meat, garlic, onion, salt, water, and consommé powder in a large soup pot. Bring to a boil, reduce the heat, and simmer for about 1 hour. Check the meat and continue cooking until the meat is fork tender and the hocks are gelatinous, about 1 hour more.

2. When the meat is completely cooked, add ¾ cup of the guajillo sauce, or more depending on the flavor and heat desired. Simmer for 10 minutes, to reduce slightly.

3. Add the hominy and continue to simmer while the hominy absorbs the flavors, about 30 minutes.

4. Before serving, remove the whole garlic and large pieces of onion. Serve with the garnishes of your choice.

GUAJILLO CHILE SAUCE

Makes about 2 cups

8 ounces dried guajillo chiles, rinsed, stems and seeds removed
1 garlic clove
Salt to taste

1. In a large saucepan, combine the chiles and 2 quarts water, bring to a simmer over high heat, and simmer for 15 minutes, or until the peppers change from a dark to lighter color and become soft. Drain, reserving about 1 cup of the cooking liquid.

2. In a blender, puree the chiles, garlic, salt, and about 1 cup of the cooking liquid on high speed until smooth. (Use just enough of the cooking liquid to make a thin puree.)

SALSA DE CHILE DE ÁRBOL

2 ounces chiles de árbol (not seeded or stemmed)
1 garlic clove, or more to taste
Salt to taste

1. In a hot, flat pan or griddle, toast the chiles on all sides until the color changes and the chiles crumble easily.

2. In a blender, puree the chiles, garlic, salt, and about 1 cup water. You can make the salsa as thin or thick as you like.

MAMBO'S

"THE NOSE KNOWS!"

We find joints on *Triple D* in a lot of cool ways. Fans write in, customers or restaurants write in, friends of friends tell my mother—you name it. But the nose knows when a joint is cooking up the real deal. So I'm sitting at a traffic light on my way to appear on *The Tonight Show with Jay Leno* and a big ole waft of fried pork comes through the window. I immediately pull into the parking lot, despite the risk of being late for the show, and found this joint. I was not disappointed.

★ TRACK IT DOWN ★

**1701 Victory Boulevard
Glendale, CA 91201
818-545-8613
www.mambosla.com**

This is the real Cuban food, made by real Cubans. Owner and chef Raul Gonzalez was taught by his wife how to cook, and he's doing roasted pork three ways, a basic sandwich, a traditional Cuban sandwich, and a roast pork dinner with white rice, plantains, beans, and mojo. He knows the way to my heart. To top it off, Tuesday night is car night, and you should see the wheels parked outside—this place has it going on.

NOW, YOU DON'T NEED THIS TO MAKE YOUR RECIPE, BUT IT SURE DOES HELP. THIS IS THE TOSTONE MAKER THE BOYS FROM MAMBO GAVE ME.

LET ME SHOW YOU MY CUBAN DANCE MOVES.

KREW NOTES

Neil "Boy Band" Martin: I wish there could be a show just about all the funny things that happen while we're shooting. Across the street from the restaurant a crew much larger than ours was shooting an episode of *Law & Order* in a strip mall. People on their set were pointing, trying to catch a glimpse of us and what we were doing. We thought it would be fun to bring out our biggest light to make our set feel like it was a true part of Hollywood. Our lights were nothing compared to those of the crew across the street, but I moved our largest piece of equipment around while Guy read his lines for the stand-up. After the second read, I decided to "bust the scene" and not get out of the way fast enough so I'd be in the shot as he walked by. Guy didn't know I was going to do it, so when I did, without missing a beat, he looked at me and made a big scene about how I mess up every take. I was really hoping it would make the end credits for the show as our "blooper moment," but it didn't.

TOSTONES RELLENOS WITH SHRIMP CEVICHE

ADAPTED FROM A RECIPE COURTESY OF RAUL GONZALEZ, MAMBO'S

Serves 2

4 lemons

3 or 4 garlic cloves, minced

Salt

8 jumbo shrimp, peeled and diced into small cubes

Canola oil, for frying

1 small tomato, diced

½ small red onion, diced

1 cup chopped fresh cilantro

2 green plantains, peeled, each sliced into 6 pieces

1. Squeeze the juice of all 4 lemons into a bowl and add the garlic, season with salt. Add the shrimp and marinate for 1 hour in the refrigerator.

2. In a medium saucepan, heat 2 inches of oil to 375°F.

3. Add the tomatoes, onion, and cilantro to the bowl and let it sit for 5 minutes.

4. Deep-fry the plantain pieces for 3 minutes, or until deep golden brown. Remove them from the oil to drain on paper towels.

5. If you have a *tostonera*, use it to press the plantain pieces into cups. If no *tostonera* is available, allow the plantains to cool slightly, then flatten them with a spatula and shape them into a cup with the back of a spoon or by hand. Refry the plantains for about 2 minutes, until crispy, and season with salt.

6. Remove the juice from the ceviche and season with salt. Stuff the center of the plantain cups with the marinated shrimp ceviche and serve any remaining ceviche alongside.

INSIDE THE MAMBO MANSION.

IT ALREADY FEELS LIKE CUBA.

ALDO'S HARBOR RESTAURANT

WHERE SCRATCH-MADE SEAFOOD STARTS AT THE DOCK

This third-generation-owned seafood joint started as a bait and tackle shop. John Olivieri's grandfather was a fisherman and a baker, and in 1977 he decided to open a restaurant. Sounds like a good recipe for success. These days John's in the kitchen and his dad, Mauro, is up the street running their bakery.

I don't have enough room here to write down how much I dig Aldo's. Do I sit here and write you an essay on the fact that they have their own bakery and make their own bread, their own pasta, and handmade raviolis (using Italian pasta machines) with house-made marinara? Or do I talk about the fresh seafood straight from the boat, cleaned on the pier right in front of the restaurant? It's all complicated by the fact that my palate was funkified by the outrageous, over-the-top cioppino, the rock cod, the shrimp, the mussels, the clams, the crab legs, the fresh calamari . . . oh, and topped off with a generous garnish of fresh lump crab. This joint is a book waiting to happen.

KREW NOTES

Jeff "Butterbean" Asell: Aldo's easily has the freshest calamari I've had.

CIOPPINO-GORGING WITH MAURO.

CIOPPINO

ADAPTED FROM A RECIPE COURTESY OF JOHN OLIVIERI, ALDO'S HARBOR RESTAURANT

Serves 2

Marinara Sauce

1 cup olive oil

¼ cup chopped garlic

2 tablespoons capers

Kosher salt

Two 14-ounce cans whole tomatoes with basil

2 tablespoons chopped fresh oregano

Freshly ground black pepper

Cioppino

2 tablespoons unsalted butter

1 teaspoon chopped garlic

1 to 2 pinches of red chile flakes

Three 4-ounce rock codfish fillets

4 large shrimp, shelled and deveined

5 mussels

4 clams

¼ cup white wine

5 or 6 calamari tubes (5 inches in length), cut into ½-inch rings

1 tablespoon lump crabmeat, for garnish

Grated Parmesan cheese, for garnish

Chopped fresh parsley leaves, for garnish

Fugasa bread or focaccia, for serving

1. To make the marinara sauce, combine the olive oil, garlic, capers, and ¼ teaspoon salt in a small saucepan over low heat, sauté until aromatic, about 5 minutes. In a large saucepan over medium heat, combine the tomatoes and oregano. Season with salt and pepper. Add the garlic mixture, lower the heat, and simmer for 3 hours. Set aside until ready to use.

2. To make the cioppino, in a 10-inch sauté pan, melt the butter over medium heat. Add the garlic and chile flakes and stir to combine, but do not brown the garlic.

3. Raise the heat to high and add the fish fillets, shrimp, mussels, and clams and cook until the mussel and clam shells open, about 5 minutes. Pour in ⅛ cup of the marinara sauce and the white wine. Stir in the calamari and cook for 2 minutes. Make sure the sauce is not too thick or thin—either cook it down a bit or add a bit more sauce if needed.

4. Transfer the cioppino to a large bowl and garnish with the crabmeat, cheese, and parsley. Serve with the bread.

LIVE CAM: THE SUPER SEAFOOD PIER IN FLAVORTOWN.

PIER 23 CAFÉ

WHERE THE CATCH OF THE DAY IS HEADIN' FOR A TACO

Do you have a restaurant in your life that is such a favorite for so long, with so many memories attached to it, that you don't remember exactly when you first went there? That's me and Pier 23. It coulda been before the *world champion* San Francisco Giants game, after a concert, or just hanging out on the pier listening to my buddy Eric Lindell play. But regardless of how I found the place, I finally had

★ TRACK IT DOWN ★

**On the Embarcadero
San Francisco, CA 94111
415-362-5125
www.pier23cafe.com**

THIS PATIO GOES OFF THE HOOK—I THINK THE FOLKS ARE IN A FLAVORTOWN FOOD COMA.

the epiphany to say, wait a second, this place should be on *Triple D*. It's got it all—the food, the music, and the party.

Flicka McGurrin bought the place more than twenty-five years ago because it was just the kinda place she liked to hang out. Same with chef Allan Sproul, so they've kept the good food and good music going. One of my favorite things about living in NoCal is the Dungeness crab, and this place does it right. Go ahead, get messy and make it. Their fish tacos start with a phone call to the fish guys, putting fresh first, then the recipe for the day. He lets the fish do the talking and serves it with fresh corn relish, salsa, and house slaw. Come to Pier 23, this bad boy's all mine. Good times.

CHEF ALLAN WITNESSED
DR. FIERI'S OPERATION.

 RESTAURANT UPDATE

Pier 23 Café has enjoyed national fame since the *Triple D* show aired. We've had hundreds of Guy's fans from all over the country come to visit and check out one of Guy's favorite spots. The whole roasted crab and the fish tacos have been flying out of the kitchen ever since, while folks constantly ask: "What was Guy's favorite dish?" You have to come in and eat to get the answer!

—FLICKA McGURRIN

WHOLE DUNGENESS CRAB

ADAPTED FROM A RECIPE COURTESY OF FLICKA McGURRIN, PIER 23 CAFÉ

Serves 2

1 Dungeness crab

¼ cup olive oil

2 tablespoons chopped garlic

2 tablespoons unsalted butter

2 tablespoons lemon juice

¼ cup white wine

¼ cup chopped fresh parsley

Sourdough bread, for serving

PIERS 22 AND 24 ARE SO JEALOUS!

LET ME COUNT THE WAYS I DIG PIER 23 . . .

1. To cook the crab, bring a large pot of water to a boil. Add the crab and cook for 10 to 12 minutes, until just cooked through. Set aside to cool a bit.

2. Clean and separate the crab by cutting the body in half. Remove the legs and reserve. To remove the outer shell, grab the apron on the underside of the crab and pull away from the crab and separate the carapace from the body with the other hand. Remove the greenish fingerlike gills from both sides of the crab. Pull off any loose webbing or particles. Cut each crab in half again.

3. In a sauté pan, heat the oil over medium-high heat. Add the garlic and cook for 30 seconds, then add the crab and cook for 3 to 5 minutes, stirring occasionally, until the garlic starts to turn golden brown (do not cover). Stir in the butter, lemon juice, and wine and simmer for 2 to 3 minutes. Garnish with the parsley. Serve with the bread.

NORTH END CAFFE

KEEPIN' IT FRESH AND KEEPIN' IT REAL

Chef John Atkinson bought a one-way ticket to Rome to follow his passion for Italian food, then came back to open this joint on one of my favorite beaches in Southern California, Manhattan Beach. So he's got fresh linguine tossed with pecorino-laced carbonara, but he's also got his take on fusion. Check out his Monte Cristo egg roll with kalua pork. That's right, pork cooked in banana leaves with some smoked salt . . . and the whole deal is served with a wasabi mojo and teriyaki sauce. There's money and then there's *bank*—and this qualifies. John totally commits himself, just like his idol Mario Batali.

KREW NOTES

Mike "Father Time" Morris: A little place above the surf of Manhattan Beach, California, with the best egg roll ever. The owner, John, was heavily influenced by Mario Batali—and we called Batali while we were taping.

FESTIVUS MAXIMUS

Every year for the last ten years there's been a celebration in January around *somebody's* birthday called Festivus Maximus. And it involves a good three to five days of poetry, yoga, long walks on the beach. . . . I'm just kidding. It involves friends, family, food, fun, and a little bit of partyin'. Anyhow, since *Triple D* has been on, various buddies from the road have attended the festivities and brought some of their world-class food. Each year it gets bigger and bigger, so special thanks to Niko and Sikey from Voula's, Mike from Hodad's, Luigi from Luigi's Pizzeria, Gorilla from Gorilla Barbeque, Bob from Chaps Pit Beef, and John from North End Caffe. Heck, I don't know if anyone shows up cause it's my birthday anymore. I think they just come for the food.

BRUTHAS FROM ANOTHA MUTHA!

KALUA PIG MONTE CRISTO EGG ROLLS

ADAPTED FROM A RECIPE COURTESY OF JOHN ATKINSON, NORTH END CAFFE

Makes 12 egg rolls

12 traditional egg roll wrappers or 24 lumpia (rice-based) wrappers

¼ cup rice flour

12 thin slices Swiss cheese

12 thin slices Black Forest ham

1½ cups shredded Kalua Pork (recipe follows)

3 cups shredded Napa cabbage

2 large egg whites

1 gallon clean frying oil, such as canola or peanut oil

Baking soda (for fire safety)

Wasabi Mojo (recipe follows)

1. Place an egg roll skin on a clean surface dusted with a small amount of rice flour. Make sure one of the four points is facing you.

2. Center 1 slice of Swiss cheese on the lower half of the wrapper, followed by 1 slice of ham. Place about 2 tablespoons of the pork in the center of the ham. Top with a bit of shredded cabbage.

3. Using a pastry brush, paint a 1-inch border of egg white on the 2 edges of egg roll wrapper facing away from you.

4. Using both hands, roll the corner nearest you over the filling while tucking the outside corners toward the center. Continue rolling until the roll is closed and sealed. Gently firm up the roll, making sure the ends are tightly tucked in (or they will open when frying). (If using a lumpia egg roll wrapper, repeat the rolling process with an additional wrapper so the finished product is two-ply. Lumpia wrappers are thinner than traditional egg roll wrappers and this helps with issues of breakage.)

5. Repeat with the rest of the wrappers and filling, making sure to wipe your working board of any excess egg white as you go, as it is very sticky.

6. Dust the finished egg rolls with a bit of rice flour, cover, and refrigerate for about 30 minutes before frying. Fry them within 24 hours, or freeze them if you like.

7. Heat the frying oil in a deep fryer to 350°F. Or, if you do not have a deep fryer, fill a Dutch oven with 2½ inches of oil (make sure not to fill within 4 inches of the top of the pot). Place the pot over medium-high heat. Test the oil with a little bit of rice flour. If the flour bubbles from the heat, the oil is ready.

8. Place just a few egg rolls in pot at a time, making sure the oil level doesn't get close to the top of pot. Fry the egg rolls, turning often, until golden brown on all sides, about 2 minutes. Place on cooling rack and continue cooking the rest of the egg rolls.

9. Should you have an accidental oil spill or flare up, cover the pot with a lid and turn off the heat source. Cover the fire with a liberal amount of baking soda. Never try to put out an oil fire with water—it is *no bueno*!

10. When the cooked egg rolls are cool enough to touch, cut them on a bias to show the layers of filling and amaze your family and friends! Serve with Wasabi Mojo.

MANHATTAN BEACH KULINARY GANGSTA!

COOK'S NOTE: With leftover pork, make Hawaiian-style "sloppy Joes" by tossing the meat with a little water and teriyaki sauce and warming it on the stovetop or in the microwave. Place on a soft burger bun. Top with Swiss coleslaw made with extra cabbage and wasabi mojo. Now you have two dishes from one shopping trip!

KALUA PORK

Makes 8 cups shredded pork

One 8- to 12-pound pork butt
1 whole banana leaf (available at Asian or Latin markets or online), cut in half
½ cup liquid smoke
⅓ cup salt

1. Preheat the oven to 225°F.

2. Rinse and drain the pork butt and pat it dry. Place half the banana leaf on the bottom of a large baking dish. Place the pork butt in the baking dish and cover it with the liquid smoke.

3. Rub the salt onto one side of the meat. Flip the meat over so the salted side is on the bottom (if the salt comes in contact with the foil while roasting, it will eat it through).

4. Top the pork butt with the remaining banana leaf half. Add 1 cup water to the baking dish and cover it tightly with foil.

5. Roast until the meat is easily shredded with your fingers or a fork, 8 to 12 hours, about 1 hour per pound.

6. Remove the pork from the baking dish, reserving 1 cup of the roasting liquid. Discard the banana leaf, foil, and remaining roasting liquid.

7. Cool the pork slightly, then shred it with your fingers and a fork, removing any large fat deposits and sinewy meat. Toss with a small amount of the reserved baking liquid (it will be salty, so proceed with caution). When the pork is seasoned as you like it, set it aside to cool thoroughly.

WASABI MOJO

Makes a bit more than 1 cup

1 cup mayonnaise (such as Hellmann's)

1 teaspoon minced garlic

2 teaspoons wasabi powder

1 tablespoon toasted sesame oil

2 tablespoons honey

1 teaspoon ground ginger

1 teaspoon lemon juice

1 tablespoon teriyaki sauce

In a small bowl, combine all the ingredients. Cover and let rest in the refrigerator for at least 30 minutes before serving.

YOU SHOULD SEE US DO THE KALUA PORK CANCAN.

CAFÉ CITTI

LOVE THE FOOD AND LOVE THE FAMILY

When I opened my first restaurant, Johnny Garlic's in Santa Rosa, one night I had a late table with this tall guy, his beautiful wife, and their kids. I went out to ask how their meal was—of course he said great—and he told me about a restaurant he owned called Café Citti. We became good buds and helped each other out. I once lent him a dishwasher, and he hosted a couple of my holiday parties. Then one day it dawned on me . . . we have to put Café Citti on

★ TRACK IT DOWN ★

9049 Sonoma Highway
Kenwood, CA 95452
707-833-2690
www.cafecitti.com

Triple D. (Note to self: Way to screw it up again, Guy. As if Café Citti, located in the heart of the wine country, wasn't already busy enough . . . wow, the place is double packed because of *Triple D.* But that doesn't matter—it's still worth the wait.)

Chef Luca Citti, Linda, and the kids make you feel like you're at home, and together they've brought Northern Italy to Northern California—they make the ravioli fresh every day. Luca even picks his own porcini for his off-the-hook porcini polenta.

THE ITALIAN CHEF PAINTS HIS MASTERPIECE ON THE CANVAS OF THE PLATE.

IT'S A FAMILY AFFAIR.

KREW NOTES

Liz "Erd" Pollock: There's nothing like watching Guy connect with another Italian chef. Luca wasn't just Italian; he used old family recipes made from the best ingredients, never wasted anything, and made authentic gourmet Italian affordable to everyone. All things that Guy himself is passionate about. Brother from another mother there.

Matt "Beaver" Giovinetti: This chef is not just a glorified cook. He's an artist taking care with each and every step to each and every dish. Although we eat quite well while we're on location, the family still made the crew a special dinner and treated us like royalty. The homemade ravioli are killer!

 RESTAURANT UPDATE

Being a part of *Diners, Drive-ins and Dives* was a great experience. Guy's support of our little family business put us on the destination map, and we will be eternally grateful!

Since the show aired we've made thousands of raviolis and have gathered many friends and families at the table. You can get that the place will be jumping whenever the show airs, but it's well worth the wait—just ask the locals.

—LINDA CITTI

POLENTA AI FUNGHI PORCINI

ADAPTED FROM A RECIPE COURTESY OF CHEF LUCA CITTI, CAFÉ CITTI

Serves 4 to 6

Polenta

1 tablespoon coarse salt

2½ cups coarse polenta

½ cup (1 stick) unsalted butter

1 cup heavy cream

1 cup grated Parmigiano-Reggiano cheese

Sauce

2 tablespoons unsalted butter

1 tablespoon chopped garlic

½ cup finely chopped fresh porcini mushrooms

Salt and freshly ground black pepper

¼ cup dry Marsala wine

1½ cups heavy cream

1 tablespoon finely chopped fresh flat-leaf parsley

Canola oil, for frying

Shaved Parmigiano-Reggiano cheese, for garnish

1. To make the polenta, bring 8 cups water to a boil in a large heavy saucepan. Add the salt. Let it boil for 2 minutes, then remove the pan from the heat and add the polenta by the handful, whisking constantly. Continue to add the polenta slowly, controlling the flow to a thin stream through your fingers to avoid forming lumps. Return the pan to the stove and bring to a low simmer. Continue cooking for about 40 minutes, stirring constantly. The polenta will be done when it cleanly pulls away from the sides of the pan. Stir in the butter, cream, and cheese. Carefully pour the polenta onto a rimmed 12 x 18-inch baking sheet. Spread it out evenly and let it cool until firm to the touch, about 1 hour and 30 minutes.

2. To make the sauce, in a large sauté pan over high heat, combine the butter, garlic, and mushrooms and sprinkle with salt and pepper. Cook without stirring until the water from the mushrooms has been released and evaporates. Add the Marsala and begin stirring with a wooden spoon. Once the ingredients are incorporated, add the cream, reduce the heat to medium, and continue cooking until the cream is reduced by half and has a thick consistency. Remove from the heat and keep covered. Set aside.

3. Prepare a deep fryer or in a large deep pot, heat about 2 inches of canola oil over high heat to 350°F. Meanwhile, slice the cooled polenta into the desired size and shape. Once the oil has reached frying temperature, add the polenta, in batches, and deep-fry until the edges are golden brown, about 5 minutes.

4. When ready to serve, stir the parsley into the sauce. Arrange the polenta on serving plates and spoon the sauce over the top. Garnish with the shaved cheese. Serve immediately.

THIS JOINT GETS SO PACKED . . . THIS MUST BE A PICTURE AT 7 A.M.

SCHELLVILLE GRILL

SONOMA MEETS TUSCANY

𝑂𝓃 𝒯𝓇𝒾𝓅𝓁𝑒 𝒟 we have met a lot of chefs, some characters, and a few crazies. But at the Schellville Grill we met all three in one: a crazy character who's a chef. Call him Matthew, Matt, Matheo, whatever, but don't call him late for his plane to Italy. He spends his off-season there, cooking his way through the country—and rumor has it he just went to gelato

★ TRACK IT DOWN ★

**22900 Broadway
Sonoma, CA 95476
707-996-5151
www.schellvillegrill.com**

school. Then he comes back to the wine country to serve folks up some of the most real-deal food I've ever had.

Chef Matthew Nagan does Italian classics as well as West Coast favorites like smoked tri-tip sandwich. He uses three different kinds of wood—soaked hickory in water, grapevines off the vineyards, and stays from wine barrels— then throws it together with some fruit-laden barbecue sauce. It's righteous barbecue. Or there's the chipotle, chicken, and mushroom Yahoo Burger—it defies description, but try it; it's the bounty of the county. And his lasagna is a bit of Tuscan Bolognese and grilled veggies meet Roman bechamel meets . . . Matthew. It's just outstanding.

P.S. Thank goodness for Matthew's sister Emily for keeping the place somewhat normal and making killer desserts.

KREW NOTES

Mike "Father Time" Morris: Owner Matthew lives in California part of the year and Tuscany, Italy, the other part. Great lasagna. Told us he had to develop a system to handle all the new business. A great guy.

LIVE CAM: WE MUST BE DISCUSSING SOMETHING REALLY IMPORTANT . . . NEITHER ONE OF US IS LAUGHING, JOKING, OR OUTTA CONTROL. A FIRST!

INDIVIDUAL LASAGNAS

ADAPTED FROM A RECIPE COURTESY OF MATTHEW NAGAN, SCHELLVILLE GRILL

You can use whatever veggies you want in this recipe. Roast them on the grill or in the oven. We use eggplant, zucchini, yellow squash, spinach, and mushrooms. Use your creativity, taking into account where you live and the season. Chef Matt says, "Get jiggy with it, have some fun!"

Makes 10 individual servings

Equipment

Pasta cutter size: 2¾ to 3 inches wide

10 ramekins: 2 to 3 inches high x 3¾ to 4½ inches wide

2 cups spinach, roughly chopped

Olive oil

Kosher salt

3 large portobello mushrooms

1 eggplant, sliced lengthwise into ¼-inch-thick strips

1 zucchini, sliced lengthwise into ¼-inch-thick strips

1 yellow squash, sliced lengthwise into ¼-inch-thick strips

Roasted Tomato Béchamel (recipe follows)

Ragu (recipe follows)

Fresh pasta, cut into thirty 2¾- to 3-inch rounds (recipe follows)

4 cups shredded mozzarella cheese

1. Preheat a grill on high heat.

2. In a medium sauté pan over medium heat, cook the spinach in 1 teaspoon olive oil for 1 to 2 minutes, until wilted. Season with salt. Reserve in a medium bowl.

3. Brush the mushrooms, eggplant, zucchini, and squash with olive oil and season with salt. Grill the vegetables for 2 to 3 minutes per side, until tender. Dice the vegetables; mix the eggplant, zucchini, and squash in a bowl and add the mushrooms to the spinach.

4. Preheat the oven to 350°F.

5. Place the ramekins on a large baking sheet and add 1 tablespoon béchamel to the bottom of each ramekin so the pasta doesn't stick. Then start layering in the vegetables, ragu, cheese, and pasta, dividing the ingredients evenly among the 10 ramekins. Push down on the ingredients as you go. One layering suggestion: béchamel, pasta, squash mixture, ragu, cheese, pasta, béchamel, mushroom-spinach mixture, cheese, pasta, béchamel, squash mixture, pasta, ragu, and top with cheese. However you want to layer it—it's up to you!

6. Bake for about 20 minutes, until the cheese is golden brown and bubbling around the edges.

COOK'S NOTE: The ragu and béchamel can be made a day ahead. The ramekins can be assembled in the morning and baked later in the day. You can start with the ragu first and then work on other recipes while it cooks.

ROASTED TOMATO BÉCHAMEL

Makes 2 to 3 cups

3 Roma tomatoes

½ teaspoon kosher salt, plus more to taste

1 tablespoon olive oil

1½ teaspoons balsamic vinegar

3 tablespoons unsalted butter

3 tablespoons all-purpose flour

2 cups whole milk

⅛ teaspoon ground nutmeg

Freshly ground black pepper

1. Preheat the oven to 450°F.

2. Place the tomatoes on a baking sheet and sprinkle with the salt. Drizzle with the olive oil and vinegar. Roast the tomatoes for 15 minutes, or until slightly charred and soft.

3. Meanwhile, in a saucepan over medium heat, melt the butter, then add the flour and whisk for 2 minutes. Slowly whisk in the milk. Reduce the heat to medium-low and continue to cook for 5 to 7 minutes, whisking often. Do not boil.

4. Puree the tomatoes in a blender and stir them into the béchamel. Season with the nutmeg and salt and pepper to taste.

RAGU

Makes 5 to 6 cups

½ cup olive oil
¾ pound ground beef
¼ pound lean ground pork
1 medium carrot, finely chopped
1 medium red onion, finely chopped
1 celery stalk, finely chopped
1 garlic clove, finely chopped
A handful of fresh parsley, basil, marjoram, thyme, and rosemary, finely chopped
One 28-ounce can diced Roma tomatoes
¼ cup tomato paste
1 beef bouillon cube
1 dried or fresh bay leaf
2 tablespoons cognac
Salt and freshly ground black pepper

1. In a large saucepan over medium-high heat, heat ¼ cup of the olive oil, add the beef and pork and brown for about 5 minutes. Remove with a slotted spoon and reserve. Add the remaining ¼ cup olive oil, the carrot, onion, celery, garlic, and herbs and sauté until the vegetables are soft and golden, about 5 minutes.

2. Return the browned meat to the pan and add the diced tomatoes, tomato paste, bouillon, bay leaf, and cognac. Season with salt and pepper. Reduce the heat to a simmer and cook for at least 2 hours, until thickened.

PASTA

Makes about 40 pasta rounds

4 cups all-purpose flour, plus more for dusting

4 large eggs, lightly beaten

Scant ¼ cup olive oil

1. Place the flour in a stainless-steel bowl and make a well in the center. Drop the eggs, oil, and ¼ cup water into the well and start to mix with your hands. Make sure to keep all your fingers together, like little scoopers; that will keep the dough from getting in between your fingers. When all ingredients are mixed together, drop the dough onto a floured surface and knead for 4 to 5 minutes, until the dough is smooth. Wrap the dough in plastic wrap and let it rest for 30 minutes.

2. Roll the pasta to about ⅛ inch thick and cut it into forty 2¾- to 3-inch rounds.

COOK'S NOTE: You can substitute store-bought fresh pasta or wonton wrappers if you don't have the time to make fresh pasta.

MATTHEW IS ALSO A MAGICIAN FOR LITTLE KIDS'
BIRTHDAY PARTIES . . . NOT REALLY!

PAUL'S COFFEE SHOP

THE SEMPER FINER DINER

The Semper Finer Diner! Man, this joint should serve as a recruiting station for all the branches of the military, because you get a proud mix of veterans and their families enjoying some real-deal diner food and military specialties. And you know this joint is legit and the commitment is there when they're serving SOS on a mess hall metal tray—ooh rah!

This military take on comfort food is served up by former marine Phil Martinez (who bought the place from the original owner, Paul). Veterans get to keep the tray—and he tells them to bring their tray back on Veterans Day to get a free SOS. He's got cheeseburgers, pot roast, and Korean barbecue. Wait, what? That's right. He does a little bit of everything to accommodate the different ethnic communities in the neighborhood. (He got the recipe for the Korean barbecue from his waitress Suzie's mother.) That's hospitality, Marine-style. Thanks for servin' our country, Phil.

> ★ TRACK IT DOWN ★
>
> **16947 Bushard Street**
> **Fountain Valley, CA 92708**
> **714-965-3643**
> **www.semperfinerdiner.com**

THE MILITARY'S CULINARY HEADQUARTERS.

FREEDOM AIN'T FREE

Anybody who knows me knows that I am a huge fan of our armed forces. The commitment made, the effort that's taken, and the risks encountered by the brave men and women of this country are what keeps us a free nation. The families, the children, and the loved ones who participate in supporting our soldiers are amazing. It's an honor as a dad, a chef, and a host of *Triple D* to have so many soldiers and their families comment on the impact *Triple D* makes. We all should serve our country in one form or another, and to think that my cooking or this show could make someone feel better or remind them of good times is amazing. Thank you all so much for the unwavering commitment to keeping our country free. 'Cause as we all know, freedom ain't free.

 RESTAURANT UPDATE

Thanks to *Diners, Drive-ins and Dives*, guests have been pouring in from all over for a taste of Paul's Coffee Shop. Before ordering, most ask, "What did Guy eat?" Thank you, Food Network and Guy Fieri!

—PHIL MARTINEZ

SOS

ADAPTED FROM A RECIPE COURTESY OF PHIL MARTINEZ, PAUL'S COFFEE SHOP

Serves 6 to 8 servings

1½ pounds ground beef

½ cup (1 stick) unsalted butter

1 cup all-purpose flour

½ tablespoon chicken base

½ tablespoon seasoned salt, preferably Lawry's

½ teaspoon granulated garlic

4 cups 2% milk

1 teaspoon ground black pepper

16 slices white bread, toasted

Home fries or hash browns, for serving

1. Brown the ground beef in a large skillet over medium heat for 15 minutes, stirring occasionally. Set aside.

2. Melt the butter in a large saucepan over low heat, being careful not to burn it. Slowly whisk in the flour to make a roux. You're looking for a thick consistency and a blond color to the flour. Add the chicken base, seasoned salt, and granulated garlic. Slowly whisk in the milk. Turn the heat to high and bring to a boil. Let it boil for 2 to 3 minutes, then lower the heat to medium. Simmer for 10 to 15 minutes, until the mixture gets thick, whisking periodically.

3. Whisk in the black pepper and browned beef. Adjust the seasoning if needed.

4. Put the toast on serving plates and ladle the SOS over the top of the toast. Serve with home fries or hash browns.

MAMA COZZA'S

SINCE 1965—OLD-SCHOOL ITALIAN FOR THREE GENERATIONS

When I recommend joints to you, they gotta be the real deal, and when a buddy recommends a joint to me, ohhh boy, they'd better be on point and have it straight. Don't sell me some bag of beans, telling me, "Oh, you went on a bad night" or "That isn't what it used to be." If you're going to send me, it'd better be correct, and my buddy Gary Maggetti told me Mama Cozza's is the joint.

You got it right, Gary. This is the Italian restaurant everybody wants to have down the street. They make the sauce, they make the dough, they make the sausage—this is it. If the walls could talk in Mama Cozza's, OMG would you have a *New York Times* best-seller on your hands.

You'll find serious Italian comfort food at this place, plus a few things you won't find anywhere else. For example, Dick Domery was an old friend of Frank Cozza Jr.'s father, Frank Sr. One day he came in and said he was tired of red clam sauce and asked them to throw in some sausage and extra garlic. So Frank Jr. said okay, and Domery Sauce was born. It's some of the best clam sauce I've ever had. But there are twenty scratch-made sauces, and they'll still

> ★ TRACK IT DOWN ★
>
> **2170 West Ball Road**
> **Anaheim, CA 92804**
> **714-635-0063**
> **www.mamacozzas.com**

THE MAGGETTI MEN HOLDING COURT AT MAMA COZZA'S.

do anything you'd like. You never know, it might just end up on the menu. This is a joint where friends of friends meet friends. When you go in there, without question, you gotta try the Domery Sauce. PS—Tell Senior I said what's up . . . What a great dude.

KREW NOTES

Neil "Boy Band" Martin: The two common things that appear in each segment of the show are Guy and the '68 Camaro. People drive by, see the car, and know that we're there. People just love that car, and a lot of times if they can't get a picture with Guy, they'll stand next to the car and grab a photo.

FRANK SR.: SON, WHAT IN HECK ARE YOU TALKING ABOUT? OF COURSE I KNOW WHERE FLAVORTOWN IS.

A new precedent was set for us at Momma Cozza's when people got a little out of control. We did our scene with the car out front, then came inside to wrap out the shoot with customers and owners. After that, Guy was done for the day. There had to have been seventy people out front waiting to get a picture or an autograph, and unfortunately, there isn't enough time for it all when Guy has a schedule to keep. He drove away, and as I went back inside to help move lights around for the remainder of the shoot, I felt my phone ringing in my pocket. Guy was calling, and he wasn't happy. He wanted to know where Fraggle was, and when I said I didn't know, he told me to get outside right away and kick all those people out of the Camaro. My jaw dropped when I walked out the door to find ten people *inside* the Camaro (which seats four) and another fifteen standing around it waiting to get in. It was hard to maintain my cool as I told people picture time was over and everyone needed to get out of the car immediately. Now the car gets packed in its trailer the minute we're done shooting with it.

 ## GUY ASIDE: THE DOCTOR WAS IN

One night I was at Mama Cozza's having dinner with my family, and I'd really not been feeling well all week. Frank Sr. noticed how sick I was and got concerned. Turns out he's great friends with the internist for two Anaheim sports teams, the Angels and the Ducks. So one of his daughters-in-law drove me to this doctor's office at 11 pm, where he met me, gave me a shot and medicine—and I was better the next day. We call that kulinary gangsta alla Mama Cozza!

MAMA COZZA'S PASTA WITH DOMERY SAUCE

ADAPTED FROM A RECIPE COURTESY OF MAMA COZZA'S

Serves 4

Salt
½ pound Italian sausage, casings removed
2 tablespoons olive oil
½ teaspoon dried basil
½ teaspoon dried oregano
2 tablespoons finely chopped garlic (from about 3 cloves)
Freshly ground black pepper
One 14-ounce can baby clams in juice (or, if available, fresh clams with 1 cup clam juice)
32 ounces your favorite spaghetti sauce
1 pound your favorite pasta

1. Bring a large pot of salted water to a boil for the pasta.

2. In a 14-inch sauté pan over medium heat, brown the sausage in the olive oil, breaking it up into bite-size crumbles, about 5 minutes. Discard the oil from the pan. Add the basil, oregano, garlic, and a couple shakes of black pepper. Give a quick stir and cook for 2 minutes more. Add the clams, clam juice, and spaghetti sauce and bring the mixture to a simmer. Turn off the heat.

3. Cook the pasta as directed on the package. Add it to the Domery Sauce and serve.

CATELLI'S

THE THIRD GENERATION'S STILL ROCKIN' RAVIOLI

I said it all in the introduction of the show—besides my own kids, nothing makes me more proud than to see one of the guys that I worked with and helped develop move on to open his own restaurant. And in this case, not just his own restaurant but a killer Italian restaurant that keeps his family legacy alive. Nick and his sister chef Domenica are rockin' the house with some of the best meatballs you'll ever try and handmade ravioli that'll knock you off your feet.

★ TRACK IT DOWN ★

**21047 Geyserville Avenue
Geyserville, CA 95441
707-857-3471
www.mycatellis.com**

BUSINESS IS SO GOOD THAT THIS IS NICK'S NEW HOT ROD.

When Nick Catelli got his first job with me at Johnny Garlic's he was a dishwasher—but not a very good one. His productivity was so low that I was going to have to relieve him of his position. So, as I sat there explaining this to him, he responded with, "You want me to wash the dishes faster? Oh, that's how I did it when I worked for my dad. Give me a second chance." He went downstairs that afternoon and did the work of two men and never stopped. Then he became a prep cook, a line cook, a waiter, a bartender, a kitchen manager, and a dining room manager. Congratulations, Nick—you did it!

LIVE CAM: NICK SERVES IT UP TO HIS FAMILY.

Nick and Domenica's grandparents opened this place in 1935. The family lost the business in 1991, but the brother and sister resolved to reopen it one day. Domenica calls it Italian-influenced California cooking, but I just call it time to mangia.

KREW NOTES

Neil "Boy Band" Martin: At the end of the day of taping, since Nicholas was living upstairs above the kitchen, Guy thought it would be hilarious to put our stencil on the ceiling right above his bed. Guy tagged it, and then asked me to tell Nicholas that he wanted to run tape on something we "forgot to cover." So Guy had Nicholas give us a tour like it was *MTV Cribs.* When Guy asked him to take us into his room, Nicholas looked uncomfortable but did it anyway, showing us around without noticing the bright yellow caricature of Guy's head right above his bed. After about a minute, Guy finally pointed it out to him. We flipped on the lights, and all Nicholas could do was smile and say, "Nice . . ." I only wonder if Guy's smiling face is still looking down at him every night.

JACK'S MEATBALL SLIDERS

ADAPTED FROM A RECIPE COURTESY OF DOMENICA CATELLI, CATELLI'S

This recipe was named for Jack Monroe of Covelo, California, who raises the organic beef that is used in the beef sliders.

Makes about 33 meatballs

1 pound ground beef

1 pound ground sausage (preferably spicy pork)

½ cup finely chopped onion

¼ cup minced garlic

2 tablespoons chopped fresh thyme

1 tablespoon chopped fresh parsley, plus more for garnish

1 large egg

½ cup grated Parmesan cheese, plus more for garnish

1 cup panko breadcrumbs

12 ounces ricotta cheese

2 tablespoons kosher salt

Olive oil

3 cups Domenica's Basic, Best-Ever Tomato Sauce (recipe follows), heated

33 small potato buns (slider size), toasted

1. Preheat the oven to 450°F.

2. In a large bowl, mix the beef, sausage, onion, garlic, thyme, parsley, egg, Parmesan cheese, breadcrumbs, ricotta cheese, and salt with your hands. Form 1½-inch balls out of the meat mixture. Heat a large ovenproof skillet (preferably cast-iron) with a bit of olive oil. Working in batches, add the meatballs and brown on all sides, about 4 minutes. Return all the meatballs to the skillet and place in the oven to finish cooking for 10 minutes.

3. Toss the meatballs with the tomato sauce. Place on the toasted slider buns, sprinkle with Parmesan cheese and parsley, and serve.

DOMENICA'S BASIC, BEST-EVER TOMATO SAUCE

Makes about 3 cups

4 or 5 garlic cloves, chopped (about ¼ inch)

½ teaspoon red pepper flakes

2 tablespoons premium low-acid extra virgin olive oil, such as Lucini or California Olive Ranch

One 28-ounce can organic crushed tomatoes

½ teaspoon salt

In a large saucepan over medium heat, sauté the garlic and pepper flakes in the oil for 1 minute. (Do not brown the garlic.) Stir in the tomatoes and salt. Bring the sauce to a boil, reduce the heat to low, and simmer, stirring occasionally, for 15 minutes.

LIVE CAM: BRUTHA FROM ANOTHA MUTHA AND SISTA FROM ANOTHA MISTA!

MAC'S FISH AND CHIP SHOP

AS GOOD AS YOU'LL GET IT ACROSS THE POND

I gotta be honest, I'm not a big fan of fish and chips. Why? First and foremost, I've had them in England, and there aren't many places in the States that I think really rock the house in the traditional style. You can't freeze the fish, you can't use processed premixed batter, you gotta do it

<table>
<tr><td>★ TRACK IT DOWN ★</td></tr>
</table>

★ TRACK IT DOWN ★

503 State Street
Santa Barbara, CA 93101
805-897-1160
www.macssb.com

SMILE, HONEY—WE JUST MADE GUY AND HUNTER EAT HAGGIS! HA HA.

real deal. So I found a joint in Santa Barbara that was doing it legit. Grant "Mac" MacNaughton uses sustainable wild Alaskan cod, his beer batter is thin and crispy just like it should be, and his chips (fries) are traditional thick-cut style. Doesn't get better than that. Or try their toad in the hole—that's bangers and mash over my all-time favorite, Yorkshire pudding with brown gravy.

These cats were doing such real-deal food from across the pond that I got myself into a little bit of a pickle . . . and had to face the haggis. Even Mac says, "Haggis is the stuff they normally throw away." But it's a traditional Scottish dish, so he honors his father's side of the family with this menu item. It was mind over matter—but not as scary as I thought. People who like it call it spicy, creamy, rich, and buttery—I don't want to tell you what I call it . . . ha ha.

> **HUNTER, GUY'S SON:** My dad takes me down to Santa Barbara and I think, *This is cool.* He asks me, "You want some fish and chips?" and I think, *Even cooler.* But then what does he end up feeding me? Ground-up liver, ground-up tongue, and ground-up heart that's coated and fried. So I said, "Dad, you say you want me to taste everything once. . . . Well, that was my *once.*"

KREW NOTES

Kerry "Gilligan" Johnson: Haggis and Hunter—great shoot! Can we show that on television?!

Matt "Beaver" Giovinetti: We meet so many great people shooting *DDD.* But once in a while, we meet our brother from another mother. Mac is that guy. From day one we all had a great rapport, laughing, joking, and poking fun at one another. Guy and Mac had excellent chemistry, and we could have done an entire half hour of outtakes. I'm pretty much a no-seafood dude, but I'd eat these fish and chips every day. They have a real British-made machine that cuts real British-style chips. Very cool!

Kate "Mrs. Bunny" Gibson: This was a terrific place, and Mac and his wife were lovely hosts to all of us. However, at Mac's, Guy had to make a dish that was probably the most dreaded in *DDD* history, haggis. We had about twenty pounds of cooked offal meat that smelled just like you would expect it to smell. And yet Mac's meat grinder was the size of a tabletop pencil sharpener. Guy stood there patiently while an entire hotel pan's worth of stinky offal meat passed through that tiny grinder. It was a sight to see . . . and smell.

RESTAURANT UPDATE

Since appearing on the show, we've been visited by tens of thousands of excited *Triple D* fans saying, "Guy sent us"—from Anchorage to Key West and beyond. In fact, we're getting more mileage out of our appearance than Guy's '68 Camaro!

—GRANT "MAC" MACNAUGHTON

TRADITIONAL BRITISH FISH AND CHIPS

ADAPTED FROM A RECIPE COURTESY OF GRANT MACNAUGHTON, MAC'S FISH AND CHIP SHOP

Authentic British fish and chips consist of a high-quality flaky white fish deep-fried in a thin, crispy batter and served on a bed of large, twice-cooked chips (think fat fries). The key to avoiding an overly greasy product is to use a fry pot large enough that the addition of the fish doesn't reduce the oil temperature too much. Realistically, in a home environment, this will mean cooking each fish individually, but the results will be well worth the staggered serving required. Remember, never leave oil unattended and never fill any cooking vessel more than halfway with oil. Use canola oil or any oil with a high smoke point and relatively neutral flavor, such as vegetable or soybean oil.

Serves 6

Twice-cooked chips

12 large russet potatoes

Enough canola oil to fill your largest cooking pot or deep fryer halfway

Salt

Dry dredge

2 cups all-purpose flour

1 tablespoon kosher salt

1 tablespoon freshly ground black pepper

Beer batter

3 cups all-purpose flour

3 tablespoons paprika

3 tablespoons kosher salt

One 12-ounce bottle lager beer (the lighter and fizzier the better)

MAC DADDY FISH AND CHIPS.

Fish

3 pounds skinless, boneless large-flake white fish (we use wild Alaskan cod because of its quality and sustainability)

Enough canola oil to fill your largest cooking pot or deep fryer halfway

Kosher salt

Good-quality malt vinegar, for serving

1. To make the chips, peel the potatoes and cut them about ½-inch x ½-inch by the natural length of the potato. Set the potatoes aside in a bowl of water.

2. Heat the oil to 275°F in a large pot or deep fryer. Thoroughly drain the chips and add them to the oil, working in batches to avoid overcrowding the pan. Fry the chips until they are soft to squeeze but not yet browned, about 10 minutes. Spread them on a paper towel–lined baking sheet and refrigerate overnight.

3. Heat the oil to 375°F in a large pot or deep fryer.

4. For the dry dredge, thoroughly mix the flour, salt, and pepper in a shallow bowl and set aside.

5. To make the beer batter, thoroughly mix the flour, paprika, and salt in a shallow bowl. While constantly whisking, add enough beer to stiffen up the mix. While still continuing to whisk, add cold water until the batter has the consistency of heavy cream and contains no lumps.

6. Fillet the fish into six 8-ounce portions, removing any bones, skin, or blood lines that are present.

7. Fry the chips, in batches if necessary, until golden brown and crispy on the outside but still fluffy on the inside, about 5 minutes. Sprinkle the chips with salt while hot.

8. Dip the fish into the seasoned flour, tapping off any excess. Then dip the fish into the batter and briefly allow the batter to drain off. Gently place the fish into the oil, allowing the fish to float away from you. Fry in batches if necessary. The fish is ready when it is golden brown and trying to float, 5 to 7 minutes.

9. Remove the fish from the oil with a fish spatula and drain it on a cooling rack. Serve the fish on a bed of chips with lashings of salt and vinegar.

TIOLI'S CRAZEE BURGER

BURGERS FROM ALL WALKS . . . AND FLIGHTS AND WATERS

Tioli's in San Diego was one of the first locations where we used a car besides my Camaro. Instead we shot with my '65 Shelby Cobra. (Carroll Shelby was a buddy of mine, a great man—even signed my car—and we miss him.) This place was all about burgers—all kinds of burgers: gator

★ TRACK IT DOWN ★

**4201 30th Street
San Diego, CA 92104**
619-282-6044
www.crazeeburger.com

LOTHAR AND WOLFGANG PUT THE CRAZEE IN THE NAME!

> The dude sitting here was an old manager of mine named Michael Osterman. I hadn't seen him in fifteen years, and he came down to see the show. After we reconnected I ended up hiring him, and he's now the food and beverage director for all my restaurants in California.

ME AND MICHAEL OSTERMAN.

burger, kangaroo burger; they've even got ostrich burger. My favorite line: "Do you get any tater with that gator? James Spader likes gator." (*Ha ha ha*, I kill me.)

Don't let the name confuse you. This was an Italian restaurant when the original owners bought it, then they turned it into a burger joint. Lothar and Wolfgang, two fine dining restaurant guys from Germany (two names ya gotta love), were the guys who created this place. But new owners Garrett and Peter are keeping it real. (Lothar and Wofgang have since moved on to start two different restaurants, one in Brazil and one in the Philippines, respectively.)

 RESTAURANT UPDATE

On May 1, 2011, Peter Cortese (my business partner and one of my best childhood friends) and I took over Crazee Burger here in North Park. We both work here at the restaurant all week managing the day-to-day operations. Although we have increased the quality of the buns, produce, and meat, the menu has all the same recipes and ingredients. We recently finished our remodel and now have twelve new beers on tap and new hardwood floors (instead of the old carpet).

—GARRETT BERNARD

TURKEY BURGERS
WITH ORANGE MUSTARD GLAZE

ADAPTED FROM A RECIPE COURTESY OF TIOLI'S CRAZEE BURGER

Serves 6

Seasoning mixture

1 tablespoon coarse kosher salt

½ teaspoon ground paprika

½ teaspoon freshly ground black pepper

½ teaspoon granulated garlic

3 pounds ground turkey (white and dark meat)

Glaze

2 tablespoons vegetable oil

½ cup diced yellow onion

2 garlic cloves, minced

¼ cup diced jalapeños, with seeds

One 9-ounce jar orange marmalade with peel

1 tablespoon Dijon mustard

¼ teaspoon ground black pepper

⅛ teaspoon chili powder

6 hamburger buns or Kaiser rolls

Garnishes

Romaine lettuce leaves

Thinly sliced red onion

Tomato slices

Kosher pickles

1. Combine all the seasoning mixture ingredients in a small bowl. Form 6 turkey patties approximately 8 ounces each and sprinkle on both sides with the seasoning mixture.

2. To make the glaze, heat the vegetable oil in a medium skillet over medium-high heat. Add the onion, garlic, and jalapeños and sauté until the onion is translucent, about 10 minutes. Add the marmalade, mustard, pepper, and chili powder and cook for about 2 minutes, until fully combined. Reserve until ready to use.

3. Set up a grill and grill the turkey patties first on very high heat, until nice markings are shown, then reduce the flame to medium. Cook the patties until well done (165°F), about 12 minutes, flipping after 5 minutes. At the same time, grill the hamburger buns on both sides.

4. Serve the hamburger as an open-faced patty with glaze on one side and garnishes on the other.

TRY TO KEEP A SERIOUS FACE—THESE ARE SERIOUS BURGERS . . .

LAUER-KRAUTS

HOME OF THE KILLER KRAUT

Oh, I hate it when I get schooled. Hate it, hate it, hate it. I mean, come on, it's sauerkraut. We've all had it—pungent, sour, needs to be rinsed the majority of the time. Most people don't care for it very much, but here I was on *Triple D* going to visit a joint that dedicates not only their name but their entire menu to this cabbage creation. If you think all kraut is created equal, you gotta check this joint out.

★ TRACK IT DOWN ★

**26 South 6th Street
Brighton, CO 80601
303-654-9700
www.lauer-krauts.com**

These are fourth-generation German family recipes that Robin Lauer-Trujillo serves up right. The kraut burger is baked in a homemade bread pocket—it's like a meat pretzel, moist, soft, and doughy. Where have these been all my life? A Lauer-Kraut original. And they do a bean and noodle soup with homemade fettucine cooked in a broth that starts with a ham bone—great flavor and definitely something I'd have again.

KREW NOTES

Liz "Erd" Pollock: Even the sauerkraut is from scratch? Are you kidding me? Guy and the whole crew treasure places like this that can't help but make amazing food because it's the only way their family has ever known. These are the places everyone needs to know about, and thanks to Guy, now they do.

Ron "Fraggle" Gabaldon: I'm always amazed at the generosity of our restaurant owners. As part of the crew we're always offered T-shirts, ball caps, and usually our own weight in great food. Guy, however, usually has his eye on something, and it's not a T-shirt. Shooting at Lauer-Krauts, we watched the process of making their fantastic sauerkraut, which starts with shredding the cabbage in a device called a hobel (pronounced hoo-vel). It's an old-fashioned mandolin that's basically a wooden box that rides along a plank with blades in the middle, and from the look of the one we were using, and the similar hobels hanging on the walls, these were tools that stayed in a family for generations. Guy can't resist that kind of history in a kitchen utensil and gave me the task of finding one he could take back to his kitchen. This wouldn't be easy, and I knew it, and Guy knew it, but he also knew I would make a big deal out of finding one—calling antiques shops, asking the owners and family where to find one, calling more antique shops, asking the owners again. Eventually the family simply took one off of the wall and presented it to him as a gift. The family members even signed it for him.

RESTAURANT UPDATE

Since the airing of our episode, all I can say is, "Thank you for the amazing blessing." The physical appearance of Lauer-Krauts has not changed, but what goes on in the kitchen certainly has. I never dreamt we would be chopping so much cabbage and onions, but I'm thankful every day to do so. It's a great feeling to know that my rent is paid, the lights are on, and my ladies' checks won't bounce. We've also had the great fortune of seeing visitors from every state in the Union, plus Canada, Europe, Asia, and Australia. We've met so many wonderful people and have had such a blast doing so. After filming, Guy was able to spend a couple of minutes with me to give me some advice. Boy, am I thankful for that advice. Everything he said to me has come true to the letter. So thanks again to everyone involved—we're more grateful than words can ever express. The next venture for Lauer-Krauts is a food truck. Coming soon . . .

—ROBIN LAUER-TRUJILLO

THE LITTLE GUY TO THE LEFT IS GOING TO BE THE NEXT
BIG SHOT IN THE KRAUT EMPIRE.

GUY'S FUNKY KULINARY KOLLECTION

Just ask my wife, Lori —I'm addicted to collecting culinary equipment, the odder the better, and the more history to it, the more I need it. Here's a taste of the tools of the trade that I've been lucky enough to be given while on the road with *Triple D.* These are some of my most prized possessions.

- Nutmeg grinder from the 1800s from Terry's Turf Club in Cincinnati

- Super-old cast-iron skillet, never washed, from Prince's Hot Chicken Shack in Nashville

- Italian meat grinder from Di Pasquales' in Baltimore

- Falafel maker from The Original Falafel Drive-In in San Jose

- Tostone maker from Mambo's in Glendale, California

- Eastern European butcher knife from Forte in Las Vegas

- Pizza peel from Vito and Nick's on the South Side of Chicago

- Cabbage mandoline (hobel) from Lauer-Krauts in Brighton, Colorado

- Brazilian spice rack from Derek Boone, an owner of Swagger Fine Spirits & Food in Kansas City

- Himalayan salt blocks from Café Rakka in Nashville

- Custom-made double-wide fork for pressing the edges of ravioli closed from Drew Abruzzese of Pineville Tavern in Pineville, Pennsylvania

- Gyro cooker from George and Themis Boretos of the Greek Corner in Boston

- Largest wok ever seen on earth, sourced from Andy Ricker of Pok Pok from an Asian cooking supply store in Portland, Oregon

- Half-gallon beer stein in the shape of a boot from Harry Kempf of Chicago Brauhaus, Chicago

- And last but not least, and the biggest—all the way from Oahu, shipped via storage container, the twenty-foot-long huli huli chicken machine from Reno Henriques, the chef of Fresh Catch in Hawaii

ORIGINAL LAUER-KRAUT BURGERS

ADAPTED FROM A RECIPE COURTESY OF MAMA LORI LAUER, "THE BOSS," LAUER-KRAUTS

Serves 18

Burger filling

1 ¾ pounds 80/20 ground chuck

1 ½ medium yellow onions, cut into ¼-inch dice

2 teaspoons coarsely ground black pepper

1 medium head green cabbage, cut into ¼-inch pieces

½ cup Lauer Kraut (recipe follows) or bagged sauerkraut (never canned)

1 teaspoon salt

Bread dough mix

2 tablespoons active dry yeast

1 tablespoon sugar

¾ cup powdered milk

8 cups all-purpose flour, plus more for dusting

2 teaspoons salt

¾ cup shortening

3 large eggs

1 teaspoon vegetable oil

1 large egg, beaten, for brushing

Pickles, for serving

1. To make the burger filling, brown the ground chuck in a large skillet over medium heat for about 3 minutes, crumbling the meat as it browns. Add the onions and 1 teaspoon of the pepper and sauté until the onions are slightly translucent, about 3 minutes. Stir in the chopped cabbage, kraut, salt, and the remaining 1 teaspoon pepper. Cook for 10 minutes, stirring occasionally, then set aside to cool.

2. To make the dough, combine the yeast and sugar with 1 cup warm water in a small bowl. Set aside for 3 to 4 minutes to let the yeast activate. Put the powdered milk in medium bowl and add 2 cups water. Add the yeast mixture to the powdered milk mixture and stir to combine.

3. In a large bowl, combine the flour and salt. Cut the shortening into the flour by hand until evenly distributed and the mixture large resembles crumbs. Make a well in the flour mixture and add the eggs. Pour the yeast–powdered milk mixture in as well. Work together, still with your hands, until the mixture comes away from the bowl (you may need a touch more flour or water), about 3 minutes. The dough will be very sticky. Oil the dough lightly on each side, cover, and let rise for 10 minutes. Punch the dough down and let rise for another 15 minutes.

4. Preheat the oven to 350°F.

5. To assemble the burgers: Dust the work surface with flour. Begin to roll the dough into an 18 x 4-inch log. Divide the log into 18 equal portions (divide the dough in half, then divide each half into thirds, then divide each of those sections into thirds). Roll each piece of dough into an 8 x 8-inch square. Turn a square over and add a full cup of the burger filling mixture to the center of the dough. Bring the opposite corners of the square together, then bring the other 2 opposite corners together so that all 4 corners are drawn together. Pinch together each of the 4 seams and the top of the dough. When you think the dough is sealed, push down slightly on the burger. This will release any extra air and help you find any place you missed sealing the burger. Turn the sealed pocket over and place on a parchment-lined baking sheet. Repeat with the remaining dough and filling.

6. Brush the tops lightly with the beaten egg. Bake for about 20 minutes, rotating the baking sheet halfway through, until the burgers are golden brown. Serve with a pickle on the side.

LAUER KRAUT

ADAPTED FROM A RECIPE COURTESY OF MAMA LORI LAUER, "THE BOSS," LAUER-KRAUTS

Makes about 5 gallons

50 pounds fresh cabbage, cored and quartered
Salt

1. Shred the cabbage finely (we use Grandpa Lauer's hobel [cabbage shredder]).

2. Put several large handfuls of freshly shredded cabbage into a stone crock.

3. Add a good handful of salt to the cabbage and begin to mash the salt into the cabbage by hand until you get a good froth and juice forms to coat the cabbage. Continue adding cabbage and mashing, adding salt as needed. You want to taste the salt, but do not oversalt.

I'M IN A FULL-BLOWN HOBEL TRANCE.

4. When the crock is full of cabbage, weight it down (we put a plate upside down on the top of the kraut, then fill a couple of gallon bags of water and lay them on top). Drape a towel over the entire crock.

5. Let the mashed cabbage and salt sit in the crock for a minimum of 28 days in a room temperature environment. After 28 days it is fermented enough. We then bag it in freezer bags, in the amounts we want to use it, and freeze it until we need it. You can also refrigerate it for up to 3 weeks if covered in brine.

COOK'S NOTE: This makes an enormous (restaurant quantity) amount of sauerkraut! Note the quantity as well as the time needed for the fermentation.

TOCABE: AN AMERICAN INDIAN EATERY

CULTURAL HERITAGE AT ITS FINEST . . . AND MOST DELICIOUS

We recognize so many cultures and cuisines in this country: Mexican, German, Irish, Italian, Russian, Cuban, you name it. But there's one cuisine that I don't think gets nearly the appreciation and representation that it should, and that's Native American. I say this especially after eating at Tocabe. It's not just the handcrafted food and the unique dishes with outstanding flavor—a lot of it has to do with the energy and attitude. As I told the owner, Ben Jacobs, when we talked about him offering up this precious family recipe, it's not just the recipe that defines his restaurant, it's the entire experience.

Osage Nation tribal member Ben Jacobs and his college buddy Matt Chandra opened this place to share the food that Ben grew up loving, from sweet corn soup to chicken Indian tacos. The tacos have a base of fry bread that starts with honey water and is just the bomb, and their hominy salsa is completely off the hook. Or try their blueberry sauced bison ribs—huge flavor.

★ **TRACK IT DOWN** ★

**3536 West 44th Avenue
Denver, CO 80211
720-524-8282
www.tocabe.com**

KREW NOTES

Anthony "Chico" Rodriguez: Like Martin's Bar-B-Que and Rainbow Drive-In, the guys at Tocabe have become incredible friends, and it all began when they surprised us with this welcoming ceremony. Ben Jacobs, a co-owner, performed a cedar smoking ceremony or a cleansing ceremony, in which each person lets go of any bad things or feelings that might be affecting them and is helped to be open to good and positive things. They used an eagle feather to help fan the smoke over each person as they cleansed their body and spirit with the smoke. It's believed that the eagle flies closest to Wa-kon-tah (God) and therefore is sacred and holds special powers. The smoking also served to prepare the space for a positive outcome—ridding it, too, of any negative feelings. By taking the smoke in your hands and rubbing it over your body, you're opening your heart to good influences. Ben told me that the ceremony was performed to honor Guy and all of us on the *DDD* crew as guests and to help to create positive energy among new friends.

LIVE CAM: BEN JACOBS IN TRADITIONAL OSAGE NATION DRESS.

Mike "Father Time" Morris: Here you find a movie-star good-looking Native American owner out to change people's perception of what his culture is like and what they eat.

Ryan "Donny" Larson: It was my third trip out with *DDD*, and I was still the new guy on set. We were shooting in the kitchen, and Guy tossed an empty bowl at me while I was standing behind a light stand. I reached around it and caught it. He was impressed, and so was I. From that moment I was officially part of the crew.

 RESTAURANT UPDATE

Since airing on *Triple D* we've gone from eight employees to twenty-three and holding strong. Fans have visited from every edge of the United States and even abroad, and we've received fan e-mails from all over the States as well as Canada, Scotland, England, South Africa, Dubai, and Costa Rica, just to name a few.

—BEN JACOBS

GREEN CHILE STEW

ADAPTED FROM A RECIPE COURTESY OF BEN JACOBS, TOCABE: AN AMERICAN INDIAN EATERY

Serves 4 to 6

1 pound russet potatoes (about 2 medium potatoes), peeled and cut into ½-inch cubes

½ pound ground beef

Kosher salt and freshly ground black pepper

⅓ cup all-purpose flour

¾ cup mild green chiles (preferably fresh, or frozen or canned), cut into small dice

½ cup hot green chiles (preferably fresh, or frozen or canned), cut into small dice

1½ cups corn kernels (preferably fresh, or frozen or canned)

1 to 2 teaspoons green chile powder

Grated cheese and sour cream, for serving, optional

1. Place 4 cups water and the potatoes in a stockpot and bring to a boil over medium heat. Cook the potatoes until fork-tender but not falling apart, about 15 minutes, then remove the pot from the heat.

2. In a sauté pan over medium heat, cook the ground beef, sprinkling lightly with salt and pepper and stirring occasionally. When the pink is cooked out of the beef, about 10 minutes, turn off the heat. Slowly mix the flour into the beef to make a roux; stir it in completely until no dry flour remains. (Depending on the fat ratio of the beef, you may need to add more or less flour. The more flour you use, the thicker your stew will be.)

3. Add the beef to the stockpot with the cooked potatoes. If the meat is in large pieces, break them up with a spoon. Once the meat is fully broken down, add the green chiles, corn, 2 teaspoons salt, 2 teaspoons pepper, and the green chile powder. Mix well and place the stockpot over medium heat. Bring the stew to a boil, then reduce the heat to a simmer and cook until thickened, about 15 minutes. Serve in bowls with cheese or sour cream, if using.

OSAGE HOMINY SALSA

ADAPTED FROM A RECIPE COURTESY OF BEN JACOBS, TOCABE: AN AMERICAN INDIAN EATERY

LET THE POSITIVE ENERGY FLOW.

Makes about 5 cups

Three 15-ounce cans hominy

½ large red onion, diced

½ cup chopped fresh cilantro leaves

1½ large garlic cloves, diced

½ to 1 serrano chile, diced

1 cup dried cranberries, chopped

1½ teaspoons ground cumin

1 tablespoon chili powder

1 tablespoon sugar

2½ teaspoons kosher salt

Pinch of ground black pepper

¼ cup lemon juice

¼ cup canola oil

1 tablespoon white vinegar

1. Rinse the hominy well and place it in a large bowl. Add the onion, cilantro, garlic, chile, cranberries, cumin, chili powder, sugar, salt, and pepper.

2. In a small bowl, whisk the lemon juice, canola oil, and vinegar. Pour the dressing over the hominy mixture and mix thoroughly with a large spoon or by hand. Refrigerate for no less than 1 hour before serving, or overnight to marry the flavors fully.

3. Serve the hominy salsa as a side dish or as a relish for an Indian taco; eat it within 24 to 48 hours.

BAR GERNIKA

BASQUE IN GOOD OLD COUNTRY COOKING

$𝒜𝓈$ $𝒶𝓃$ $𝑒𝓍𝒸𝒽𝒶𝓃𝑔𝑒$ $𝓈𝓉𝓊𝒹𝑒𝓃𝓉$ in France I'd been to some Basque restaurants, and upon seeing that there was one in Boise, I admit I was surprised. But I came to understand that Boise has one of the largest Basque settlement areas in the country—they came over from the area bordering France and Spain as sheepherders in the late 1800s. The current owner, Jeff May, worked with the original Basque owner, then bought the place. It's amazing to me that Basque food is

★ TRACK IT DOWN ★

**202 South Capitol Boulevard
Boise, ID 83702
208-344-2175
www.bargernika.com**

not more widely appreciated. We've shot a couple Basque-style joints on *Triple D*, and it's good, rustic, simple, flavorful food.

Of course, in a sheepherding community you'll find lamb on the menu, from lamb stew to lamb kabobs and the popular lamb grinder with Swiss, peppers, mushrooms, onions, and au jus, plus other traditional Basque foods, like solomo (roast pork) sandwiches, croquettas, garlic soup, and that old favorite: beef tongue. You know I've gotta love the food at a place to go out on a limb and eat beef tongue. I'm not a big tongue fan, but the way they cook it and the time and attention to detail given to the recipe was worth the risk. Regulars actually call in ahead of time to reserve their order for the Saturday tongue special. There wasn't anything I tried there that I didn't really dig.

KREW NOTES

Bryna "The Pirate" Levin: We made some typical Basque dishes at Bar Gernika, which were interesting, but everyone we talked to kept touting the tongue. So we decided we had to make it, even though Guy was already wrapped. Tongue is not appealing, especially when you see it whole and raw. But by the time it had been braising in liquid for hours and the gnarly taste-bud-covered skin had been removed and the meat was thinly sliced, it looked like any other meat. And it was delicious, so delicious that we wanted Guy to come back and try it. So the next day on his way to the airport Guy agreed to make a tongue-tasting pit stop. He told me, "This better be worth a special trip." All I can say is, he may not list tongue as one of his favorite foods, but he didn't regret stopping by for a bite.

 ## RESTAURANT UPDATE

Being associated with *DDD* has not only had great benefit for us, but for our fourteen staff members as well. We are so grateful for the exposure and the business it continues to bring us.

I asked the staff for their best memories of Guy's visit, and the first thing they mentioned was actually something that happened more recently. One late afternoon, shortly after a re-run of our episode had aired, Drew Barrymore came in, plopped down on a bar stool, and simply said, "I'll have what Guy had!" I told the boys that I thought you weren't looking for adolescent fantasy stories, but for actual stories about the filming here. They said, "Yeah, but we have Guy to thank for that...."

We were also able to show off a little of the Basque culture to Guy. He really seemed to like our indoor fronton (ball court). It's a traditional Basque game from the old country, akin to jai alai. The fronton is about a hundred years old and was built in the middle of an old Basque sheepherders' boarding house, where our office is located.

—JEFF MAY

Awesome!
G

UP IN FLAMES IN THE KITCHEN.

SOLOMO WITH PIMIENTOS (ROAST PORK SANDWICH WITH PEPPERS)

ADAPTED FROM A RECIPE COURTESY OF JEFF MAY, BAR GERNIKA

The peppers used in the marinade are traditional dried Basque txorizero (pronounced choricero) peppers. We have a local urban farm grow them for us. They're a sweeter pepper and can be substituted at home with dried New Mexico or California chiles. The pepper sauce is also terrific in tomato sauce or added to soup.

Makes 6 sandwiches

Pepper sauce

2 ounces dried txorizero peppers (or dried New Mexico chiles)

Solomo

2 pounds center-cut boneless pork loin

2 teaspoons kosher salt

½ teaspoon granulated garlic

Olive oil, for cooking

Pimientos

Four 4-ounce jars sliced pimientos or roasted red peppers

1 tablespoon olive oil

1 garlic clove, chopped

½ teaspoon sugar

½ teaspoon salt

2 fresh, firm, crusty baguettes, sliced through the middle and cut into thirds to make 6 sandwiches

1. FOR THE PEPPER SAUCE: In a heatproof bowl, reconstitute the dried peppers by pouring enough hot water over them to cover. Let them stand, covered, until softened, about 30 minutes. Put the peppers in a food processor with 2 to 3 tablespoons of the soaking liquid and puree. Run through a food mill or a mesh strainer to smooth out the sauce.

2. FOR THE SOLOMO: Trim the excess fat along the top and sides of the pork loin. Sprinkle the loin with the salt and granulated garlic. Rub ¼ cup of the pepper sauce marinade all over the pork. Roll it up in plastic wrap and marinate for 24 hours in the refrigerator.

3. FOR THE PIMIENTOS: If using whole pimientos, remove them from the can and reserve the canning juice. Slice them lengthwise into 1-inch-wide pieces. Set aside. In a medium saucepan, heat the olive oil over medium heat. Add the garlic and cook until it begins to turn golden, 2 to 3 minutes. Add the pimientos and all of the canning juice, then add the sugar and salt. Mix well and simmer for about 20 minutes, until the liquid changes to a nice orange color.

4. Slice the pork loin into ¼- to ½-inch-thick slices, to end up with 12 slices. Preheat a flat-top grill (a cast-iron skillet or other heavy skillet will do just fine) over medium-high heat and add 1 tablespoon of oil. Cook half the pork slices for 3 to 4 minutes in all, turning once and splashing about 1 teaspoon of liquid from the pimiento mixture on each side. Reduce the heat to medium if necessary. Repeat with more oil and the second batch of pork.

5. Place 2 slices of pork (and its juices) and some pimientos in each piece of baguette to make 6 sandwiches.

YOU DON'T NEED YOUR PASSPORT FOR THIS INTERNATIONAL FLAVOR.

WESTSIDE DRIVE IN

GOURMET FOOD SERVED OUT OF A 1950S LANDMARK

Like I say, if it's funky I'll find it, and here in Boise they've got a joint where they serve fresh-caught fish and prime rib out of a drive-in. But it's not just prime rib—it gets slathered in bacon fat before it cooks. Chef Lou Aaron grew up about six blocks from this 1950s landmark, and he'd come by all the time for shakes. So after twenty-seven years as a chef, he jumped at the chance to buy the joint.

★ TRACK IT DOWN ★

1939 West State Street
Boise, ID 83702
208-342-2957
www.cheflou.com

Don't let the little drive-in building fool ya. Yes, that's where you're picking the food up, but this dude has a full-blown commercial kitchen right next door. So he can cook anything you like. Make sure you bring your appetite, and you gotta try the tender, meaty finger steaks. It's a staple in Boise, everyone has got their own twist, but they all serve 'em up with a spicy cocktail sauce. I know it's funky, but ya gotta try it.

KREW NOTES

Matt "Beaver" Giovinetti: A drive-in with killer prime rib and au jus you could eat by itself, and they do actual baked potatoes. Amazing.

★ RESTAURANT UPDATE

After Guy's visit to the Westside, our sales went up 50 percent, and sales have consistently been up every month since. It was such a blessing for him to choose us! We have had fans of the show visit from almost all fifty states, and we have filled up four guest books! We've since expanded (Guy's suggestion) and opened up Westside Drive In number two at 1113 Parkcenter Boulevard in February 2012. It has been received very well too! Thanks, Guy.

—LOU AARON

LOU INTRODUCES ME TO A FINE SPECIMEN: THE FRIED FINGER STEAK.

FINGER STEAKS WITH COCKTAIL SAUCE

ADAPTED FROM A RECIPE COURTESY OF LOU AARON, WESTSIDE DRIVE IN

Serves 2 to 3

1½ cups all-purpose flour, plus 1 cup seasoned with 2 teaspoons ground black pepper, 2 teaspoons granulated garlic, and 1 tablespoon seasoning salt

½ cup cornstarch (¼ cup if you want the finger steaks less crispy)

1 tablespoon chicken base

1 tablespoon granulated garlic

2 teaspoons ground black pepper

2 teaspoons baking powder

A few drops of yellow food coloring, optional

4 cups vegetable shortening, such as Crisco

1 pound sirloin, cut into 3 x ½-inch strips

Cocktail Sauce (recipe follows), for serving

1. To make the batter, in a large bowl, mix together the 1½ cups unseasoned flour, the cornstarch, chicken base, granulated garlic, black pepper, and baking powder. Slowly pour in 2 cups water, whisking constantly until all the water is incorporated into the mixture. Mix until smooth. Stir in the yellow food coloring, if using, and set aside.

2. In a high-sided 10-inch skillet or a deep fryer, heat the shortening to 350°F (or medium-high heat if you don't have a thermometer or fryer).

3. Coat a few of the sirloin strips in the seasoned flour. Shake off the excess. Drop the strips in the batter a few at a time. Pick the strips up, let them drip a bit, and then lay them in the hot oil. Turn after 25 to 30 seconds. Fry for 25 to 30 seconds more. Remove the finger steaks with a slotted spoon. Lay them on a paper towel–lined plate to drain off the excess grease. Repeat with the rest of the finger steaks. Serve with cocktail sauce.

COCKTAIL SAUCE

Makes 1 cup

1 cup chili sauce

1 tablespoon horseradish sauce

2 tablespoons lemon juice

Combine all the ingredients in a bowl. Store refrigerated.

EVEN THE HOT RODS EAT AT THIS DRIVE-IN!

STANDARD DINER

THERE AIN'T NOTHIN' STANDARD ABOUT THE STANDARD DINER

Originally an old Texaco gas station, circa 1938, this building was transformed into a diner in 2006. It's one of those places off Route 66 with a real-deal back story. Owner Matt DiGregory bought a 1969 Cadillac convertible from a classic car dealership that was here in 1990, and he remembers thinking the place would make a really great restaurant. So sixteen years later he bought the building and opened up the Standard Diner. That's just how interesting this place is. Plus, they're doing old-school diner food in a contemporary cooking style. It's not just meatloaf, it's meatloaf wrapped in bacon. And they've got a bourbon butter-slathered burger, tempura-fried ahi tuna, fried game hen on sweet potato pies, and even a roasted beet stuffed with fontina cheese. Yes, this is all happening in a diner. But as Matt clarifies, standard means a benchmark that all others are compared to.

NOTHIN' STANDARD HERE.

★ TRACK IT DOWN ★

320 Central Avenue SE
Albuquerque, NM 87102
505-243-1440
www.standarddiner.com

THE "NEW" DEFINITION OF "FILLING STATION."

SIDENOTE: This was the first time that I ever saw the sign UNATTENDED CHILDREN WILL BE GIVEN AN ESPRESSO AND A FREE PUPPY.

KREW NOTES

Mike "Father Time" Morris: You come to this huge, classic-looking diner to put the comfort food feed-bag on. Ten minutes before Guy walked in, the chef went to the cooler to get some logs of ground beef wearing a beautiful white chef's jacket. Of course the meat leaked, and when he came to the set, he had huge blood streaks across his chest. Thankfully, there was a dry cleaner across the street, so some promises of *DDD* show swag brought us a nicely cleaned white chef's jacket in the nick of time. Whew.

 RESTAURANT UPDATE

Wow, the fans of *DDD* are amazing. Not a day goes by when we don't have at least a few guests come to Standard Diner as a result of the show. Our best visit was from a private pilot and his wife, who flew to Albuquerque all the way from San Francisco just to have lunch and dinner with us and then flew back. Now that's dedication!

—MATT DiGREGORY

BACON-WRAPPED MEATLOAF
WITH RED WINE GRAVY

ADAPTED FROM A RECIPE COURTESY OF MATT DiGREGORY, STANDARD DINER

Serves 4

1 large yellow onion, finely diced

2 teaspoons olive oil

2 large eggs

2 tablespoons soy sauce

1 tablespoon dark brown sugar

2 tablespoons golden raisins, chopped

1 tablespoon Worcestershire sauce

1 tablespoon yellow mustard

½ cup ketchup

⅛ teaspoon dried rosemary

⅛ teaspoon dried sage

⅛ teaspoon dried thyme

⅛ teaspoon dried parsley

2½ pounds Angus reserve ground beef

¼ cup breadcrumbs

Salt and freshly ground black pepper

½ pound sliced applewood-smoked bacon

Red Wine Meatloaf Gravy (recipe follows)

1. Preheat the oven to 350°F.

2. In a medium sauté pan over medium heat, sweat the onion with the olive oil until softened, 5 to 8 minutes. Remove from the heat to cool.

3. In a medium bowl, beat the eggs, then add the soy sauce, brown sugar, raisins, Worcestershire sauce, mustard, ketchup, and herbs and mix together. Mix in the onions.

4. Place the ground beef in a stand mixer and mix on medium speed. Add the egg mixture and breadcrumbs and mix until incorporated. Season with salt and pepper.

5. Layer the bacon shingle-style across a piece of parchment paper. Place the meatloaf mixture in the center and roll it into a bacon-wrapped log by lifting up the sides of the parchment, making sure that the bacon overlaps the meatloaf.

6. Wrap the parchment-wrapped log in foil and twist each end until snug. Place the meatloaf on a baking sheet.

7. Bake the meatloaf for 30 minutes. Remove from the oven, remove the foil and parchment, and bake for another 15 minutes, or until the internal temperature reaches 165°F.

8. Cut the meatloaf into 4 pieces and serve with the gravy.

RED WINE MEATLOAF GRAVY

Serves 8 to 10

½ cup diced yellow onion

2 celery stalks, diced

2 garlic cloves, minced

2 tablespoons olive oil

1 cup red wine

½ cup (1 stick) unsalted butter

½ cup all-purpose flour

2 cups beef stock

1 cup chicken stock

1 fresh thyme sprig

Salt and cracked black pepper

1. In a large sauté pan over medium-high heat, sauté the onion, celery, and garlic in the olive oil for 3 minutes, or until softened. Add the red wine and cook, stirring, until the liquid has reduced to a syrup, about 15 minutes.

2. In another sauté pan, melt the butter over medium heat. Sprinkle the flour over the butter and cook for 2 minutes, whisking. Whisk in the beef and chicken stock, add the thyme, and bring to a boil.

3. In a slow stream, whisking constantly, pour the stock mixture into the wine and onion mixture. Simmer for 10 minutes, or until thickened to your liking. Strain, then season with salt and pepper. Serve over meatloaf.

THE COFFEE CUP

KILLER CHILE VERDE AND THE FASTEST EGG MAN IN THE WEST

This was one of the first times we shot *Triple D,* and I wanted to cover Vegas because I'm a UNLV guy (I've even got an honorary doctorate!). I wanted to show that there's more to Las Vegas than just the Strip, and coming out to Boulder City was part of that. The Coffee Cup's got some history. Open since the 1930s, it helped feed all the guys while they were building the Hoover Dam.

★ TRACK IT DOWN ★

**512 Nevada Way
Boulder City, NV 89005**
702-294-0517
www.worldfamouscoffeecup.com

From omelets to French toast to peanut butter waffles, this place has something for everybody. Carri and Al Stevens run the Coffee Cup with their daughter, Lindsay. They bought the place fire-sale-style over the course of two days when they heard their favorite joint was available. There was no time to think. Al was in restaurant supply and Carri had been a waitress, but they'd never run a restaurant. And they've been making it work ever since.

TONGUE TWISTER

There's a line in this show that goes, "So are all the other omelets," but I couldn't say it when I was doing the voice-over in the booth. I couldn't get it; it was too tongue tying for me. So I made up a word: *soarealltheotheromelets,* like when you're a kid saying the alphabet and you get to *el-em-en-oh-pee.* It became a long-running joke between me and the technician at the studio—whenever a word became difficult for me, he would say, *"Soarealltheotheromelets."*

JOE HERMAN AND THE EGG CRACK ATTACK

While I was there I heard a rumor that Joe Herman, the cook, could crack 180 eggs in 190 seconds. Amazing, and true, but you have to hang out in the kitchen to see it.

KREW NOTES

Anthony "Chico" Rodriguez: The Coffee Cup was the *first ever* shoot of the series. Now, we'd shot the pilot the summer and fall before and used multiple different muscle cars in the show, but this was the series and we were now using the famous red Camaro. These were the old days of the show when the crew was very small and Bunny and I did everything, so the night before the shoot, we washed it, waxed it, buffed it, gassed it, and got it totally ready.

Well, we thought we did. It comes time to do the stand-up on this beautiful day on this very first shoot of this new series on Food Network. We pull the Camaro out, we drive it down the street, and we hit the button for the top to come down. Nothing. We hit it again. Nothing . . . we hit it over and over and over again. *Nothing.* You see, we did everything the night before, *except* lower the top. So we found a local antique car shop and had the top removed—yes, taken out of the car. But now the cover was sunken down. Luckily it was January and chilly even in California. If you look closely, you might be able to tell that under the cover instead of the top there were some of Bunny's and my blankets and sweatshirts. Shhh . . . don't tell anyone.

IT'S A KNOCKOUT??

There was a pipe coming out in the kitchen and I was trying to get the shot, coming around a corner, and hit my head square on that pipe. I was still standing up, but I was literally out of consciousness, seeing stars, for I don't know how long. Full-blown cartoon. *Boiiiiiiiiing!* It's the hardest I've ever been hit on the head.

 RESTAURANT UPDATE

DDD fans, you rock, and Guy, you rock! We now have the most fun and energetic fans and customers from all over the globe who visit and bring business to our beautiful small town. We can't say thank you enough!

—THE CREW AT THE COFFEE CUP

PORK CHILE VERDE

ADAPTED FROM A RECIPE COURTESY OF AL STEVENS, THE COFFEE CUP

You can serve this in an omelet, with warm corn tortillas or rice and beans, or on top of huevos rancheros.

Serves 5 to 6

3¾ pounds lean pork, diced

One 21-ounce can green enchilada sauce

Leaves of ⅓ bunch of fresh cilantro

⅓ large onion, chopped

⅓ bunch of green onions, chopped

1 jalapeño, seeded and chopped

3 tablespoons canned diced green chiles

Granulated garlic, to taste

Freshly ground black pepper

In a large saucepan over low heat, simmer the pork with 3 cups water, covered, until tender, about 2 hours, skimming occasionally. Drain the pork and return it to the pan. Add the remaining ingredients and cook over medium heat until the vegetables are tender and the flavors are nicely melded, about 35 minutes. Serve hot.

FORTE EUROPEAN TAPAS BAR & BISTRO

COMFORT FOOD VIA BULGARIA

Back in the day, when I went to UNLV (yes, the home of the 1990 NCAA champions, the Runnin' Rebels! Shameless plug) and worked in the meat purveyor industry, I gotta tell ya, there were a lot of sports bars, quite a few Mexican restaurants, some fine dining, and that was about it unless you were on the Strip. There wasn't a lot going on. But now you go back to Vegas and ho ho! It's like everybody realized what a killer town Vegas is. If you want it, you can now find it, like

★ TRACK IT DOWN ★

4180 S. Rainbow, Suite 806
Las Vegas, NV 89103
702-220-3876
www.barforte.com

Forte: amazing Eastern European food by a real-deal female entrepreneur. The food's outrageous, the art is really cool, and Nina Manchev's the bomb . . . that is, if she doesn't talk about, mention, reference, or describe the complete undermining and duping of the host of one of Food Network's top shows, *DDD*. As long as she keeps it secret, she's the bomb . . . hint, hint . . .

Nina opened the place while attending UNLV to serve up something a little different to the Vegas community. So on the corner of Flamingo and Rainbow, you can take a trip to Bulgaria right here in Vegas. (You thought it was all stromboli and chicken wings, didn't you?) She's got richly seasoned homemade sausage recipes that have been passed down through generations, including one for cured sausage that dates back to Roman times, and her Thracian clay pot is chock full of charcuterie. Plus, there's more familiar Eastern European comfort food favorites like goulash and stroganoff. You gotta check it out.

KREW NOTES: THE FORTE PRANK

It was a lighting bolt of an idea in Flavortown that pranked the un-prankable mayor, Guy Fieri. It all started as the crew was setting up equipment for Guy's arrival at Forte in Las Vegas (go Rebels!). Big Bunny was tuning his ears and setting up his audio gear for the day's work ahead when he chuckled to himself with this thought: *Wouldn't it be funny if we told Guy that Nina (the owner of Forte) and her family don't speak English?!* There was a moment of silence as the wheels of the old Flavortown prank mill began to churn. Chico called Boy Band and Father Time over to tell them the idea and asked Boy Band to get Nina and her father, Stephan. It started out simple: "You guys don't speak English." They got the idea right away, and it was game-on.

After a few minutes, Chico's mischievous brain was in full Chico mode. "Wait a second, if they aren't going to be speaking English, why don't they argue about something, too?!" So he told them, with a crooked smile, "Right after Guy starts talking to Nina on camera, Stephan, you should interrupt the scene and start arguing, about *anything* . . . argue about the morning paper or what color the sky is, it'll all be in Bulgarian, so Guy won't know the difference." It was decided that when the joke went on long enough, Father Time would signal Chico and he would simply slap the prep table with his hand and say "OK" to end it.

It wasn't long before Guy arrived at Forte. Father Time went up to him as he always does to give him the daily rundown for the shoot. He slips in how Nina and her family are really great people, and added, "She doesn't speak English very well, but you're really good at dealing with this." Not too much, because Guy can smell a practical joke a mile away. Father Time set the stage for what was to be the best "I got you" moment in the history of *DDD*.

While Guy finished getting the rundown from Father Time, Bunny, Chico, Boy Band, and the Iceman had a conversation just within earshot of Guy, talking about how great Nina was, despite her language barrier, just to seal the subtle expectations that Father Time had already laid out.

"Let's head into the kitchen and get this thing going," Father Time said, and it was as if the crew was at the Indianapolis 500 and heard, "Gentlemen, start your engines." The crew took their places in the kitchen, knowing they had the best seats in the house for what would be TV magic.

The cameras started rolling and the shoot began. Iceman was the designated camera-cover-guy, shooting the behind the scenes of this soon-to-be-legend. Guy and Nina begin cubing a pork butt for some sausage that Forte makes in-house. Guy decided to break the language barrier by talking about the old knives she was using. Nina began to speak in broken English, playing her part perfectly. Guy listened to her struggling to connect the words and shot the crew a look that said, "This is going to be a really long shoot, and what have you guys done to me?"

After a few unproductive minutes, Boy Band dropped the hammer and got Stephan to loudly interrupt the shoot. This led to him and Nina having a heated argument in Bulgarian, with Stephan storming back

THIS IS JUST WRONG . . . HA HA HA. DUPED!

out into the dining room. A frustrated Boy Band said, "I'll handle it" and followed him out of the kitchen. Out there, Boy Band told Stephan he did great, but now he wanted him to walk into the scene behind Guy and Nina.

Boy Band returned to his post on set and told Father Time, Guy, and the crew that everything was fine now, he had it handled. Guy was in the middle of this TV nightmare, struggling to have a conversation with Nina about her family. Then Stephan stomped in and Guy decided to put an end to this misery. He politely introduced himself and tried to explain to Stephan using hand gestures that Stephan had to be quiet, there was a TV shoot going on. The argument between Nina and her dad then began again, louder and more intense. Stephan stormed out of the kitchen once again, even more agitated this time, yelling about something none of us understood, all of this on camera. Guy was struggling with how to handle this awkwardness, when Stephan once again came back into the scene, angrier this time. Guy gave him a look. Boy Band walked into the scene and put his arm around Stephan's shoulder to escort him out into the dining room.

There they both started laughing hysterically. Boy Band told him, "Now let me have it! Yell at me as loud as you can about whatever you want, as long it's in Bulgarian." He did, and Boy Band said, "Now go back in the kitchen and I'm going to follow you in." As Boy Band reentered the kitchen, flustered, he threw his arms up and said to Father Time, "I don't know what to do—I can't communicate with this guy."

HE WEARS STRIPES LIKE A PRANK PIRATE!

By now Guy is clearly confused; this is one of the most awkward positions he's ever been in on *DDD*. When Boy Band and Stephan were staging their shouted argument in the dining room (which Guy can hear), Nina explained to Guy in Bulgarian that Stephan thought he was going to be cooking, and that his ego was bruised over the situation.

Father Time felt the awkwardness had now reached its crescendo, so he whispered to Chico, "That's it."

Chico tapped the table and said, "OK," the prearranged code word to tell Nina to end it. She had been speaking Bulgarian to Guy, and midsentence switches to English with absolutely *no* accent and says, "So we've been living here twenty years and speak perfect English." The look on Guy's face was priceless, totally confused, and you could see the wheels turning. At first he didn't get it, until Stephan casually looked at him and said, "What's up, man?!" Laughter erupted and Guy screamed, "No way!" By far the best reaction to any prank in the history of the show.

We tried to keep shooting over the next thirty minutes, but Guy kept losing it when Nina would talk to him with no accent at all. The crew, used to these on-set pranks, kept laughing and laughing, messing up the shots. Guy, who is the king of practical jokes, calmly and coolly looked each member of the crew in the eye and put a price on their head: "You're dead, you're dead," and so on. Boy Band got it four months later with a cream pie to the face. The rest of the crew still sleeps with one eye open, waiting for the other shoe to drop.

This was one of the most fun *DDD* shoots to be on, one that shows the camaraderie of Guy and the road crew. As soon as Tim McOsker, our executive producer, heard about it, he said he wanted it in the show, and it's proven to be one of the most popular segments ever. The crew loves doing the show, and this prank shows it.

RESTAURANT UPDATE

Being a part of the *Triple D* family has been an indescribably astounding experience. It has been so wonderful to share our culture with all the amazing fans of *Diners, Drive-Ins and Dives,* and really expose people to what Eastern European food is all about.

—NINA MANCHEV

THIS GIRL NINA CAN PULL A PRANK—AND SHE WILL PAY THE PRICE . . . HA HA.

STUFFED SWEET PEPPERS

ADAPTED FROM A RECIPE COURTESY OF NINA MANCHEV, FORTE EUROPEAN TAPAS BAR & BISTRO

Serves 8

Yogurt sauce

3 cups thick European-style yogurt

1 cup chopped fresh dill

3 tablespoons minced garlic

1 tablespoon kosher salt

Dash of extra-virgin olive oil

Stuffed sweet peppers

2 tablespoons extra-virgin olive oil

1 onion, finely chopped

1 carrot, finely grated

3 pounds ground pork

1 cup cooked jasmine or other rice

½ cup dried savory

1 bunch fresh dill, finely chopped

1 tablespoon plus 1 teaspoon kosher salt

1 tablespoon ground black pepper

Pinch of Hungarian or Spanish paprika

8 equal-size bell peppers, tops cut off, cored, and seeded

1. For the yogurt sauce, combine all the ingredients in a large bowl. Set aside.

2. Preheat the oven to 400°F. Heat the olive oil in a sauté pan over medium heat. Add the onion and cook until softened, about 4 minutes. Add the carrot and cook, stirring occasionally, until softened, about 3 minutes. Transfer the onion mixture to a large bowl and cool. Fold the pork into the mixture. Add the rice, savory, dill, salt, pepper, and paprika and mix well.

3. Fill the peppers with the pork mixture, slightly rounded on the top. Place the peppers on a rimmed baking sheet. Add enough water to barely cover the bottom of the baking sheet. Cover with foil and bake for about 55 minutes until the peppers are tender and the pork is cooked through. Uncover the foil and continue baking for 5 to 10 more minutes, until the pork mixture is lightly browned. Serve the peppers with the yogurt sauce.

COOK'S NOTE: The yogurt sauce is very garlicky; you can cut back on the garlic if you prefer. And you can also make the recipe with 30 sweet mini bell peppers if you like. Cook for 30 minutes covered and 3 minutes uncovered.

WHAT, ME? I DIDN'T DO IT!

CATTLEMEN'S STEAKHOUSE

DID SOMEONE SAY BEEF COUNTRY?

In the historic district of Oklahoma City called Stockyard City, you'll find this hundred-year-old joint. They specialize in aged, hand-cut steaks—always have and always will. When owner Dick Stubbs bought it more than twenty years ago, he brought in restaurant buddy David Egan to keep this place authentic. They didn't want to be run outta town. All steaks are seasoned up the Cattlemen's way with Cattlemen's seasoning, then cooked on a 650°F grill. The meat speaks for itself, super-tender with delicious au jus.

Having a little meat background myself, I really appreciate a restaurant that cuts its own meat. I'm talking band saw and everything. But when you go to the old school steakhouses you've got to be prepared to enjoy (and appreciate) some of the cultural classics like brains and eggs and lamb fries as well. Oh, by the way, let me tell you, *I gots to try 'em all.*

★ TRACK IT DOWN ★

**1309 S. Agnew Avenue
Oklahoma City, OK 73108
405-236-0416
www.cattlemensrestaurant.com**

KREW NOTES

Matt "Beaver" Giovinetti: Guy has a really amazing life. He's part chef, rock star, actor, stand-up comic, inspirational speaker, and television personality. What I think is so great about *DDD* is at times we get to see all of those facets of his life in one place. Guy is one of the funniest people I've ever known. He knows what's funny, his ability to improvise is unmatched, and his sense of timing is incredible. At Cattlemen's Steakhouse Guy and the chef had a hysterical time making the brains and eggs. As if eggs weren't enough, we had to throw in the brains! You can imagine Guy tackling this dish—the looks, the groans, the theatrics! After much teasing, Guy finally takes a bite. He looks around frantically for something to drink but doesn't find anything. Looking around further, he sees a plate of fried somethings in the food warmer next to the line. He grabs one and takes a bite. It's just as bad—it's lamb fries (lamb testicles). Guy created this entire comical scene on the fly, and it's something I'll never forget.

YOU TRY IT AND HAVE SOMEONE PHOTOGRAPH YOUR EXPRESSION . . .

 RESTAURANT UPDATE

Working with Guy was a real pleasure. Having a food service background, he was a true professional to work with. He understood and appreciated what we were doing. Our restaurant attracts a lot of out-of-town visitors, and the most frequent question is, "Is this where Guy Fieri was?" A popular experience is when visitors (both locals and travelers) have their picture taken next to the wall where Guy's picture is spray-painted. Having been featured on the show has given our (102-year-old) restaurant just one more stamp of credibility.

—DAVID EGAN,
DIRECTOR OF OPERATIONS,
CATTLEMEN'S STEAKHOUSE

I ALWAYS TWEAK OUT WHEN I SEE MEAT CUT WITH A BAND SAW.

CATTLEMEN'S LAMB FRIES

ADAPTED FROM A RECIPE COURTESY OF CATTLEMEN'S STEAKHOUSE

Serves 4

12 ounces frozen lamb testicles
1 cup cracker meal
Canola oil, for frying
Salt
Cocktail sauce and lemon wedges, for serving

1. Buy whole lamb testicles from a butcher and freeze them if they're not already frozen; they won't slice properly if you start from a thawed state.

2. Peel away the outside membrane on the testicles. With a sharp, serrated knife, slice the testicles very thinly (about ⅛ inch thick). The testicles may be sliced a couple of hours ahead and refrigerated or used right away.

3. Roll the slices in the cracker meal, making sure the whole surface is covered.

4. In a deep skillet, heat about ½ inch of oil to 360°F.

5. Drop the breaded lamb testicles slices into the hot oil and fry for 4 to 5 minutes, turning once or twice to ensure uniform browning.

6. Place the fried testes onto paper towels to absorb the oil. Season with salt and serve *immediately*! This is not a dish that can be held warm for a long time. They must be served hot.

7. Serve with your favorite cocktail sauce and a squeeze from a fresh lemon wedge.

CATTLEMEN'S BRAINS AND EGGS

ADAPTED FROM A RECIPE COURTESY OF CATTLEMEN'S STEAKHOUSE

Serves 2

2 tablespoons unsalted butter

6 ounces cleaned calf brains (find them at a butcher shop)

Salt and freshly ground black pepper

6 large eggs

1. Melt the butter in a nonstick sauté pan over low heat. Add the brains and cook until they are firm to the touch, about 6 minutes, stirring occasionally with a wooden spoon or rubber spatula and breaking them up as they cook. Season with salt and pepper.

2. Lightly beat the eggs in small bowl. Pour into the pan and scramble until they are done to your liking, 3 to 5 minutes.

3. Season with salt and pepper and serve immediately on warm plates.

ALL KINDS OF OLD-SCHOOL RIDES PARKED OUT FRONT.

OTTO'S SAUSAGE KITCHEN

IT'S LIKE MEAT DISNEYLAND

It's a broken record—Portland's an awesome place, particularly when it's sunny, but what makes it even more awesome is the food. You can find all kinds, but especially one of my favorites: handmade, homemade, house-cured and smoked sausage, in every way, shape, or form, not to mention the killer beef jerky. I sat outside at a picnic table and I thought I was in Germany.

In 1937, owner Jerry Eichentopf's grandfather opened the place. Now four generations strong, they're still making sausage the old-school way—and they even make their own old-fashioned

> ★ TRACK IT DOWN ★
>
> **4138 Southeast Woodstock Boulevard**
> **Portland, OR 97202**
> **503-771-6714**
> **www.ottossausage.com**

wieners here. Grilled up, their fifty kinds of sausage have snap, and they're tender, creamy, juicy, and studded with flavor. And they've also got roast beef, corned beef, and fresh smoked pastrami. All thriller, no filler.

KREW NOTES

Bryna "The Pirate" Levin: This is an amazing location that proved once and for all that a hot dog can be gourmet food—it just has to be made fresh with the right ingredients. They make the most amazing sausages and beef jerky, a favorite of Guy's that I get him every year for his birthday, shipped fresh from Portland.

Matt "Beaver" Giovinetti: You really "Otto" try this place, with old-school cured meats and a killer deli. They have one of the biggest buffalo choppers (an industrial kitchen grinder) I've ever seen.

THE FAMILY AND THEIR RACKS UPON RACKS OF SMOKED SAUSAGES.

OTTO'S BEER CHEESE SOUP

ADAPTED FROM A RECIPE COURTESY OF HEIDI EICHENTOPF,

DAUGHTER OF OWNERS JERRY AND GRETCHEN EICHENTOPF, OTTO'S SAUSAGE KITCHEN

Serves 8 to 10

½ cup (1 stick) unsalted butter

½ cup chopped carrot

½ cup chopped celery

1 medium yellow onion, chopped

½ cup all-purpose flour

One 12-ounce bottle or can of beer, such as Sierra Nevada Pale Ale or Blind Pig

2 cups chicken broth

7 ounces extra-sharp cheddar cheese, shredded

7 ounces Swiss cheese, shredded

2 cups half-and-half

1 teaspoon salt

½ teaspoon dry mustard

½ teaspoon Worcestershire sauce

1 pound smoked sausage, such as Otto's Smoked Polish Ring, cut into ¼-inch dice

1. Melt the butter in a large saucepan over medium heat. Add the carrot, celery, and onion and sauté until softened, about 10 minutes. Add the flour and cook for about 2 minutes, stirring often. While whisking constantly, slowly add the beer and let cook for 1 minute after all the beer has been added. Add the chicken broth and bring to a boil. Stirring constantly, slowly add the cheeses and cook until just boiling and smooth. Add the half-and-half, salt, dry mustard, and Worcestershire sauce. Reduce the heat to low and cook until the soup has thickened, 7 to 10 minutes.

2. Meanwhile, place the sausage in a sauté pan over medium heat and cook until heated through and lightly browned, about 5 minutes. Add the sausage to the soup, transfer to a large serving bowl, and serve hot.

WHERE PIGS FLY FOR REAL.

"HOW MUCH IS THAT DOGGIE IN THE WINDOW?" COME ON . . . SING ALONG.

BUNK SANDWICHES

HOME OF FUNKALICIOUS SANDWICHES

Reubens here are made with pork belly—need I say more? Okay, I will . . . I don't know if it's fair to call their Russian dressing Russian dressing—it should be called something sexy, like liquid Moscow. These guys are scratch-making the not-so-ordinary, from a salt cod sandwich with marinated olives and chorizo to a Vietnamese banhmi. Tommy Habetz and Nick Wood met at a fine dining joint. They always enjoyed making unusual sandwiches, so they went in together to open Bunk.

You can get the funk at Bunk. These dudes have creativity, enthusiasm, and sandwich style that's downright funkalicious.

> ★ TRACK IT DOWN ★
>
> **621 SE Morrison**
> **Portland, OR 97214**
> **503-477-9515**
> **www.bunksandwiches.com**

KREW NOTES

Anthony "Chico" Rodriguez: We show up at about six a.m. to get ready for Guy to arrive at eight a.m. to begin shooting. That day we were making a salt cod sandwich and a pork belly Reuben. Boy Band asked if they were all ready to shoot and had their mise en place set. They said, "All set." Now, *mise en place* is a French phrase meaning "everything in place," as in set up—or in our case, ready to shoot. It was at this point Butterbean heard the two owners talking:

Owner 1: "I can't believe we don't have any pork belly."
Owner 2: "It sold out as much as the cod—we have none of that here either."

It would make it tough to shoot *DDD* without the two featured items! As it turns out, not only did they not have the two main ingredients, they had *nothing* prepared. Now these are great guys, running this amazing sandwich shop, who just needed our help that day. Butterbean ran off to the store and Boy Band and I started chopping vegetables. About 7:58 a.m., as Guy is walking in the door, Neil put his knife down. The *DDD* crew gets it done—we're a great team, and sometimes that even means kitchen prep.

Neil "Boy Band" Martin: When we shoot *Diners*, we develop a very close relationship with the owners and the chefs we work with—we shoot at each location twice, sometimes three times. We cook the dishes you see in the show once without Guy (the secret is out now . . .) and again with him so we can edit the footage together and control the set. In this case, as Chico said, we did a bit more—about an hour before Guy's arrival we sent our audio tech, Jeff, to the grocery store not once, but twice, to get the produce we needed for the shoot. Rather than setting up lights, I spent my time in the kitchen chopping peppers and onions and hunting for ingredients. We still joke about it to this day, because every time we asked the owners Tommy and Nick if they had such and such ready for whatever I was prepping for, their answer was, "Totally, totally," or "Cool, cool." Amazingly enough, we got everything ready, the shot went off without a glitch, and I got to eat one of the best pork belly sandwiches I've ever had.

LIVE CAM: I'M EATING IT SO FAST THAT IT'S BLURRY!

BUNK SANDWICHES PORK BELLY REUBEN

ADAPTED FROM A RECIPE COURTESY OF TOMMY HABETZ AND NICK WOOD, BUNK SANDWICHES

Serves 4

Cured pork belly

1 cup kosher salt

1 cup sugar

1 tablespoon chopped garlic

1 teaspoon ground fennel

1 teaspoon ground nutmeg

1 teaspoon red chile flakes

1 to 2 pounds naturally raised pork belly

¼ to ½ cup molasses (depending on the size of the pork belly)

Sandwich

8 slices good seeded rye bread

1 cup Russian Dressing (recipe follows)

8 slices Swiss cheese

2 cups store-bought or homemade sauerkraut

2 tablespoons unsalted butter, melted

1. To make the pork belly, in a medium bowl, combine the salt, sugar, garlic, fennel, nutmeg, and chile flakes and coat the pork belly thoroughly. Cover and cure in the refrigerator for 2 to 3 days.

2. Preheat the oven to 275°F. Brush the cured pork belly with the molasses, place it in a roasting pan, and roast for 3½ to 4 hours, until tender. If the belly starts to get too dark, cover it in foil. Take it out of the oven and let it rest for at least 30 minutes. Slice ¼ inch thick.

3. To make the sandwiches, spread Russian dressing on one side of each bread slice. Place a slice of Swiss cheese on each bread slice. Add a couple of slices (2 ounces) of roasted pork belly to 4 of the bread slices and top with the sauerkraut. Top each of the 4 sandwiches with one of the remaining slices of bread with Swiss. Lightly brush melted butter on the outside of the sandwiches.

4. Heat a panini press or griddle over medium heat. Add the sandwiches to the press or griddle and cook until the cheese is melted, 4 to 6 minutes. Cut the sandwiches in half and serve.

RUSSIAN DRESSING ← Liquid Moscow

Makes about 3 cups

1 cup mayonnaise

1 cup ketchup

1 tablespoon grainy mustard

1 hard-boiled egg, peeled and chopped

2½ tablespoons bacon fat

1 tablespoon Tabasco sauce or other hot sauce

1½ tablespoons Worcestershire sauce

1 tablespoon red wine vinegar

½ cup chopped pickles

Salt and freshly ground black pepper, to taste

Combine all the ingredients thoroughly in a large bowl. Transfer the dressing to a container or bottle, cover, and refrigerate for at least 2 hours.

POK POK

SOUTHEAST ASIAN THAT KNOWS NO BOUNDARIES

You gotta love Portland: really cool people live there, like my goddaughters Sophia and Emma (shameless shout-out), there's great weather (when it's not raining), and then there's the awesome, awesome food. Like this joint, Pok Pok—Andy Ricker should be the ambassador of righteous Southeast Asian food to America. The dude knows no boundaries. Food processor? Never. He takes out a mortar and pestle, along with the coconut milk grinder he acquired just for one authentic dish. You want the real-deal experience without the twenty-hour plane ride? You gotta check out Pok Pok.

> ★ TRACK IT DOWN ★
>
> **3226 SE Division Street**
> **Portland, OR 97202**
> **503-232-1387**
> **www.pokpokpdx.com**

Andy does his best to get people to try something different, and there's no better place to do just that. Northern Thai drinking food? Check. Coconut curry soup made using an imported Thai coconut milk machine? Check. Sour-spicy green papaya salad? You know he's got that—it's called pok pok. But you have to try the Vietnamese chicken wings—some regulars call it meat candy. They're off the hook.

While I hung out with Andy I recognized he had all the coolest Asian ingredients and cooking equipment, and I pride myself on my arsenal of equipment and well-stocked pantry. So he took me to his local Asian market hot spot, and yes, I shipped home five boxes of $400 worth of Asian culinary ingredients and equipment I didn't have . . . Lori was thrilled.

KREW NOTES

Bryna "The Pirate" Levin: I think this was an eye-opening experience for a lot of the crew and for Guy. Pok Pok serves up incredibly authentic Thai food of a kind not often found outside of Thailand. The chef, Andy Ricker, won a James Beard Award the year after we shot with him and has gone on to get lots of national attention for his cooking. He cooked with ingredients I'd never seen, using cooking methods and vessels we'd never encountered. Guy was completely intrigued, and at the Asian market after the shoot Guy bought a wok that had to be four feet across. Not sure how that one made its way back to Santa Rosa, but Guy was pretty pleased with his purchase.

Matt "Beaver" Giovinetti: Chef Andy probably knows more about authentic Thai and Vietnamese food than anybody in the United States. The dude does everything from scratch, including making coconut milk with that machine he imported from Thailand. If it's not authentic, Andy doesn't do it.

LIVE CAM: DOESN'T MATTER, ANDY—YOU MAY BE THE OWNER, BUT I WAS IN LINE FIRST!

LIVE CAM: CHEF ANDY AND ME IN THE CHICKEN WING COCKPIT.

LIVE CAM: THE COCONUT MILK MACHINE, A TRUE FLAVORTOWN CULINARY WEAPON.

VIETNAMESE CHICKEN WINGS

ADAPTED FROM A RECIPE COURTESY OF ANDY RICKER, POK POK

Makes about 16 pieces

½ cup Vietnamese fish sauce

½ cup sugar

8 garlic cloves, minced, soaked in ¼ cup water for 30 minutes

2 pounds chicken wings (separate the drum from the rest of the wing, leaving the wing tip on)

Rice bran oil or vegetable oil, for frying

1 cup rice flour

¼ cup packaged tempura flour

Cucumber, pickled vegetables, and lettuce, for serving

1. In a bowl, whisk the fish sauce and sugar to dissolve the sugar. Squeeze the garlic through a piece of cheesecloth into the fish sauce mixture, reserving the garlic, and whisk again. Set aside half of the liquid, add the wings to the other half, and toss to coat. Cover and refrigerate for at least 4 hours or overnight to marinate, tossing the wings occasionally.

2. Heat ¼ cup rice bran oil in a wok over low heat. Add the minced garlic and cook until crispy and light brown, 3 to 4 minutes. Strain, then drain on paper towels.

3. In a large, thick-bottomed pot, heat 3 inches of oil to 350°F.

4. Drain the wings in a colander. Combine the rice flour and tempura flour in a shallow bowl, add the wings, and turn to coat. Knock off the excess flour and fry the wings in batches until golden and cooked through, 8 to 10 minutes. Drain the wings on paper towels.

5. In a wok, cook the reserved marinade over medium-high heat until syrupy, 1 to 2 minutes. Put the wings in the pan with the reduced marinade and toss, adding the fried garlic so it coats the wings.

6. Remove from the pan and serve immediately, with cucumber, pickled vegetables, and lettuce.

NOBLE PIG SANDWICHES

THE BEST THINGS BETWEEN SLICED BREAD

I lay claim to the knuckle sandwich . . . it's my brand, my logo, hell, even my tattoo, so when I find out that two dudes in Austin have opened up a sandwich joint and one of their menu items is the knuckle sandwich, I tell you what, they'd better deliver the real deal. (jk.) Now, fortunately things didn't get messy . . . the guys were great

★ TRACK IT DOWN ★

**11815 620 North, Suite 4
Austin, TX 78750
512-382-6248
www.noblepigaustin.com**

CAN YA FEEL THE POWER OF THE KNUCKLE SANDWICH? I CAN!

SEEEEEE? IT SAYS KNUCKLE SANDWICH . . . I GOT DIBS.

and the knuckle sandwich was the bomb. And they even legitimized their piracy of my beloved knuckle sandwich with the offering of the duck pastrami. Shut the front door, it was killer. So, I guess for now we'll kind of call you guys at the Noble Pig charter members of the Knuckle Sandwich Krew. Dues are due December first.

Brandon Martinez and John Bates are house smokin', curing, and butchering just about everything for a sandwich. They met up at culinary school and decided to get serious about sandwiches. Bread's baked fresh daily, and like I said, regular pastrami isn't good enough for these guys—they have to make it with duck. Darn good duck—perfect balance of salt, smoke, and fat that melts in your mouth. And that roast beef, cheddar, and horseradish knuckle sandwich requires a fork and knife . . .

Noble Pig Sandwiches does pig three ways—pulled pork, ham, and bacon—and did I mention that they cure their own bacon for all their sandwiches? They're the pig mafia.

KREW NOTES

Ryan "Donny" Larson: Noble Pig had a disco ball hanging in the kitchen. We thought it would only be right to shut off the lights and have it going when Guy came in. He gave us a short dance routine, and it ended up making the show! Guy: They promised it wouldn't air . . . They will pay!!

Matt "Beaver" Giovinetti: Smoked. Duck. Pastrami. Three of my favorite words. Eccentric dudes making eccentric food.

KNUCKLE SANDWICH

ADAPTED FROM A RECIPE COURTESY OF BRANDON MARTINEZ AND JOHN BATES, NOBLE PIG SANDWICHES

Serves 1

4 ounces sliced Roast Beef (recipe follows)

¼ cup warm Au Jus (recipe follows), plus more for dipping

1 hoagie roll or baguette, cut in half lengthwise

3 tablespoons Horseradish Sauce (recipe follows)

1 or 2 slices sharp cheddar cheese

¼ cup caramelized onions

Heat the sliced roast beef and au jus in a skillet over medium-high heat. Stuff the bread with the horseradish sauce, cheese, caramelized onions, and hot roast beef. Then, to take the sando over the top, dunk the whole thing in au jus. Serve with a knife and fork.

ROAST BEEF

4 to 8 sandwiches worth of beef, depending on the size of your roast

At Noble Pig Sandwiches they use the knuckle, which is the old-school butcher's term for the bottom of the inside round.

1½ pounds beef, such as the inside round or center-cut beef tenderloin roast

3 to 4 tablespoons vegetable oil

3 tablespoons salt

1 tablespoon freshly ground black pepper

2 tablespoons granulated garlic

1. Preheat the oven to 400°F.

2. Rub the beef with the oil, salt, pepper, and granulated garlic. Don't be shy with the seasoning—it needs lots of flavor. Place the beef in a roasting pan and roast until the internal temperature reaches 135°F, 30 to 45 minutes. Make sure to save the pan drippings for the au jus. Let the meat rest for about 15 minutes, then slice it for your sandos.

AU JUS
Makes about 1 quart

Pan drippings from the roast beef

2 tablespoons fresh thyme leaves

2 tablespoons granulated garlic

1 teaspoon freshly ground black pepper (if you love black pepper, go for a full tablespoon)

1 tablespoon brown sugar

¼ cup red wine vinegar

Salt to taste

In a medium saucepan over medium heat, combine all the ingredients and 1 quart water and bring to a simmer. Cook for 15 minutes and adjust the seasoning to your taste. The jus should be clear, brown, and brothy.

MY KULINARY ROCK IMPRESSION OF THE GREAT GENE SIMMONS.

HORSERADISH SAUCE
Makes about 2¼ cups

¼ pound fresh horseradish

Canola oil, if needed

2 cups mayonnaise

1 teaspoon cayenne pepper

⅛ teaspoon smoked paprika

1 lemon

Salt and freshly ground black pepper

Peel the horseradish and grind it to a fine consistency in a food processor. You may need to add a little oil to help the horseradish grind. In a medium bowl, combine the ground horseradish, mayonnaise, cayenne, and paprika. Zest and juice the lemon, then add the zest and juice to the bowl. Mix together and season with salt and pepper.

RAINBOW DRIVE-IN

A DRIVE-IN IN PARADISE

As if going to Oahu in Hawaii isn't great enough in itself—I mean you've got Diamond Head, snorkeling at Hanauma Bay, and visiting the North Shore—then going to the Rainbow Drive-In just pushes it all over the top. This place is amazing. Even before I went there, Jim Gusukuma and his crew were banging out 1,200 plate lunches a day—which is more than 400,000 a year. Stop, stand in line, and get ready to wow your taste buds. This is a drive-in in paradise.

Plate lunches started being served to the workingman out of lunch wagons and Rainbow was one of the first that went bricks and mortar. Since 1961 they've been serving up Hawaiian specialties with 2 scoops of rice, a scoop of macaroni salad, and then whatever main dish you choose, like barbecued steak, shoyu chicken, or mahi mahi. Then there's the loco moco—rice, hamburger, and fried eggs with gravy on top. Even their gravy starts with homemade chicken stock—and they serve about 300 gallons a week, easily. Another best-seller is their chili plate with 2 hot dogs; it's spicy, creamy, and dynamite. It's classic Hawaiian fast food.

> ★ TRACK IT DOWN ★
>
> **3308 Kanaina Avenue**
> **Honolulu, HI 96815**
> **808-737-0177**
> **www.rainbowdrivein.com**

KREW NOTES

Anthony "Chico" Rodriguez: Recently I took my family to Hawaii on vacation to Oahu, which was followed up by a *DDD* shoot. I have gotten to meet many great people over the years of *DDD* and the owner of Rainbow, Jim Gusukuma, has become a great friend. Jim hung out a few times with my family while we were on vacation and took the time to teach my daughters how to surf, which they still talk about to this day! All told, I was on the island of Oahu for eighteen days—and I ate at Rainbow eighteen times.

When we shot there, we were told we were going to make a chili plate of homemade chili and macaroni salad with rice. By the description I thought to myself, *Can that really be that good?* Let me confirm: I had it every day of the trip and am planning my next visit to Oahu, with many stops at Rainbow for good food and great friends.

Jeff "Butterbean" Asell: I noticed when I went back to Rainbow that they put the menu on flat panel TVs so Guy couldn't manipulate prices by just moving numbers around. Good move! Cuz he's been known to play jokes by changing the letters on the menu board.

 RESTAURANT UPDATE

In 2011 Rainbow Drive-In celebrated its fiftieth anniversary, selling some of its popular plate lunches at rollback prices to thank its longtime—and loyal—customers. The iconic local eatery also opened a logo store next door, added a few more parking stalls, and installed digital menu boards—all ushering in the next fifty years in Hawaii.

—JIM GUSUKUMA

THE MAYOR OF FLAVORTOWN ISLAND!

SHOYU CHICKEN

RECIPE COURTESY OF SUE MAYNARD, FORMER COOK, RAINBOW DRIVE-IN

Serves 4 to 6

2½ teaspoons finely minced garlic

1½ tablespoons Worcestershire sauce

1¼ cups shoyu soy sauce

1 cup sugar

3 tablespoons apple cider vinegar

¼ teaspoon freshly ground black pepper

2 ounces (5 tablespoons) peeled and crushed fresh ginger

5 pounds bone-in chicken thighs

3 tablespoons all-purpose flour

THE SHOYU MASTER, SUE MAYNARD.

1. Mix together the garlic, Worcestershire, soy sauce, sugar, vinegar, black pepper, and ginger in a small bowl. Heat a large sauté pan over medium heat and sear the chicken skin side down for 3 to 5 minutes. Turn the chicken skin side up and pour in the sauce. Bring to a boil, then lower the heat and simmer for 40 minutes, skimming off any fat that rises.

2. In the meantime, combine the flour and 3 tablespoons of water and whisk until smooth to make a slurry. Bring the chicken mixture to a boil again, add the flour slurry, and stir to combine. Lower the heat and simmer for 10 minutes to thicken. Arrange the chicken in a deep serving platter and cover with the sauce.

JIM TEACHING CHICO'S GIRL HOW TO SURF—OR IS CHICO'S GIRL TEACHING HIM?

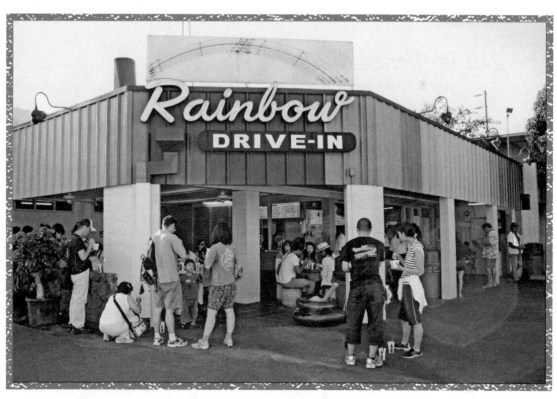

DON'T LET THIS PICTURE FOOL YOU . . . THE LINE IS WAY LONGER.

FRESH LOCAL WILD

SEAFOOD SO FRESH IT'LL SLAP YA

Located in Vancouver, British Columbia, this is a "restaurant on wheels," 'cause that's what chef Josh Wolfe likes to call it. But I prefer to call it "the caboose on the train of the Flavortown Express." Ladies and gentlemen, you're stepping into the delicious zone with this guy. I knew right off the bat I was going to overeat. He's a couple blocks from the water and uses fish he often buys straight from the fishermen. This guy's got moves so good we set them to disco music. He's a lean, mean, street vendin,' cookin' machine. His seafood is so fresh it'll slap ya. He's

LIVE CAM: ALL ABOARD THE FLAVORTOWN EXPRESS.

★ TRACK IT DOWN ★

Safest bet: Check the website
Southeast corner of Hastings and Burrard
Vancouver, BC V6R 2R6
Canada
www.freshlocalwild.com

CANADA OR BUST

Everybody was out of their minds when we found out *Triple D* was going international. I've got e-mails, Twitter posts, texts—you name it, with "you gotta come check out this joint!" Now, granted, we have a strong Food Network following in Canada, but the real question was: Is the '68 going to make it through customs? (*Ha ha ha*.) When we started looking in Vancouver, north of my home state, it didn't take us long to realize that there was a virtual cornucopia of *Triple D*–worthy joints. We came, we found, we ate, and we will be back! To my Canadian brothers and sisters, thanks for all the *Triple D* support, especially sending all the info and tips. You've got a huge country, and we want more.

Guy!

got a poutine with more seafood in it than you get at a fancy restaurant and an oyster sandwich po-boy style so good that you'd think you're in N'awlins.

My recommendation: Before you fly out to BC, get a GPS on this dude, cause he's mobile. Should be called: Fresh, Local, and Crazy.

KREW NOTES

Kerry "Gilligan" Johnson: Guy caused quite a stir on that busy corner in Vancouver!

Jeff "Butterbean" Asell: I like simple descriptive names—they nailed it at Fresh Local Wild.

Ryan "Donny" Larson: I received my yellow construction helmet here (which on occasion I still wear while shooting on set). A picture of me getting my yellow helmet made the Vancouver newspaper.

 ## RESTAURANT UPDATE

DDD has such an amazing fan base, and we're so happy Guy shared them with us! More than anything, the show brought people here that we might never have met, and it's so great that everyone comes to say hello. We look forward to meeting all of you in the seasons to come!

—JOSH WOLFE

BC SEAFOOD CHOWDER "POUTINE"

ADAPTED FROM A RECIPE COURTESY OF JOSH WOLFE, FRESH LOCAL WILD

This recipe makes a wonderful chowder. Most of the time at the restaurant, it's used over the-house-made French fries, but it's really quite versatile. Certainly you can fry your own, but even oven fries make the perfect host. Or use it as a base for a piece of seared fish, a soup, or, if thickened a little more, as a great dip for chips—think spinach and seafood dip hot out of the oven.

Serves 12 as poutine or 4 as chowder

Stock

1 teaspoon coriander seeds

1 teaspoon fennel seeds

1 teaspoon white peppercorns

4 garlic cloves, sliced

4 shallots or 1 small onion, sliced

1 tablespoon unsalted butter

2 pounds fresh clams

1½ cups dry white wine (I use sauvignon blanc)

6 to 8 sprigs fresh thyme, plus more if desired

3 bay leaves

2 pounds fresh mussels

Sauce

1 pound smoked bacon, cut into ½-inch pieces

½ cup (1 stick) plus 3 tablespoons unsalted butter

2 garlic cloves, finely chopped

2 shallots, finely diced

½ cup white wine

½ cup all-purpose flour

4 cups cold whole milk

1 cup ⅓-inch-diced carrots

1 cup ⅓-inch-diced celery

1 cup ⅓-inch-diced fennel

¼ cup finely chopped fresh flat-leaf parsley

Salt

Finely sliced chives or green onions, for garnish

French fries, for serving (optional)

1. FOR THE STOCK: Sweat the coriander seeds, fennel seeds, peppercorns, garlic, and shallots in the butter in a heavy-bottomed pot over medium heat (this will help control the heat so you don't burn the ingredients). When the shallots are translucent, about 5 minutes, add the clams, white wine, thyme, and bay leaves. Cover the pot to steam the clams, and as they begin to open, add the mussels. Simmer gently, covered, to open the mussels and remaining clams, about 3 minutes.

2. When all the shells are open, strain off the liquid and reserve, setting aside the shellfish to cool slightly until you can handle them. Shuck the meat out of all the shells, refrigerate, and reserve for the sauce. Discard the vegetables and herbs.

3. FOR THE SAUCE: Cook the bacon in the same pot over medium heat to render the fat. This will be used to make the roux later. When the bacon begins to brown, add 3 tablespoons of the butter, the garlic, and shallots. Continue to sweat over medium heat until the shallots are translucent, about 5 minutes. Add the white wine and reduce until it's almost dry, about 5 minutes. Add the reserved shellfish stock and reduce by half, about 30 minutes. Remove from the heat and set aside on the stovetop.

4. Melt the remaining ½ cup butter in a separate small saucepan or deep sauté pan over medium heat to the bubbling point and stir in the flour very well with a wooden spoon, incorporating it while removing clumps. Cook for 3 to 5 minutes while stirring regularly, to make a lightly browned roux. Add the roux to the pan with the bacon and place over medium heat. Add the cold milk to the hot roux while stirring constantly. Bring to a boil, then reduce to a simmer. You will have to monitor it carefully and stir frequently so the flour doesn't stick to the bottom (if it does, don't panic! You can remove the sauce, clean the bottom of the pot, and put it back in . . . phew!). Simmer for 10 minutes, then add the carrots, celery, and fennel, and continue cooking until the raw flour taste has been cooked out and the vegetables are tender (they will add texture to the finished chowder), about 20 minutes longer.

5. Add the reserved mussels and clams. Simmer for 1 minute to heat through and add the parsley. Season with salt, garnish with the chives, and serve immediately either as chowder or over french fries.

COOK'S NOTE: The chowder can be cooled and stored for several days before serving; add the reserved mussels and clams right before serving.

TOMAHAWK RESTAURANT

A COMMUNITY ICON SINCE 1926 THAT'S GOT THE BEEF

Thank goodness there are strict border controls between Canada and the United States, otherwise I don't think it would be too far-fetched to believe that I might make some midnight runs to the Tomahawk. They serve up perfectly cooked roast beef in their beef dip and, more important, as a supporting role in one of my favorite things from childhood: Yorkshire pudding. It's the oldest restaurant in Vancouver and still run by the same family, servin' up the real deal.

Second-generation owner Chick Chamberlain took over the place from his parents, who opened it back in 1926. They apparently made it more of a meeting place in the beginning—and didn't know how to cook. But that's all changed now, even more so with Chef Anne Zubaidi behind the stove. (I am now a disciple, because I sucked at making my Yorkshire pudding before getting schooled by Anne. Now they're puffy McMagic, not flat McTragic.) Their beef dip (tri-tip sandwich) is made with homemade beef stock and au jus . . . there are so many things that make this so right: the meat,

⋆ TRACK IT DOWN ⋆

1550 Philip Avenue
North Vancouver, BC V7P 2V8
Canada
604-988-2612
www.tomahawkrestaurant.com

the gravy, the garlic butter, the bread. Then there's the hundred-year-old recipe for steak and mushroom pie. She could feed me beef six ways to Sunday.

When I was an exchange student in France, I took a train to Brussels, then a ferry to England, and another train all the way up to Yorkshire. When I got there I met up with a girl I went to school with, Jenny Thompson, who was spending her junior year in high school with her aunt. When I arrived, exhausted from travel, she said, "Oh, sit down, my aunt will make you something awesome, some Yorkshire pudding." Yorskhire pudding? I hate pudding. I spent the next twenty-five minutes dreading what I assumed was some custard pudding thing. Yet, lo and behold, out it came, and I ate all they could make—and I've been on the quest for great Yorkshire pudding ever since.

KREW NOTES

Kate "Ask Kate" Gibson: It's always a great experience for a producer when your talent is particularly excited about the food, and man, Guy loves Yorkshire pudding. So when Anne, our chef, knew how to do it right, he went mad for the dish. The secret to the dish is getting it in the oven and not peeking (patience not being Guy's specialty), so at times we had to hold him back, but the result was worth it.

CHICK EXPLAINS HOW HE'LL AIR-DROP YORKSHIRE PUDDING TO ME IN NOR CAL!

YORKSHIRE PUDDINGS

RECIPE COURTESY OF ANNE ZUBAIDI, TOMAHAWK RESTAURANT

Makes 12 Yorkshire puddings

1¼ cups all-purpose flour

¾ cup whole or low-fat milk

2 eggs

1½ teaspoons salt

Freshly ground black pepper

2 tablespoons beef drippings, lard, or vegetable oil

1. Preheat the oven to 425°F.

2. In a large bowl, whisk together the flour, milk, ½ cup water, the eggs, salt, and pepper to taste.

3. Divide the beef drippings among the cups of a 12-cup muffin pan. Place in the oven and bake until the drippings are smoking hot.

4. Divide the batter equally among the muffin cups. Bake until golden brown and crisp, 20 to 25 minutes.

CHEF ANNE AND HER MAGIC OVEN.

THE RED WAGON CAFÉ

WHERE THE PRESIDENT OF PORK RUNS THE KITCHEN

Who knew that the folks in Vancouver would be so porktastic? I mean I am the official POP (Pal of Pork), but this guy with this menu looks like he could be running for President of Pork. It's real-deal food—the only thing I caution you is to watch out for that crazy split personality dish that disguises itself as pancakes but sneaks up on ya with killer barbecue and some righteous Jack Daniel's syrup.

Chef/owner Brad Miller takes a wild ride with creative combinations of classic foods. He does short ribs with brie, croque madames, and a crispy pork belly that takes bacon to a whole new level. This should be illegal: confited pork belly, that's then deep-fried. Served up with salsa verde, hollandaise, roasted tomato, eggs, and home fries, it's going big done right.

> ★ TRACK IT DOWN ★
>
> **2296 East Hastings Street**
> **East Vancouver, BC V5L 1V4**
> **Canada**
> **604-568-4565**
> **www.redwagoncafe.com**

KREW NOTES

Kerry "Gilligan" Johnson: Guy called Jeff Arnett, the head distiller at Jack Daniel's, to chat about the recipe mid-shoot—the chef had to love that!

Jeff "Butterbean" Asell: Pork, pancakes, and bourbon—I dream of these during tailgating season . . .

Ryan "Donny" Larson: Jack Daniel's syrup. Need I say more? I've had some in my refrigerator ever since the shoot.

PULLED PORK PANCAKES WITH JD SYRUP

ADAPTED FROM A RECIPE COURTESY OF BRAD MILLER, THE RED WAGON CAFÉ

Serves 6 (makes about 18 pancakes)

2 cups all-purpose flour

2 teaspoons baking soda

1 teaspoon salt

2 large eggs

2 cups buttermilk

Canola oil, for cooking the pancakes

Pulled pork (recipe follows)

JD Syrup (recipe follows)

Salted butter, for serving

THINGS ARE OUTTA CONTROL WITH THE JACK DANIEL'S SYRUP!

LIVE CAM: COME ON IN TO THE HOME OF THE PORKTASTIC MENU.

NOTE: You'll need a smoker for this recipe.

1. Blend the flour, baking soda, and salt in a bowl. In a separate, larger bowl, blend the egg and buttermilk. Fold the dry ingredients into the wet, taking care not to overmix. Leave the batter slightly lumpy.

2. Heat some oil in a large nonstick pan over medium heat. Ladle about ¼ cup pancake batter into the pan for each pancake, cooking 3 at a time. Cook the pancakes for about 2 minutes per side, flipping once when edges are golden and small bubbles form on top.

3. To serve, layer hot pulled pork between the 3 pancakes. Cover with JD Syrup and top with a pat of salted butter. Repeat!

PULLED PORK

As this makes more pulled pork than you need, go ahead and freeze any leftovers for future pancakes; it freezes beautifully. And you'll have more spice rub than you'll need, so you can store it in a covered jar in the refrigerator for future BBQ.

Serves 12

Spice rub

1 tablespoon ground black pepper

2 teaspoons cayenne pepper

2 tablespoons chile powder

3 tablespoons ground coriander

1 tablespoon dark brown sugar

1 tablespoon dried oregano

⅓ cup paprika

⅓ cup kosher salt

2 tablespoons ground white pepper

1 boneless pork butt, about 3 pounds

Small bag of wood chips (preferably hickory), soaked in water for 30 minutes

2 bottles or cans of your favorite beer

Your favorite BBQ sauce

1. Combine all the rub spices in a bowl and rub the pork butt with ¼ cup of the spice mixture. Wrap the pork butt in plastic wrap and refrigerate for 12 hours or overnight.

2. Unwrap the pork butt and smoke for about 1 hour. (Follow the stovetop smoker manufacturer's instructions or use an outdoor smoker.)

3. Preheat the oven to 225°F. Remove the pork butt from the smoker, place it in a roasting pan, and add the beer. Cover and braise in the oven until the pork is tender and pulls apart with a fork, about 3 hours.

4. Pull the pork and mix it with ½ cup of the braising liquid and BBQ sauce to taste.

JD SYRUP

One 12-ounce bottle pure maple syrup
Whiskey, such as Jack Daniel's

In a medium saucepan, heat the maple syrup over medium heat. Add whiskey to taste and bring to a boil for a couple of minutes. Keep warm to serve. Store leftovers in the refrigerator.

"YA SEE, GUY—PULLED PORK PANCAKES ARE YOUR FRIEND!"

MEAT & BREAD

WHERE A SMALL MENU MEETS MONSTER FLAVOR

Let's just get this straight right off the bat: Meat & Bread is not your everyday sandwich joint. You can eat there 365 days a year and eat a different sandwich every day. They make only four different types of sandwiches on a particular day, but let me just tell you this, whatever sandwich you order, they make a porchetta that you won't forgetta.

> ★ TRACK IT DOWN ★
>
> **370 Cambie Street**
> **Vancouver, BC, Canada V6B 2N3**
> **604-566-9003**
> **www.meatandbread.ca**

MEAT + BREAD = MONEY!

THESE PEOPLE NEVER LEAVE—AND FOR GOOD REASON.

It all started when owners Frankie Harrington and Cord Jarvie met in Dublin while working at a restaurant. They'd head to Sunday "carvery" or roast dinner together and think about what it would be like to put that into a sandwich, and now chef Joe Sartor does the heavy lifting in the kitchen. And for that porchetta they get the best local pork they can buy, and it's culinary gangster. It's so juicy and tender and balanced—they rock it.

KREW NOTES

Kate "Ask Kate" Gibson: This place is run by a few young guys, and the entire place is white and green, very carefully designed by an interior decorator friend of theirs, who attended our shoot that day. When we told everyone that we were about to spray-paint our traditional insignia on the wall, "Guy Ate Here," he went ballistic. So, this place is one of the only *DDD* restaurants with no spray-paint insignia on its walls.

PORCHETTA

ADAPTED FROM A RECIPE COURTESY OF MEAT & BREAD

Makes 4 sandwiches

3 pounds boneless pork middleloin, rind on (or substitute pork belly, rind on)

Salt Rub (recipe follows)

Salsa Verde (recipe follows)

½ cup chopped fresh flat-leaf parley

2 tablespoons chopped fresh rosemary

Olive oil

4 bread rolls

1. Preheat the oven to 300°F.

2. Score the rind of the pork in a crosshatch pattern. Turn the pork over and season the flesh side heavily using two thirds of the salt rub mixture. Spoon half of the salsa verde on the flesh of the pork. Evenly distribute the chopped parsley and rosemary on the flesh. Roll the pig from loin to belly in a log form and tie with butcher's twine in equal intervals. Rub the pork down with olive oil, followed by the remainder of the salt rub mixture.

3. Place the pork on a wire rack over a baking sheet and roast for 1 hour and 45 minutes, or until the internal temperature reaches 115°F. Increase the oven temperature to 450°F and roast until the pork reaches an internal temperature of 160°F and the skin is crispy, about 15 more minutes. Remove from the oven and allow the roast to rest for 20 minutes. Transfer to a cutting board and slice the pork, mixing the belly meat, crackling, and loin. Serve the meat on bread rolls and top with the remaining salsa verde.

SALT RUB

2 teaspoons fennel seeds

2 teaspoons coriander seeds

2 teaspoons dried rosemary

2 teaspoons black peppercorns

2 teaspoons red chile flakes

2 tablespoons coarse sea salt

Zest of 1 lemon

Toast the fennel seeds, coriander seeds, and rosemary in a dry skillet over medium heat for 2 minutes. Grind the toasted herbs and spices along with the peppercorns and chile flakes in a spice grinder or mortar and pestle. Mix in the sea salt and lemon zest.

SALSA VERDE

1 teaspoon fennel seeds

1 teaspoon coriander seeds

1 teaspoon red chile flakes

2 bunches fresh flat-leaf parsley, stemmed

4 garlic cloves

1 cup olive oil

Zest and juice of 2 lemons

Kosher salt

1. Toast the fennel and coriander seeds in a dry skillet over medium heat for 2 minutes. Grind the fennel, coriander, and chile flakes in a spice grinder or mortar and pestle.

2. In a food processor or blender, combine the parsley, garlic, ground fennel, coriander, and chile flakes, and the olive oil and blend until smooth. Mix in the lemon zest and juice and season with salt.

ACKNOWLEDGMENTS

GUY THANKS

My family: Lori, Hunter, and Ryder Fieri. Jim and Penny Ferry. Morgan, Jules, and Annie. The Price, Langermeier, Barrett, Bowers, Apel, Nelson, Ramsay, and Stansbury families. Donna, Jason, Shauntel, Brandon, and Jordan Brisson, Rock Star, Cowboy, Medusa, and Roxy. **The Knuckle Sandwich Team:** Reid Strathearn, Anthony Hoy Fong, Rena Brown, Ron "Turtle" Wargo, Tom Howard, Riley Lagesen. **The Krew:** My sister Ann Volkwein, writer extraordinaire. Thanks for all of your great support and excellent literary skills—and congrats on being a new mom. Dustin and Jen Rota, Ariel "The Spanyard" and Nicole Ramirez, Paul "Dirty P" and Lisa Brown, Lisa Millerick-Thompson, Jesse "Possum" and Brandi Smith, "Gorilla" Rich Bacchi, Paul "5-0" Messerschmitt, Carl "Cuban" Ruiz, Marie Kirby, Daniel "Millie" Millich, Justin "Jenkie" Kunkle, Matt Pintor, "Cowboy" Mike and Cam Barrer, Milt "Uncle Milt" Close, Brian "Bags" Baglietto, Brian Daly, Big Jon Snyder, Nico and Sikey, Mike "Part Time" Burwell, "Stretch," "Hodad," Gary Maggetti, Eric "Reno" Schweikl, Jack Levar, Chris and Amy Lands, Joe and Misty Magelitz, "Panini" Pete Bloehme, Johnny "Sizzleshanks" Quinlan, Reno "Chicken F'er" Henriques. **The Johnny Garlic's and Tex Wasabi's Team. Guy's American Kitchen & Bar NYC:** Jon Bloostein and the team. **Guy Fieri On Campus:** Tom Post, Ray Torres, Gloria Chabot, Ann Pulczinski and the team at Sodexo. **William Morris Endeavor:** Jason "The Man" Hodes, Jeff "The Big Deal" Googel, Bethany Dick, Michelle "Michi" Bernstein, Jon Rosen, Deb Shuwarger, Mark Itkin, Dorian Karchmar. Jenni, Liz, and Julia. **Sunshine Sachs:** Shawn Sachs, Pamela Spiegel, Ethan Rabin, Maggie McKeon. **William Morrow:** Cassie Jones, Kara Zauberman, Liate Stehlik, Lynn Grady, Tavia Kowalchuk, Megan Swartz, Joyce Wong, Ann Cahn, Paula Szafranski, Kris Tobiassen, Karen Lumley. **Art and illustration:** Joe Leonard, Monkey Wrench Tattoo. **Food Network:** Brooke Johnson, Bob Tuschman, Allison Page, Susie Fogelson, Brian Lando, Pat Guy, Bill Calamita, Robert Madden, Jr., Susan Stockton, Miriam Garron, Jill Novatt, Liz Tarpy, Irika Slavin, Seth Hyman, Katie Ilch, Amanda Melnick, Jessica Baumgardner, Norina Li. **Guy's Big Bite:** Mark "Dunkee" Dissin, Jeff Christian, Jenna Zimmerman, Danielle LaRosa, Santos Loo, and the *GBB* Krew. **Special mention to the rest of the supporting characters in Guy's Food Quest:** The Motley Que: Matt "Mustard" and Melissa Sprouls, Mikey Z, Riley, and Unyawn. My Sista, Rachael Ray. Jimmy John and Leslie Liataud. Marc Summers. Jeff Arnett and Jack Daniel's. Rob Myers and Myers Restaurant Supply. Marcee Katz and Chefworks. Carol Press. Gatorz Sunglasses. Pesto. Rob Weakley, Dave Bernahl and Pebble Beach Food & Wine. The cast of **Rachael vs. Guy: Celebrity Cook Off.** Sherwood and Globe Shoes. Marcel and Tera Reece. Oakland Raiders. The York family and the 49ers. Steve and Sean at Chevy. Room 101 Jewelry. Fender Guitars. Teddy "Castro" the driver. Evan Miller and Lifetime Brands. Gia Brands. Josh Solovy and Golden West/Completely Fresh Foods. Emeril and Alden Lagasse. Mario Batali. Bill Nolan. Tom Rowan. Jeff Blazy. Coach at KJ. DJ Cobra. Mike Perea. Manny "Papi" Hinojosa. Fred and Cowboy Mouth. Steve and Landyn Hutchinson. Robert Irvine. "Uncle" Bo Dietl. Eric Lindell. Brent Farris and KZST. Rob and Jocelyn and KFGY. Marcy Smothers. Pete Howe. Young's Market. Roger and Kicker. Ron Little. National Pork Board. Steve from Smash Mouth. Pat Williams. Andrea at Mugnaini. Bob Cabral, Chevy Dave, Jane and Roger Holm, the Culinary Program at Maria Carrillo High School, Phil Krohn, Cartronics. All my friends and family in Sonoma County, Ferndale, and the great US of A.

THE TRIPLE D KREW GIVES THANKS

Kat Higgins, Executive Producer. Sincerest thanks to those who have been instrumental building blocks of *DDD*, whose talent and perseverance have nurtured me and impacted the continued success of this phenomenal show. My ever-supportive family and extraordinary son, the original *DDD* team, the remarkable Citizen Pictures, and the Luke Skywalker to my Princess Leia—the outstanding Guy. I am inspired by each of you.

Anthony "Chico" Rodriguez, Director of Photography. To be part of *DDD* from the very beginning, affecting so many restaurants and lives in a positive way, has been an incredible gift. A huge thank you to Guy—our quarterback, running back, and everything along the way—for being the soul of what this show is about, but more important, for being a great friend. A thank you to Citizen for being great partners. A thank you to everyone at Match/Cut for being a team & family to be proud of. But, the biggest *thank you* there is goes to my three girls: my wife, Sarah, and my two amazing daughters, Ava and Vivian. *DDD* takes us all away from home a lot. Their love and support not only make it all possible but also makes for great hugs at the airport coming back from every trip. Sarah, Ava, and Vivian, I love you guys "bigger than space."

David "Big Bunny" Canada, Audio Tech. Thank you, *DDD* locations, Food Network, and Guy. Thank you Lori, Hunter, and Ryder for sharing your husband and dad with the *DDD* crew for all these years. My parents, for love and support, and my sister, Avery, and family for always having a welcoming home and heart. Thank you, *DDD*, for introducing me to the love of my life, and a hell of a producer, Kate Gibson. Love and respect to my road family at Match/Cut Productions and Citizen Pictures. Thank you, *DDD* fans, for keeping us on the road!

Mike "Father Time" Morris, Field Producer. Thank you to everyone who created this wonderful show, and allowed me to become part of it. Thanks to Anthony Rodriguez and David Canada, my close friends, who made the call to make it happen for me. And thanks to all at Citizen Pictures who make the magic happen every Monday night. A big thank you to our crew, my second family on the road. A real *big* thank you to my wife, Jill, and my children, who allow me to be on the road, sometimes weeks at a time, to do the job I love. And the one person without whom this would have not been possible, Guy Fieri, a great friend and the most talented person I've ever seen on TV.

Bryna "The Pirate" Levin, Field Producer. My first shoot for *DDD* was in 2007. Guy was shocked that I was missing my son's birthday for work, but my son forgave me and I'm still with the show. It's been an epic ride that I'm thrilled to be a part of. Thanks to everyone on the crew whose professionalism and friendship make it so worthwhile, thanks to Citizen Pictures for picking up the ball and running with it, and thanks in particular to Guy, the engine fueling us all. Namaste.

Kate "Ask Kate" Gibson AKA Kate Canada, Field Producer. On *DDD* I met my husband, David, my miracle and my rock. For that I'll always be thankful. Thank you to Guy, whose hard work and passion make this show great. Thank you to his amazing family for sparing him so we can explore America. Thank you to my family, for not wigging out when I announced what I wanted to do when I grew up. But mostly, thank you Match/Cut, my close friends, and steadfast crew who make every day of work a joy.

Liz "Erd" Pollock, Field Producer. Endless appreciation to my unconditionally loving family: Russ, JoAnn, John, and Adrian. To Lori, Hunter, and Ryder; thanks for sharing Guy with us all these years. To the *DDD* crew and Citizen Pictures, thanks for your unwavering support, both professionally and personally. Lastly, here's to Guy, who takes time out for me and for all of us even when he's spinning busy. Cheers, Guy!

Matt "Beaver" Giovinetti, Director of Photography. My deepest gratitude, love, and thanks to my mom, Martha-Lee Ellis. You have always loved, supported, and believed in me. *DDD* is the greatest job with the best field team ever assembled. I'm grateful to and love you all. Thanks to David and Anthony at Match/ Cut. I've grown personally and professionally with you guys over the years—many more to come! Thanks to Guy Fieri for all the years, thanks to Mike Morris for all the beers.

Neil "Boy Band" Martin, Associate Producer. *Triple D* has been an amazing ride for me, and I feel truly blessed. I am entirely grateful for the team I work with at Citizen Pictures and Match/Cut Productions, and to Guy for being the best host in television. Most important, our incredible fans! You continue to watch even after seeing an episode a dozen times, and it never gets old. I see what you say on the Internet and it makes me realize how lucky I really am!

Jeff "Butterbean" Asell, Audio Tech. My appreciation goes first off to my cherished wife, Michelle. Her love and patience make my long road trips manageable, and they're my reason to rush home. The fans are the reason we still get to run around the country and shoot a fantastic show with crews that are more like family. We get to meet sensational chefs who are part of an experience we find to be precious. To Guy, and all who make *DDD*, I love you.

Ryan "Donny" Larson, Cameraman. Dear Minnesota, Minneapolis, Nike sneakers, art, photography, Sriracha, Bic lighters, Advil, coffee, Pepto-Bismol, rainbows, orange Trident, yellow helmets, cheeseburgers, Super Glue, gaff tape, and truffle oil: thank you all for being invaluable tools in my life on the road. And to my family, my friends, my amazing girlfriend Mariah, Match/Cut Productions, Citizen Pictures, Guy Fieri, and all the incredible restaurants and every *Triple D* fan out there: Words can't express how much I appreciate each and every one of you.

Josh "The Ice Man" Bane, Cameraman. Of all the shows I've worked on throughout my career, *Triple D* has been the most fun! When you spend as much time on the road as we have, you need a strong team that you can count on. This crew embodies that mentality and commitment to quality. Many thanks to Guy, Citizen Pictures, and Match/Cut Productions for welcoming me into the family and for giving me the opportunity to be part of the most well-oiled machine on television.

Kerry "Gilligan" Johnson, Associate Producer. Thank you to the amazing *DDD* crew, everyone at Match/Cut Productions, and the field producers and team at Citizen Pictures that come together to make every shoot great. Thank you to my girlfriend, Cassie, and my family and my friends who've always been there for me. Thank you to all the amazing locations, owners, and chefs that allow us to come in and get a behind-the-scenes look at the restaurants and share their great food with our audience. And finally, thank you to Guy Fieri whose energy, creativity, and talent bring everything together to entertain us all.

Ron "Fraggle" Gabaldon, Unit Manager. I'd like to thank all the owners, managers, servers, bartenders, busboys, and dishwashers of all of our restaurants for helping us make a great show. All your hard work in preparation for the shoot and the hospitality you show us mean the world to a travel-weary crew like ours. We love what this show does for a joint, and everyone involved deserves the good that comes out of it.

Tony Carrera, Production Assistant. I'm so glad I've had the opportunity to be a part of such a great show. I want to give a big thanks to Guy, along with Citizen Pictures and Match/Cut Productions, for making all of this possible. I couldn't ask for a better group of people to work with. I can't wait for all the great food and experiences to come as we continue traveling the country for *DDD*!

RECIPE INDEX

LIST OF RESTAURANTS

Here's a list of all the terrific restaurants that have been shown on Triple D. *The restaurants in orange are featured in this book, the restaurants with an asterisk were in the first book,* Diners, Drive-ins and Dives: An All-American Road Trip . . . with Recipes!, *and the restaurants with two asterisks were in the second book,* More Diners, Drive-ins and Dives. *But you gotta visit 'em all!*

❏ **A1 DINER***
3 Bridge Street
Gardiner, ME 04345
(207) 582-4804
www.a1diner.com/menus

❏ **AFRAH**
314 E. Main Street
Richardson, TX 75081
(972) 234-9898
afrah.com

❏ **ALCENIA'S**
317 N. Main Street
Memphis, TN 38103
(901) 523-0200

❏ **ALDO'S HARBOR
RESTAURANT**
616 Atlantic Avenue
Santa Cruz, CA 95062
(831) 426-3736
www.aldos-cruz.com

ALPINE STEAKHOUSE**
❏ 4520 S. Tamiami Trail
Sarasota, FL 34231
(941) 922-3797
www.alpinesteak.com

❏ **AL'S BREAKFAST***
413 14th Avenue S.E.
Minneapolis, MN 55414
(612) 331-9991

❏ **AMATO'S CAFE****
6405 Center Street
Omaha, NE 68016
(402) 558-5010

❏ **ANCHOR BAR**
413 Tower Avenue
Superior, WI 54880
(715) 394-9747
anchorbar.freeservers.com

❏ **ARLETA LIBRARY
BAKERY AND CAFE**
5513 SE 72nd at Harold
Portland, OR 97206
(503) 774-4470
www.arletalibrary.com

❏ **ARNOLD'S COUNTRY
KITCHEN**
605 8th Avenue South
Nashville, TN 37203
(615) 256-4455

❏ **AT LAST CAFE**
204 Orange Avenue
Long Beach, CA 90802
(562) 437-4837
www.jmchefcatering.com

❏ **ATHENS FAMILY
RESTAURANT**
2526 Franklin Pike
Nashville, TN 37204
(615) 383-2848
www.athensfamilyrestaurant
.com

❏ **AT SARA'S TABLE
CHESTER CREEK CAFE**
1902 East 8th Street
Duluth, MN 55812
(218) 724-6811
www.astccc.net

❏ **AUNT MARY'S CAFE**
4307 Telegraph Avenue
Oakland, CA 94609
(510) 601-9227
www.auntmaryscafe.com

❏ **AVILA'S MEXICAN
RESTAURANT**
4714 Maple Avenue
Dallas, TX 75219
(214) 520-2700
www.avilaselranchito.net

❏ **BABY BLUES BBQ***
444 Lincoln Boulevard
Venice, CA 90291
(310) 396-7675
www.babybluesvenice.com

❏ **BACHI BURGER**
470 E. Windmill Lane
Las Vegas, NV 89123
(702) 242-2244
bachiburger.com

❏ **BACKROAD PIZZA**
1807 2nd Street
Santa Fe, NM 87505
(505) 955-9055
www.backroadpizza.com

❏ **THE BAGEL
DELICATESSEN &
RESTAURANT**
6439 E Hampden
Denver, CO 80222
(303) 756-6667
www.thebageldeli.com

❏ **BANG!**
3472 W. 32nd Avenue
Denver, CO 80211
(303) 455-1117
bangdenver.com

❏ **BAR-B-Q KING****
2900 Wilkinson Boulevard
Charlotte, NC 28208
(704) 399-8344
www.barbaking.com

❏ **BAR GERNIKA**
202 South Capitol Boulevard
Boise, ID 83702
(208) 344-2175
www.bargernika.com

❏ **THE BARKING DOG**
115 E 49th Street
Indianapolis, IN 46298
(317) 924-2233
www.barkingdogindy.com

❏ **BAYWAY DINER***
2019 S. Wood Avenue
Linden, NJ 07036
(908) 862-3207
baywaycatering.mfbiz.com

❏ **BBQ SHACK****
1613 E. Peoria Street
Paola, KS 66071
(913) 294-5908
www.thebbqshack.com

❏ **BEACH PUB**
1001 Laskin Road
Virginia Beach, VA 23451
(757) 422-8817
www.beachpubvb.com

❑ BEACON DRIVE-IN**
255 John B. White Sr.
  Boulevard
Spartanburg, SC 29306
(864) 585-9387
www.beacondrivein.com

❑ BECKY'S DINER
390 Commercial Street
Portland, ME 04101
(207) 773-7070
www.beckysdiner.com

❑ BENNY'S SEAFOOD*
2500 SW 107th Avenue
Miami, FL 33165
(305) 227-1232

❑ BEN'S BEST DELI
96-40 Queens Boulevard
Rego Park, NY 11374
(718) 897-1700
www.bensbestdeli.com

❑ BERT'S BURGER BAR
235 N. Guadalupe Street
Santa Fe, NM 87501
(505) 982-0215

**❑ BETO'S
COMIDA LATINA**
8142 Broadway Street
San Antonio, TX 78209
(210) 930-9393
www.betosinfo.com

**❑ BETTE'S
OCEANVIEW DINER**
1807 Fourth Street
Berkeley, CA 94710
(510) 644-3932
www.bettesdiner.com

❑ BIG & LITTLE'S
860 N. Orleans Street
Chicago, IL 60610
(312) 943-0000
www.bigandlittleschicago
  .com

**❑ BIG DADDY'S BBQ
& BANQUET**
107 Wickersham Street
Fairbanks, AK 99701
(907) 452-2501
www.bigdaddysbarb-q.com

**❑ BIG JIM'S IN
THE RUN****
201 Saline Street
Pittsburgh, PA 15207
(412) 421-0532
www.bigjimsrestaurant.com

**❑ BIG MAMA'S KITCHEN
AND CATERING**
3223 N. 45th Street
Turning Point Campus,
  Building A
Omaha, NE 68104
(402) 455-6262
www.bigmamaskitchen.com

❑ BIG STAR DINER
305 Madison Avenue North
Bainbridge Island, WA 98110
(206) 842-5786

❑ BIZZARRO
1307 N. 46th Street
Seattle, WA 98103
(206) 632-7277
www.bizzarroitaliancafe.com

❑ BLACK DUCK CAFE
605 Riverside Avenue
Westport, CT 06800
(203) 227-7978

**❑ BLACKTHORN RES-
TAURANT AND PUB**
2134 Seneca Street
Buffalo, NY 14210-2365
(716) 825-9327
www.blackthornrestaurant
  .com

❑ BLOW FLY INN
1201 Washington Avenue
Gulfport, MS 39507
(228) 896-9812
www.blowflyinn.com

**❑ BLUE ASH CHILI
RESTAURANT**
9565 Kenwood Road
Cincinnati, OH 45242
(513) 984-6107
www.blueashchili.com

❑ THE BLUE DOOR PUB
1811 Selby Avenue
St. Paul, MN 55104
(651) 493-1865
www.thebdp.com

❑ BLUE MARLIN
2500 North East 163rd Street
N Miami, FL 33302
(305) 957-8822

❑ BLUE MOON CAFÉ*
1621 Aliceanna Street
Baltimore, MD 21231
(410) 522-3940

❑ BLUE PLATE DINER
2041 S. 2100 Street East
Salt Lake City, UT 84108
(801) 463-1151

**❑ BLUEPLATE LUNCH
COUNTER**
308 SW Washington Street
Portland, OR 97204
(503) 295-2583
www.eatatblueplate.com

**❑ BLUE WATER
SEAFOOD MARKET AND
GRILL**
3667 India Street
San Diego, CA 92103
(619) 497-0914

**❑ BOBBY'S HAWAIIAN
STYLE RESTAURANT***
1011 Hewitt Avenue West
Everett, WA 98201
(425) 259-1338
www.bobbyshawaiian
  stylerestaurant.com

❑ BOBO DRIVE-IN**
2300 S.W. 10th Avenue
Topeka, KS 66604
(785) 234-4511

❑ BOB'S CLAM HUT
315 US Route 1
Kittery, ME 03904
(207) 439-4233
www.bobsclamhut.com/
  home.htm

❑ BOB'S TACO STATION
1901 Avenue H
Rosenberg, TX 77471
(281) 232-8555
http://bobstacos.com

❑ BOULEVARD DINER
1660 Merritt Boulevard
Dundalk, MD 21222
(410) 285-8660
boulevarddiner.com

**❑ BRANDY'S
RESTAURANT AND
BAKERY**
1500 E. Cedar Avenue
Flagstaff, AZ 86004
(928) 779-2187
www.brandysrestaurant.com

❑ BRATS BROTHERS
13355 Ventura Boulevard
Sherman Oaks, CA 91423
(818) 986-4020

❑ BREWBURGER'S
4629 S. 108th Street
Omaha, NE 68127
(402) 614-7644
www.brewburgersomaha.com

❑ THE BRICK
1727 McGee Street
Kansas City, MO 64108
(816) 421-1634
www.thebrickkemo.com

❏ **BRICK OVEN PIZZA**
800 S. Broadway
Baltimore, MD 21231
(410) 563-1600
www.boppizza.com

❏ **BRINT'S DINER**
4834 E. Lincoln Street
Wichita, KS 67218
(316) 684-0290

❏ **BROADWAY DINER**
6501 Eastern Avenue
Baltimore, MD 21224
(410) 631-5666
www.broadwaydiner1.com

❏ **BRODERS'
CUCINA ITALIANA**
2308 W. 50th Street
Minneapolis, MN 55410
(612) 925-3113
broders.com

❏ **BROKEN RECORD**
1166 Geneva Avenue
San Francisco, CA 94112
(415) 963-1713
www.brokenrecordsanfran
    cisco.com

❏ **BRO'S CAJUN
CUISINE**
3214 Charlotte Avenue
Nashville, TN 37209
(615) 329-2626
www.broscajuncuisine.com

❏ **BROWNSTONE DINER
AND PANCAKE FACTORY***
426 Jersey Avenue
Jersey City, NJ 07302
(201) 433-0471
www.brownstonediner.com

❏ **BRYANT-LAKE BOWL**
801 W. Lake Street
Minneapolis, MN 55408
(612) 825-3737
www.bryantlakebowl.com

❏ **BUBBA'S FINE DINER**
566 San Anselmo Avenue
San Anselmo, CA 94960
(415) 459-6862
www.bubbasfinediner.com

❏ **BUNK SANDWICHES**
621 SE Morrison
Portland, OR 97214
(503) 477-9515
www.bunksandwiches.com

❏ **BUN 'N' BARREL**
1150 Austin Highway
San Antonio, TX 78209
(210) 828-2829
bunnbarrel.com

❏ **BURGER ME**
10418 Donner Pass Road
Truckee, CA 96161
(530) 587-8852
www.burgermetruckee.com

❏ **BYWAYS CAFE**
1212 NW Glisan Street
Portland, OR 97209
(503) 221-0011
www.bywayscafe.com

❏ **CABBAGETOWN
MARKET**
198 Carroll Street
Atlanta, GA 30312
(404) 221-9186
www.cabbagetownmarkt.com

❏ **CABO FISH TACO**
3201 North Davidson Street
Charlotte, NC 28205
(704) 332-8868
www.cabofishtaco.com

❏ **CAFÉ CITTI**
9049 Sonoma Highway
Kenwood, CA 95452
(707) 833-2690
www.cafecitti.com

❏ **CAFE ON
THE ROUTE****
1101 Military Avenue
Baxter Springs, KS 66713
(620) 856-5646
www.cafeontheroute.com

❏ **CAFÉ PITA**
10890 Westheimer
Houston, TX 77042
(713) 953-7237

❏ **CAFE RAKKA**
71A New Shackle Island Road
Hendersonville, TN 37075
(615) 824-6264
caferakka.com/default.aspx

❏ **CAFÉ ROLLE**
5357 H Street
Sacramento, CA 95819
(916) 455-9140
www.caferolle.com

❏ **CALIFORNIA
TACOS & MORE****
3235 California Street
Omaha, NE 68131
(402) 342-0212
www.californiatacosandmore
    .com

❏ **CALIFORNIA TACOS
TO GO**
1450 Skipper Road
Tampa, FL 36613
(941) 971-8226
www.californiatacostogo.com

❏ **CANE ROSSO**
2612 Commerce Street
Dallas, TX 75226
(214) 741-1188
ilcanerosso.com

❏ **CAPONE'S PUB**
751 North 4th Street
Coeur d'Alene, ID 83814
(208) 667-4843
www.caponespub.com

❏ **CAPTAIN
CHUCK-A-MUCK'S**
21088 Marina Road
Rescue, VA 23424
(757) 356-1005
www.captainchuck-a-mucks
    .com

❏ **CASAMENTO'S
RESTAURANT****
4330 Magazine Street
New Orleans, LA 70115
(504) 895-9761
www.casamentosrestaurant
    .com

❏ **CASINO EL CAMINO**
517 E. 6th Street
Austin, TX 78701
(512) 469-9330
www.casinoelcamino.net

❏ **CASPER'S &
RUNYON'S NOOK**
492 Hamline Avenue South
St. Paul, MN 55116
(651) 698-4347
www.crnook.com

❏ **CATELLI'S**
21047 Geyserville Avenue
Geyserville, CA 95441
(707) 857-3471
www.mycatellis.com

❏ **CATTLEMEN'S
STEAKHOUSE**
1309 S Agnew Avenue
Oklahoma City, OK 73108
(405) 236-0416
www.cattlemensrestaurant
    .com

❏ **CECILIA'S CAFE**
230 6th Street S.W.
Albuquerque, NM 87102
(505) 243-7070

CEMITAS PUEBLA**
3619 W. North Avenue
Chicago, IL 60647
(773) 772-8435
www.cemitaspuebla.com

CEMPAZUCHI
1205 East Brady Street
Milwaukee, WI 53202
(414) 291-5233
www.cempazuchi.com

CENTRAL CITY CAFÉ
529 14th Street West
Huntington, WV 25704
(304) 522-6142

CHAPS COFFEE CO
4235 South Cheney
    Spokane Road
Spokane, WA 99224-9467
(509) 624-4182
www.chapsgirl.com

CHAP'S PIT BEEF*
5801 Pulaski Highway
Baltimore, MD 21205
(410) 483-2379
www.chapspitbeef.com

CHARLIE PARKER'S
700 North Street
Springfield, IL 62704
(217) 241-2104

CHARLIE'S DINER
32 W. Main Street
Spencer, MA 01562
(508) 885-4033

CHEF POINT CAFÉ
5901 Watauga Road
Wautaga, TX 76148
(817) 656-0080
www.chefpointcafe.org

CHILAM BALAM
3023 N. Broadway Street
Chicago, IL 60657
(773) 296-6901
www.chilambalamchicago
    .com

CHINO BANDIDO*
15414 N. 19th Avenue,
    Suite K
Phoenix, AZ 85023
(602) 375-3639
www.chinobandido.com

CHOP HOUSE BURGERS
1700 W. Park Row Drive #116
Arlington, TX 76013
(817) 459-3700
www.chophouseburgers.com

CHUCK'S SOUTHERN COMFORTS CAFE
6501 W. 79th Street
Burbank, IL 60459
(708) 229-8700
www.chuckscafe.com

CITRUS BREAKFAST & LUNCH
2265 W. Great Neck Road
Virginia Beach, VA 23451
(757) 227-3333
citrusvb.com

CLARKSTON UNION BAR & KITCHEN
54 S. Main Street
Village of Clarkston, MI 48346
(248) 620-6100
clarkstonunion.com

THE COFFEE CUP
512 Nevada Way
Boulder City, NV 89005
(702) 294-0517
www.worldfamouscoffeecup
    .com

COLONNADE
1879 Cheshire Bridge Road
    N.E.
Atlanta, GA 30324
(404) 874-5642
www.colonnadeatl.com

COLOSSAL CAFE
1839 East 42nd Street
Minneapolis, MN 55407
(612) 729-2377
www.colossalcafe.com

COMET CAFE
1947 N. Farwell Avenue
Milwaukee, WI 53202
(414) 273-7677
www.thecometcafe.com

COOKIE JAR RESTAURANT
1006 Cadillac Court
Fairbanks, AK 99701
(907) 479-8319
www.cookiejarfairbanks.com

COREY'S CATSUP AND MUSTARD
623 Main Street
Manchester, CT 06040
(860) 432-7755
catsupandmustard.com

COUNTER CAFE
626 North Lamar
Austin, TX 78703
(512) 708-8800
www.countercafe.com

COUNTRY CAFÉ
235 North Santa Claus Lane
North Pole, AK 99705
(907) 488-8455

THE COVE**
606 W. Cypress Street
San Antonio, TX 78212
(210) 227-2683
www.thecove.us

COZY CORNER
745 N. Parkway
Memphis, TN 38105
(901) 527-9158
www.cozycornerbbq.com

CRAZY BURGER CAFÉ & JUICE BAR
144 Boon Street
Narragansett, RI 02882
(401) 783-1810
www.crazyburger.com

CREOLE CREAMERY
4924 Prytania Street
New Orleans, LA 70115
(504) 894-8680
www.creolecreamery.com

CRYSTAL RESTAURANT
1211 Penn Avenue
Pittsburgh, PA 15222
(412) 434-0480

CULHANE'S IRISH PUB
967 Atlantic Boulevard
Atlantic Beach, FL 32233
(904) 249-9595
www.culhanesirishpub.com

DADDYPOPS DINER
232 N. York Road
Hatboro, PA 19040
(215) 675-9717

DAD'S KITCHEN
2968 Freeport Boulevard
Sacramento, CA 95818
(916) 447-3237
ilovedadskitchen.com

DANNY'S ALL-AMERICAN DINER
4406 N. Falkenburg Road
Tampa, FL 33610
(813) 740-0606
dannysallamericandiner.com

DARI-ETTE DRIVE-IN**
1440 Minnehaha Avenue East
St. Paul, MN 55106
(651) 776-3470

□ DARWELL'S CAFE**
127 E. First Street
Long Beach, MS 39560
(228) 868-8946
www.darwellscafe.com

**□ DEFONTE'S
SANDWICH SHOP
(BROOKLYN)**
379 Columbia Street
Brooklyn, NY 11231
(718) 625-8052
www.defontesinbrooklyn.com

**□ DEFONTE'S
SANDWICH SHOP**
261 Third Avenue
New York, NY 10010
(212) 614-1500
www.defontesofbrooklyn.com

**□ DELL RHEA'S
CHICKEN BASKET**
645 Joliet Road
Willowbrook, IL 60527
(630) 325-0780
www.chickenbasket.com

**□ DEWESE'S
TIP TOP CAFE***
2814 Fredericksburg Road
San Antonio, TX 78201
(210) 732-0191
www.tiptopcafe.com

□ THE DINER
213 E Main Street
Norman, OK 73069
(405) 329-6642

□ THE DINING CAR*
8826 Frankford Avenue
Philadelphia, PA 19136
(215) 338-5113
www.thediningcar.com

□ DI PASQUALE'S**
3700 Gough Street
Baltimore, MD 21224
(410) 276-6787
www.dispasquales.com

□ DISH
1220 Thomas Avenue
Charlotte, NC 28205
(704) 344-0343
www.eatatdish.com

**□ DISH CAFE &
CATERING**
855 Mill Street
Reno, NV 89502
(775) 348-8264
www.dishcafecatering.com

**□ DIXIE QUICKS
MAGNOLIA ROOM****
1915 Leavenworth Street
Omaha, NE 68012
(402) 346-3549
www.dixiequicks.com

□ DMK BURGER BAR
2954 N. Sheffield Avenue
Chicago, IL 60657
(773) 698-6482
www.dmkburgerbar.com

□ DONATELLI'S**
2692 East County Road E.
White Bear Lake, MN 55110
(651) 777-9199
www.donatellis.com

□ DON CHOW TACOS
West Los Angeles area
Santa Monica, CA
www.donchowtacos.com

**□ DONNIE MAC'S
TRAILER PARK CUISINE**
1515 West Grove Street
Boise, ID 83702
(208) 384-9008
www.donniemacgrub.com

**□ DOR-STOP
RESTAURANT**
1430 Potomac Avenue
Pittsburgh, PA 15216
(412) 561-9320
www.dor-stoprestaurant.com

□ DOT'S BACK INN*
4030 Macarthur Avenue
Richmond, VA 23227
(804) 266-3167

**□ DOTTIE'S TRUE
BLUE CAFE**
28 Sixth Street
San Francisco, CA 94103
(415) 885-2767
dotties.biz

**□ DOUGH PIZZERIA
NAPOLETANA**
6989 Blanco Road
San Antonio, TX 78213
(210) 979-6565
www.doughpizzeria.com

□ DOUMAR'S
1919 Monticello Avenue
Norfolk, VA 23517
(757) 627-4163
www.doumars.com

□ DUARTE'S TAVERN*
202 Stage Road
Pescadero, CA 94060
(650) 879-0464
www.duartestavern.com

□ DULUTH GRILL
118 S. 27th Avenue West
Duluth, MN 55806
(218) 726-1150
www.duluthgrill.com

□ EARL'S DRIVE IN
12139 Olean Road
Chaffee, NY 14030-9767
(716) 496-5125

**□ THE EARLY
BIRD DINER**
1644 Savannah Highway
Charleston, SC 29407
(843) 277-2353
www.earlybirddiner.com

□ EISHEN'S
108 2nd Street
Okarche, OK 73762
(405) 263-9939

□ EL BOHIO
1127 Harry Wurzbach
San Antonio, TX 78234
(210) 822-8075

□ 11TH STREET DINER
1065 Washington Avenue
Miami Beach, FL 33139
(305) 534-6373
www.eleventhstreetdiner.com

**□ ELF'S DEN
RESTAURANT & LOUNGE**
14 Miles Richardson Highway
North Pole, AK 99705
(907) 488-3268

**□ EL INDIO MEXICAN
RESTAURANT***
3695 India Street
San Diego, CA 92103
(619) 299-0333
www.el-indio.com

□ ELK PUBLIC HOUSE
1931 West Pacific Avenue
Spokane, WA 99204
(509) 363-1973
www.wedonthaveone.com

**□ EMILY'S
LEBANESE DELI**
641 University Avenue N.E.
Minneapolis, MN 55416
(612) 379-4069
www.emilyslebanesedeli.com

**□ EMMA JEAN'S
HOLLAND BURGER CAFÉ***
17143 D Street (Route 66)
Victorville, CA 92394
(760) 243-9938
www.hollandburger.com

EVELYN'S DRIVE-IN*
2335 Main Road (Route 77)
Tiverton, RI 02878
(401) 624-3100
www.evelynsdrivein.com

EVEREADY DINER*
4189 Albany Post Road
(Route 9 North)
Hyde Park, NY 12538
(845) 229-8100
www.theevereadydiner.com

FAB HOT DOGS
19417 Victory Boulevard
Reseda, CA 91335
(818) 344-4336
www.fabhotdogs.com

FALCONETTI'S
1812 Commercial Drive
Vancouver, BC, V5N 4A5
(604) 251-7287
www.falconettis.com

THE FARMER'S SHED
2514 Augusta Highway
Lexington, SC 29072
(803) 996-0700
www.farmersshed.com

**FLAKOWYTZ
OF BOYNTON**
7410 West Boynton
    Beach Boulevard
Boynton Beach, FL 33437
www.flakowitzofboynton.com

**FLIP FLOPS
GRILL & CHILL**
2217 Upton Drive #814
Virginia Beach, VA 23454
(757) 427-3547
www.flipflopsvb.com

THE FLY TRAP*
22950 Woodward Avenue
Ferndale, MI 48220
(248) 399-5150
www.theflytrapferndale.com

**FOOLISH CRAIG'S
CAFE**
1611 Pearl Street
Boulder, CO 80302
(303) 247-9383
www.foolishcraigs.com

FOREIGN & DOMESTIC
306 E. 53rd Street
Austin, TX 78751
(512) 459-1010
fndaustin.com

**FORTE EUROPEAN
TAPAS BAR & BISTRO**
4180 S. Rainbow, Suite 806
Las Vegas, NV 89103
(702) 220-3876
www.barforte.com

**FOUR KEGS
SPORTS PUB***
267 N. Jones Boulevard
Las Vegas, NV 89107
(702) 870-0255
www.fourkegs.com

FRANKS DINER*
508 58th Street
Kenosha, WI 53140
(262) 657-1017
www.franksdinerkenosha.com

FRED'S TEXAS HOUSE
915 Currie Street
Ft. Worth, TX 76107
(817) 332-0083
www.fredstexascafe.com

FRESH LOCAL WILD
Burrard Street & W. Hastings
    Street
Vancouver, BC, V6R 2R6
(604) 808-1800
www.freshlocalwild.com

FUEL CANTINA
211 Rutledge Avenue
Charleston, SC 29403
(843) 737-5959
www.fuelcharleston.com

G & A RESTAURANT**
3802 Eastern Avenue
Baltimore, MD 21224
410) 276-9422
www.gandarestaurant.com

**GAFFEY STREET
DINER**
247 N. Gaffey Street
San Pedro, CA 90731
(310) 548-6964
www.gaffeystreetdiner.com

**GALEWOOD
COOKSHACK**
Various locations
Chicago, IL
(773) 470-8334
www.galewoodcookshack.com

**GALWAY BAY
IRISH PUB**
63 Maryland Avenue
Annapolis, MD 21401
(410) 263-8333
www.galwaybayannapolis.com

GARIFUNA FLAVA
2516-2518 W. 63rd Street
Chicago, IL 60629
(773) 776-7440
www.garifunaflava.com

GATSBY'S DINER
2598 Alta Arden Expressway
Sacramento, CA 95825
(916) 977-0102
www.gatsbysdiner.com

GAZALA'S PLACE
709 9th Avenue
New York, NY 10036
(212) 245-0709
www.gazalasplace.com

GEORGE'S PLACE
301 Beach Drive
Cape May, NJ 08204
(609) 884-6088

GEORGIA'S GREEK
323 NW 85th Street
Seattle, WA 98117
(206) 783-1228
www.georgiasgreek
    restaurant.com

GERACI'S
2266 Warrensville Center
    Road
Cleveland, OH 44118
(216) 371-5643
www.geracisrestaurant.com

**GERMAINE'S LUAU,
WAHIAWA, HI**
444 Hobron Lane, Suite 501
Honolulu, HI 96815
(808) 947-1244
www.germainesluau.com

GET FRESH CAFE
2500 Church Street
Norfolk, VA 23504
(757) 966-6577
www.5ptsfarmmarket.org

GIUSEPPE'S
2824 E. Indian Road
Phoenix, AZ 85016
(602) 381-1237
www.giuseppesrestaurant.com

GIUSTI'S
14743 Walnut Grove-Thornton
    Road
Walnut Grove, CA 95960
(916) 776-1808
www.giustis.com

THE GLASS ONION
1219 Savannah Highway
Charleston, SC 29407
(843) 225-1717
www.ilovetheglassonion.com

GLENN'S DINER
1820 W. Montrose Avenue
Chicago, IL 60613
(773) 506-1720
www.glennsdiner.com

GLORIA'S CAFE
10227 Venice Boulevard
Los Angeles, CA 90034
(310) 838-0963
www.gloriascafela.com

GOLD 'N SILVER INN
790 West 4th Street
Reno, NV 89503
(775) 323-2696
www.goldnsilverreno.com

THE GOLDEN BEAR
2326 K Street
Sacramento, CA 95816
(916) 441-2242
www.goldenbear916.com

GOOD DOG BAR & RESTAURANT
224 South 15th Street
Philadelphia, PA 19102-3806
(215) 985-9600
gooddogbar.com

GORDY'S HI-HAT
415 Sunnyside Drive
Cloquet, MN 55720
(218) 879-6125
www.gordys-hihat.com

GORILLA BARBEQUE**
2145 Coast Highway
Pacifica, CA 94044
(650) 359-7427
www.gorillabbq.com

GRAMPA'S BAKERY AND RESTAURANT
17 SW First Street
Dania Beach, FL 33004
(954) 923-2163
www.grampasbakery.com

GREEK CORNER RESTAURANT
2366 Massachusetts Avenue
Cambridge, MA 02140
(617) 661-5655
www.greekcorner.us/index
.html

GREEN MESQUITE
1400 Barton Springs Road
Austin, TX 78704
(512) 479-0485
www.greenmesquite.net

GRINDER'S PIZZA
417 East 18th Street
Kansas City, MO 64108
(816) 472-5454
www.grinderspizza.com

GROVERS BAR AND GRILL
9160 Transit Road
East Amherst, NY 14051
(716) 636-1803

GRUBSTAKE
1525 Pine Street
San Francisco, CA 94109
(415) 673-8268
www.sfgrubstake.com

GUMBO SHACK
212½ Fairhope Avenue
Fairhope, AL 36532
(251) 928-4100
www.guysgumbo.com

HACKNEY'S ON HARMS*
1241 Harms Road
Glenview, IL 60025
(847) 724-5577
www.hackneys.net

HANK'S CREEKSIDE RESTAURANT**
2800 4th Street
Santa Rosa, CA 95405
(707) 575-8839
www.sterba.com/sro/creek
side

HANK'S HAUTE DOGS
324 Coral Street
Honolulu, HI 96813
(808) 532-4265

2330 Kalakaua Avenue
Honolulu, HI 96815
(808) 532-4265
www.hankshautedogs.com

HAPPY GILLIS CAFE & HANGOUT
549 Gillis Street
Kansas City, MO 64106
(816) 471-3663
www.happygillis.com

HAROLD'S RESTAURANT*
602 Limestone Street
Gaffney, SC 29340
(864) 489-9153
www.haroldsrestaurant.com

HARRY'S ROADHOUSE**
96 B Old Las Vegas Highway
Santa Fe, NM 87505
(505) 989-4629

HARVEY'S HOT DOGS II
3205 Stamford Road
Portsmouth, VA 23703
(757) 483-0613

HAUS MURPHY'S**
5739 W. Glendale Avenue
Glendale, AZ 85301
(623) 939-2480
www.hausmurphys.com

HAVANA HIDEOUT
509 Lake Avenue
Lake Worth, FL 33460
(561) 585-8444
www.havanahideout.com

THE HIGHLANDER**
931 Monroe Drive NE
Atlanta, GA 30308
(404) 872-0060
www.thehighlanderatlanta
.com

HIGHSTOWN DINER
151 Mercer Street
Highstown, NJ 08520
(609) 443-4600

HIGHWAY INN
94-226 Leoku Street
Waipahu, HI 96797
(808) 677-4345
www.myhighwayinn.com

HILDEBRANDT'S
84 Hillside Avenue
Williston Park, NY 11596
(516) 741-0608
www.hildebrandtsrestaurant
.com

HILLBILLY HOT DOGS*
6591 Ohio River Road
Lesage, WV 25537
(304) 762-2458
www.hillbillyhotdogs.com

HILLS' RESTAURANT AND LOUNGE
401 W Main Avenue
Spokane, WA 99201
(509) 747-3946
www.hillsrestaurantand
lounge.com

HOB NOB HILL**
2271 1st Avenue
San Diego, CA 92101
(619) 239-8176
www.hobnobhill.com

HODAD'S*
5010 Newport Avenue
Ocean Beach, CA 92107
(619) 224-4623

❏ HONEY'S SIT-N-EAT
800 North 4th Street
Philadelphia, PA 19123
(215) 925-1150
www.honeys-restaurant.com

❏ HONKY TONK BBQ
1213 W. 18th Street
Chicago, IL 60608
(312) 226-7427
www.honkytonkbbqchicago
.com

❏ HOPFLEAF BAR
5148 N. Clark Street
Chicago, IL 60640
(773) 334-9851
hopleaf.com

❏ HRD COFFEE SHOP
521 #A 3rd Street
San Francisco, CA 94107
(415) 543-2355
www.hrdcoffeeshop.com

❏ HULLABALOO DINER
15045 FM 2154
Wellborn, TX 77845
(979) 690-3002
www.hullabaloodiner.com

❏ INDY'S HISTORIC STEER-IN RESTAURANT
5130 E 10th Street
Indianapolis, IN 46219
(317) 356-0996
www.steerin.net

❏ INGRID'S KITCHEN
3701 North Youngs Boulevard
Oklahoma City, OK 73112-
7555
(405) 946-8444
www.ingridskitchen.com

❏ IRAZU
1865 N. Milwaukee Avenue
Chicago, IL 60647
(773) 252-5687
www.irazuchicago.com

❏ IRON BARLEY*
5510 Virginia Avenue
St. Louis, MO 63111
(314) 351-4500
www.ironbarley.com

❏ JAKE'S GOOD EATS
12721 Albemarle Road
Charlotte, NC 28227
(704) 545-4741
www.jakesgoodeats.com

❏ JAMAICA GATES CARIBBEAN CUISINE
1020 W. Arkansas
Arlington, TX 76013
(817) 795-2600
www.jamaicagates.com

❏ JAMAICA KITCHEN
8736 Sunset Drive
Kendall Lakes, FL 33173
(305) 596-2585
www.jamaicakitchen.com

❏ JAMAICAWAY
900 Rosa L Parks Boulevard
Nashville, TN 37208
(615) 255-5920
www.jamaicawaycatering.com

❏ JAMIE'S BROADWAY GRILLE
427 Broadway
Sacramento, CA 95818
(916) 442-4044
www.jamiesbroadwaygrille
.com

❏ JAX AT THE TRACKS
10144 West River Street
Truckee, CA 96160
(530) 550-7450
www.jaxtruckee.com

❏ JAY BEE'S
15911 Avalon Boulevard
Gardena, CA 90247
(310) 532-1064
www.jaybeesbbq.com

❏ JEFFERSON DINER
5 Bowling Green Parkway
Lake Hopatcong, NJ 07849
(973) 663-0233
www.jeffersondiner.com

❏ JERSEY'S CAFE
13710 North Meridian Street
Carmel, IN 46032
(317) 846-7760
www.jerseyscafe.com

❏ J.J.MCBREWSTER'S
3101 Clays Mill Road #301
Lexington, KY 40503
(859) 224-0040
jjmcbrewsters.com

❏ JIMMY'S DOWN THE STREET
1613 E. Sherman
Coer d'Alene, ID 83814
(208) 765-3868
www.jimmysdownthestreet
.com

❏ JIMTOWN STORE
6706 Highway 128
Healdsburg, CA 78213
(707) 433-1212
jimtown.com

❏ JOE'S CABLE CAR
4320 Mission Street
San Francisco, CA 94112
(415) 334-6699
www.joescablecarrestaurant
.com

❏ JOE'S FARM GRILL*
3000 E. Ray Road
Gilbert, AZ 85296
(480) 563-4745
www.joesfarmgrill.com

❏ JOE'S GIZZARD CITY*
120 W. Main Street
Potterville, MI 48876
(517) 645-2120
www.gizzardcity.com

❏ JOE SQUARED PIZZA
133 W. North Avenue
Baltimore, MD 21201
(410) 545-0444
www.joesquared.com

❏ JOE TESS PLACE
5424 S. 24th Street
Omaha, NE 68102
(402) 733-4638
www.joetessplace.com

❏ JOEY K'S RESTAURANT & BAR
3001 Magazine Street
New Orleans, LA 70115
(504) 891-0997
www.joeyksrestaurant.com

❏ JOHN MULL'S MEATS AND ROAD KILL GRILL
3730 Thom Boulevard
Las Vegas, NV 89130
(702) 645-1200
johnmullsmeats.com

❏ JOHNNY'S BAR-B-Q
5959 Broadmoor
Mission, KS 66201
(913) 432-0777
www.johnnysbbqkc.com

❏ JOHNNY GARLIC'S
1460 Farmers Lane
Santa Rosa, CA 95405
(707) 528-6368
www.johnnygarlics.com

❏ JOHN'S OF 12TH STREET
302 E. 12th Street
New York, NY 10003
(212) 475-9531
www.johnsof12thstreet.com

❏ JOSE'S REAL CUBAN FOOD
8799 Cortez Road W.
Bradenton, FL 34210
(941) 795-4898
josesrealcubanfood.com

❏ **J.T. FARNHAM'S***
88 Eastern Avenue
(Route 133)
South Essex, MA 01929
(978) 768-6643

❏ **KATIE'S RESTAURANT**
3701 Iberville Street
New Orleans, LA 70119
(504) 488-6582
www.katiesinmidcity.com

❏ **KEEGAN'S
SEAFOOD GRILLE***
1519 Gulf Boulevard
Indian Rocks Beach, FL 33785
(727) 596-2477
www.keeganseafood.com

❏ **KELLY O'S DINER****
1130 Perry Highway #28
Pittsburgh, PA 15237
(412) 364-0473
www.kellyos.com

❏ **KELLY'S DINER****
674 Broadway
Somerville, MA 02144
(617) 623-8102
www.kellysdiner.com

❏ **KENNY AND ZIGGY'S**
2327 Post Oak Boulevard
Houston, TX 77056
(713) 871-8883
www.kennyandziggys.com

❏ **THE KITCHEN**
529 S. A Street
Oxnard, CA 93030
(805) 385-8980
thekitchenona.com

❏ **KRAMARCZUK'S**
215 East Hennepin Avenue
Minneapolis, MN 55414
(612) 379-3018
www.kramarczuk.com/restau
rant/restaurant.html

❏ **KRAZY JIM'S
BLIMPY BURGER**
551 S. Division Street
Ann Arbor, MI 48104
(734) 663-4590
www.blimpyburger.com

❏ **KUMA'S CORNER**
2900 W. Belmont Avenue
Chicago, IL 60618
(773) 604-8769
www.kumascorner.com

❏ **LA CAMERONERA**
1952 West Flagler Street
Miami, FL 33135
(305) 642-3322
www.garciabrothersseafood
.com

❏ **LA CARAQUENA**
300 W. Broad Street
Falls Church, VA 22040
(703) 533-0076
www.lacaraquena.com

❏ **LA PIAZZA AL FORNO**
5803 W Glendale Avenue
Glendale, AZ 85301
(623) 847-3301
www.lapiazzaalforno.com

❏ **LA PINES CAFE**
1061 Robert Road
Slidell, LA 70458
(985) 641-6196
www.lapinescafe.com

❏ **LA TEXANITA**
1667 Sebastopol Road
Santa Rosa, CA 95407
(707) 527-7331
www.latexanita.com

❏ **LAKE EFFECT DINER**
3165 Main Street
Buffalo, NY 14214
(716) 833-1952
www.curtinrestaurants.com/
lake-effect-diner.html

❏ **LANDMARK
RESTAURANT DINER**
4429 Central Avenue
Charlotte, NC 28205
(704) 532-1153
www.landmarkdinercharlotte
.com

❏ **LANKFORD GROCERY**
88 Dennis Street
Houston, TX 77006
(713) 522-9555
www.lankfordgrocery.com

❏ **LAUER-KRAUTS**
26 South 6th Street
Brighton, CO 80601
(303) 654-9700
www.lauer-krauts.com

❏ **LEAPING
LIZARDS CAFE**
4408 Shore Drive
Virginia Beach, VA 23455
(757) 460-5327
www.theleapinglizard.com

❏ **LEONARD'S PIT
BARBECUE**
5465 Fox Plaza Drive
Memphis, TN 38115
(901) 360-1963
www.leonardsbarbecue.com

❏ **LEO'S BBQ**
3631 N. Kelley Avenue
Oklahoma City, OK 73111
(405) 424-5367

❏ **LIBERTY ELM DINER**
777 Elmwood Avenue
Providence, RI 02907
(401) 467-0777
www.libertyelmdiner.com

❏ **LITO'S MEXICAN
RESTAURANT**
514 E. Haley Street
Santa Barbara, CA 93103
(805) 962-1559
www.litosmexfoodsb.com

❏ **THE LITTLE
DEPOT DINER**
1 Railroad Avenue
Peabody, MA 01960
(978) 977-7775
www.thelittledepotdiner.com

❏ **LITTLE TEA SHOP**
69 Monroe Avenue
Memphis, TN 38103
(901) 525-6000

❏ **LO BELLO'S
SPAGHETTI HOUSE**
809 5th Avenue
Coraopolis, PA 15108
(412) 264-9721
www.lobellosspaghettihouse
.com

❏ **THE LOBSTER SHANTY**
25 Front Street
Salem, MA 01970
(978) 745-5449
www.lobstershantysalem.com

❏ **LOLA'S—A LOUISIANA
KITCHEN**
241 W. Charleston, Suite 101
Las Vegas, NV 89102
(702) 227-5652
lolaslasvegas.com

❏ **LONE STAR
TAQUERIA****
2265 Fort Union Boulevard
Salt Lake City, UT 84121
(801) 944-2300

❏ **LOS TAPATIOS**
354 N. White Road
San Jose, CA 95127
(408) 729-6199

❏ **LOS TAQUITOS**
4747 East Elliot Road #17
Phoenix, AZ 85044
(480) 753-4361
www.ltgrill.com

LOUIE AND THE REDHEAD LADY
1851 Florida Street
Mandeville, LA 70448
(985) 626-6044
www.louieandtheredhead
   lady.com

LOUIE MUELLER BARBECUE*
206 W. Second Street
Taylor, TX 76574
(512) 352-6206
www.louiemuellerbarbecue
   .com

LOUIS' BASQUE CORNER
301 E. 4th Street
Reno, NV 89501
(775) 323-7203
www.louisbasquecorner.com

LOUIS FAMILY RESTAURANT
286 Brook Street
Providence, RI 02906
(401) 861-5225
www.louisrestaurant.org

LUCKY'S CAFE
777 Starkweather Avenue
Cleveland, OH 44113
(216) 622-7773
www.luckyscafe.com

LUKE'S INSIDE OUT
1109 S. Lamar Boulevard
Austin, TX 78704
(512) 589-8883
www.lukesinsideout.com

MAC AND ERNIE'S ROADSIDE EATERY*
Williams Creek Depot FM 470
Tarpley, TX 78883
(830) 562-3250
www.macandernies.com

MAC'S FISH AND CHIP SHOP
503 State Street
Santa Barbara, CA 93101
(805) 897-1160
www.macssb.com

MAD GREEK'S DINER
72112 Baker Boulevard
Baker, CA 92309
(760) 733-4354

MAGNOLIA CAFE**
1920 S. Congress Avenue
Austin, TX 78704
(512) 445-0000

2304 Lake Austin Boulevard
Austin, TX 78703
(512) 478-8645
www.themagnoliacafe.com

MAGNOLIA PANCAKE HAUS
606 Embassy Oaks
San Antonio, TX 78216
(210) 496-0828
www.magnoliapancakehaus
   .com

MAHONY'S PO-BOY SHOP
3454 Magazine Street
New Orleans, LA 70115
(504) 899-3374
www.mahonyspoboys.com

MAINE DINER
2265 Post Road
Wells, ME 04090
(207) 646-4441
www.mainediner.com

MAMA'S 39TH STREET DINER
3906 Waddell Street
Kansas City, MO 64111
(816) 531-6422

MAMA COZZA'S
2170 West Ball Road
Anaheim, CA 92804
(714) 635-0063
www.mamacozzas.com

MAMA E'S WINGS & WAFFLES
3838 Springlake Drive
Oklahoma City, OK 73111
(405) 424-0800

MAMBO'S
1701 Victory Boulevard
Glendale, CA 91201
(818) 545-8613
www.mambosla.com

MANCI'S ANTIQUE CLUB**
1715 Main Street
Daphne, AL 36526
(251) 626-9917
www.manci.net

MAPLE & MOTOR
4810 Maple Avenue
Dallas, TX 75219
(214) 522-4400
www.mapleandmotor.com

MARIA'S TACO XPRESS*
2529 S. Lamar Boulevard
Austin, TX 78704
(512) 444-0261
www.tacoxpress.com

MARIETTA DINER*
306 Cobb Parkway South
Marietta, GA 30060
(770) 423-9390
www.mariettadiner.net

MARLA'S CARIBBEAN CUISINE
3761 Bloomington Avenue S.
Minneapolis, MN 55407
(612) 724-3088
www.marlascuisine.com

MARLOWE'S RIBS
4381 Elvis Presley Boulevard
Memphis, TN 38116
(901) 332-4159
www.marlowesmemphis.com

MARTIN'S BAR-B-QUE JOINT
7238 Nolensville Road
Nolensville, TN 37135
(615) 776-1856
www.martinsbbqjoint.com

MASSEY'S RESTAURANT
1805 8th Avenue
Fort Worth, TX 76110
(817) 921-5582

MATTHEWS CAFETERIA**
2229 Main Street
Tucker, GA 30084
(770) 939-2357
www.matthewscafeteria.com

MATT'S BIG BREAKFAST**
801 N. 1st Street
Phoenix, AZ 85004
(602) 254-1074
www.mattsbigbreakfast.com

MAUI'S DOG HOUSE
806 New Jersey Avenue
Wildwood, NJ 08260
(609) 846-0444
www.mauisdoghouse.com

MEAL TICKET
1235 San Pablo Avenue
Berkeley, CA 94706
(510) 526-6325
www.mealticketrestaurant.com

MEAT & BREAD
370 Cambie Street
Vancouver, BC
   V6B 2N3
(604) 566-9003
www.meatandbread.ca

MELT BAR AND GRILLED
14718 Detroit Avenue
Lakewood, OH 44107
(216) 226-3699
www.meltbarandgrilled.com

MEMPHIS TAPROOM
2331 E Cumberland Street
Philadelphia, PA 19125
(215) 425-4460
www.memphistaproom.com

MERRITT CANTEEN INC.
4355 Main Street
Bridgeport, CT 06606
(203) 372-1416
www.merrittcanteen.com

METRO DINER
3302 Hendricks Avenue
Jacksonville, FL 32207
(904) 398-3701
www.metrodiner.com

METRO 29 DINER
4711 Lee Highway
Arlington, VA 22207
(703) 528-2464

MICHIGAN BREWING CO.
1093 Highview Drive
Webberville, MI 48892
(517) 521-3600
www.michiganbrewing.com

MIKE'S CHILI PARLOR*
1447 N.W. Ballard Way
Seattle, WA 98107
(206) 782-2808
www.mikeschiliparlor.com

MIKE'S CITY DINER**
1714 Washington Street
Boston, MA 02118
(617) 267-9393
www.mikescitydiner.com

THE MODERN
337 13th Avenue N.E.
Minneapolis, MN 55413
(612) 378-9882
www.moderncafeminnea
    polis.com

MOGRIDDER'S*
565 Hunts Point Avenue
Bronx, NY 10474
(718) 991-3046
www.mogridder.com

MOM'S TAMALES
3328 Pasadena Avenue
Los Angeles, CA 90031
(323) 226-9383
www.momstamales.com

MOMOCHO
1835 Fulton Road
Cleveland, OH 44113
(216) 694-2122
www.momocho.com

MONTE CARLO STEAKHOUSE*
3916 Central S.W.
Albuquerque, NM 87105
(505) 836-9886

MONUMENT CAFE
500 S. Austin Avenue
Georgetown, TX 78627
(512) 868-5932
www.themonumentcafe
    .com/#/cafe

MOOCHIE'S MEAT-BALLS AND MORE**
232 E. 800 South
Salt Lake City, UT 84111
(801) 596-1350
(801) 364-0232
www.moochiesmeatballs.com

MORIN'S HOMETOWN BAR AND GRILLE
16 S. Main Street
Attleboro, MA 02703
(508) 222-9875
www.morinsdiner.com

MOROCCAN BITES
5714 Evers Road
San Antonio, TX 78238
(210) 706-9700
www.moroccanbitescuisine
    .com

MOSEBERTH'S FRIED CHICKEN
1505 Airline Boulevard
Portsmouth, VA 23707
(757) 393-1721
www.moseberths.com

MR. BARTLEY'S BURGER COTTAGE
1246 Massachusetts Avenue
Cambridge, MA 02138
(617) 354-6559
www.mrbartley.com

MULBERRY CAFE
64 Jackson Avenue
Lackawanna, NY 14218
(716) 822-4292
www.mulberryitalian
    ristorante.com

MUNCH'S RESTAURANT & SUNDRIES
3920 6th Street South
St. Petersburg, FL 33705
(727) 896-5972
munchburger.com

MURPHY'S BAR & GRILL
2 Merchant Street
Honolulu, HI 96813
(808) 531-0422
murphyshawaii.com

MUSTACHE BILL'S DINER**
8th Street and Broadway
Barnegat Light, NJ 08006
(609) 494-0155

NADINE'S BAR AND RESTAURANT**
19 S. 27th Street
Pittsburgh, PA 15203
(412) 481-1793
www.nadinesbar.com

NAGLEE PARK GARAGE
505 East San Carlos Street
San Jose, CA 95112-2104
(408) 286-1100
www.nagleeparkgarage.com

NAKED CITY PIZZA
3240 S. Arville Street
Las Vegas, NV 89102
(702) 243-6277
www.nakedcitylv.com

NANA ORGANIC
3267 S. Halsted Street
Chicago, IL 60608
(312) 929-2486
www.nanaorganic.com/live/

NIC'S GRILL
1201 N. Pennsylvania Avenue
Oklahoma City, OK 73107
(405) 524-0999

NICKEL DINER
524 Sputh Main Street
Los Angeles, CA 90013
(213) 623-8301
www.nickeldiner.com

NICO'S PIER 38
1133 N. Nimitz Highway
Honolulu, HI 96817
(808) 540-1377
www.nicospier38.com

NIKO NIKOS
2520 Montrose Boulevard
Houston, TX 77006
(713) 528-1308
www.nikonikos.com

900 GRAYSON
900 Grayson Street
Berkeley CA 94710
(510) 704-9900
www.900grayson.com

NOBLE PIG SANDWICHES
11815 620 N., Suite 4
Austin, TX 78750
(512) 382-6248
www.noblepigaustin.com

THE NOOK
492 Hamline Avenue South
St. Paul, MN 55116
(651) 698-4347

NORTH END CAFFE
3421 Highland Avenue
Manhattan Beach, CA 90266
(310) 546-4782
www.northendcaffe.net

NORTHERN WATERS SMOKEHAUS
Dewitt-Seitz Marketplace
Duluth, MN 55802
(218) 724-7307
www.northernwatersmoke
haus.com

NORTON'S PASTRAMI & DELI
18 W. Figueroa Street
Santa Barbara, CA 93103
(805) 965-3210
www.nortonspastrami.com

NYE'S POLONAISE ROOM
112 East Hennepin Avenue
Minneapolis, MN 55414
(612) 379-2021
www.nyespolonaise.com

O'ROURKE'S DINER
728 Main Street
Middletown, CT 06457
(860) 346-6101
www.orourkesdiner.com

THE OINKSTER
2005 Colorado Boulevard
Eagle Rock, CA 90041
(323) 255-6465
www.theoinkster.com

THE OLD COFFEE POT RESTAURANT
714 Saint Peter Street
New Orleans, LA 70116
(504) 524-3500
www.letseat.at/theold
coffeepot

OOHHS & AAHHS GOURMET DELI
1005 U Street NW
Washington, DC 20001
(202) 667-7142
www.oohhsnaahhs.com

THE ORIGINAL FALAFEL'S DRIVE-IN*
2301 Stevens Creek Boulevard
San Jose, CA 95128
(408) 294-7886
www.falafeldrivein.com

THE ORIGINAL VITO & NICK'S PIZZERIA**
8433 S. Pulaski Road
Chicago, IL 60652
(773) 735-2050
www.vitoandnick.com

OTTO'S SAUSAGE KITCHEN
4138 SE Woodstock Boulevard
Portland, OR 97202
(503) 771-6714
www.ottossausage.com

OVER EASY
4037 N. 40th Street
Phoenix, AZ 85018-5204
(602) 468-3447
www.eatatovereasy.com

PAGODA RESTAURANT
431 North Santa Claus Lane
North Pole, AK 99705
(907) 488-3338
pagodanorthpole.com

PAM'S KITCHEN
5000 University Way
Seattle, WA 98105
(206) 696-7010
www.pams-kitchen.com

PANINI PETE'S*
42½ S. Section Street
Fairhope, AL 36532
(251) 929-0122
www.paninipetes.com

PANOZZO'S ITALIAN MARKET
1303 S. Michigan Avenue
Chicago, IL 60605
(312) 356-9966
panozzos.com

PARADISE PUP**
1724 S. River Road
Des Plaines, IL 60018
(847) 699-8590

PARASOL'S**
2533 Constance Street
New Orleans, LA 70130
(504) 897-5413

PARKETTE DRIVE IN
1230 E. New Circle Road
Lexington, KY 40505
(859) 254-8723
www.theparkette.com

PARKVIEW NITECLUB
1261 West 58th Street
Cleveland, OH 44102
(216) 961-1341
www.parkviewniteclub.com

PAT'S BARBECUE**
155 W. Commonwealth
Avenue
Salt Lake City, UT 84115
(801) 484-5963
www.patsbbq.com

PATRICK'S ROADHOUSE
106 Entrada Drive
Los Angeles, CA 90402
(310) 459-4544
www.patricksroadhouse.info

PAUL'S COFFEE SHOP
16947 Bushard Street
Fountain Valley, CA 92708
(714) 965-3643
www.semperfinerdiner.com

PAWLEY'S FRONT PORCH
827 Harden Street
Columbia, SC 29205-1001
(803) 771-8001
www.pawleysfrontporch.com

PEACEFUL RESTAURANT
532 W. Broadway
Vancouver, BC, V5Z 1E9
(604) 879-9878
www.peacefulrestaurant.com

PECAN LODGE
1010 S. Pearl Expy. Dallas
Farmers Market, Shed 2
Dallas, TX 75201
(214) 748-8900
www.pecanlodge.com

PENGUIN DRIVE-IN*
1921 Commonwealth Avenue
Charlotte, NC 28205
(704) 375-6959

PEPE'S AND MITO'S
2911 Elm Street
Dallas, TX 75226
(214) 741-1901
www.pepesandmitos.com

PERFECTLY FRANKS
118 N. Main Street
Summerville, SC 29483
(843) 871-9730

**PETE'S
BREAKFAST HOUSE**
2055 E. Main Street
Ventura, CA 93001
(805) 648-1130
www.petesbreakfasthouse
.com/index.html

**PICABU
NEIGHBORHOOD BISTRO**
901 W 14th Avenue
Spokane, WA 99204
(509) 624-2464
www.picabu-bistro.com

PIER 23 CAFÉ
On the Embarcadero
San Francisco, CA 94111
(415) 362-5125
www.pier23cafe.com

PINE STATE BISCUITS
3540 SE Belmon
Portland, OR 97214
(503) 236-3346
www.pinestatebiscuits.com

PINEVILLE TAVERN
Route 413 Durham Road
Pineville, PA 18946
(215) 598-3890
www.pinevilletavern.com

THE PITSTOP
1706 Sunrise Highway
Merrick, NY 11566
(516) 223-7799
www.pitstopeats.com

PIZZA JUNCTION
1269 Erie Avenue
North Tonawanda, NY 14120
(716) 692-6366
www.thepizzajunction.com

PIZZA PALACE*
3132 E. Magnolia Avenue
Knoxville, TN 37914
(865) 524-4388
www.visitpizzapalace.com

PIZZALCHIK
7330 W. State Street
Boise, ID 83714
(208) 853-7757
www.pizzalchik.com

PIZZERIA LOLA
5557 Xerxes Avenue South
Minneapolis, MN 55410
(612) 424-8338
www.pizzerialola.com

PIZZERIA LUIGI**
1137 25th Street
San Diego, CA 92102
(619) 233-3309
www.pizzerialuigi.com

PODNAH'S PIT
1469 NE Prescott Street
Portland, OR 97211
(503) 281-3700
www.podnahspit.com

POK POK
3226 SE Division Street
Portland, OR 97202
(503) 232-1387
www.pokpokpdx.com

**POKE STOP
AT MILILANI**
95-1840 Meheula Parkway
Mililani, HI 96789
(808) 626-3400
www.poke-stop.com

POLISH VILLAGE CAFE
2990 Yemans Avenue
Hamtramck, MI 48212
(313) 874-5726
www.thepolishvillagecafe
.com

POLKA RESTAURANT
4112 Verdugo Road
Los Angeles, CA 90065
(323) 255-7887
www.polkacatering.com

**PORTHOLE
RESTAURANT**
20 Custom House Wharf
Portland, ME 04101
(207) 780-6533
www.portholemaine.com

**PRINCE
LEBANESE GRILL**
502 W Randol Mill Road
Arlington, TX 76011
(817) 469-1811
www.princelebanesegrill.com

PSYCHO SUZI'S*
2519 Marshall Street N.E.
Minneapolis, MN 55418
(612) 788-9069
www.psychosuzis.com

PUTAH CREEK CAFE
1 Main Street
Winters, CA 95694
(530) 795-2682
www2.buckhornsteakhouse
.com

Q FANATIC BBQ
180 Miller Road
Champlin, MN 55316
(763) 323-6550
www.qfanatic.com

Q RESTAURANT
225 Clement Street
San Francisco, CA 94118
(415) 752-2298
www.qrestaurant.com

**QUAHOG'S
SEAFOOD SHACK**
206 97th Street
Stone Harbor, NJ 08084
(609) 368-6300
www.quahogsshack.com

RAINBOW DRIVE-IN
3308 Kanaina Avenue
Honolulu, HI 96815
(808) 737-0177
www.rainbowdrivein.com

RAMONA CAFE*
628 Main Street
Ramona, CA 92605
(760) 789-8656
www.ramonacafe.com

R&R TAQUERIA
7894 Washington Boulevard
Elkridge, MD 21075
(410) 799-0001
www.rrtaqueria.com

RED ARROW DINER*
61 Lowell Street
Manchester, NH 03101
(603) 626-1118
www.redarrowdiner.com

THE REDHEAD
349 E. 13th Street
New York, NY 10003
(212) 533-6212
www.theredheadnyc.com

RED IGUANA**
736 W. North Temple
Salt Lake City, UT 84116
(801) 322-1489
www.rediguana.com

RED LION
2316 South Shepherd Drive
Houston, TX 77019
(713) 529-8390
www.redlionhouston.com

**THE RED
WAGON CAFÉ**
2296 E. Hastings Street
Vancouver, BC V5L 1V4
(604) 568-4565
www.redwagoncafe.com

❑ **RICK AND ANN'S**
2922 Domingo Avenue
Berkeley, CA 94705-2454
(510) 649-8538
www.rickandanns.com

❑ **RICK'S PRESS ROOM**
130 East Idaho Avenue
Meridan, ID 83642
(208) 288-0558
www.rickspressroom.net

❑ **RICK'S WHITE
LIGHT DINER**
114 Bridge Street
Frankfort, KY 40601
(502) 330-4262
www.rickswhitelightdiner.com

❑ **RIGOLETTO ITALIAN
BAKERY & CAFE**
2181 Upton Drive, Suite 414
Virginia Beach, VA 23454
(757) 427-3999
www.rigolettoitalianbakery
.com

❑ **RINCON CRIOLLO**
40-09 Junction Boulevard
Corona, Queens, NY 11368
(718) 458-0236
www.rinconcriollo.wix.com

❑ **RINO'S PLACE**
258 Saratoga Street
East Boston, MA 02128
(617) 567-7412
www.rinosplace.com

❑ **RITZ DINER****
72 E. Mount Pleasant Avenue
Livingston, NJ 07039
(973) 533-1213

❑ **RIVERSHACK TAVERN***
3449 River Road
Jefferson, LA 70121
(504) 834-4938
www.therivershacktavern.com

❑ **RJ'S BOB-BE-QUE
SHACK**
5835 Lamar Avenue
Mission, KS 66062
(913) 262-7300
www.rjsbbq.com

❑ **ROBERTO'S
AUTHENTIC
MEXICAN FOOD**
39510 North Daisy Mountain
    Drive, Suite 170
Anthem, AZ 85086
(623) 465-1515
www.robertosaz.com

❑ **ROCCO'S CAFÉ**
1131 Folsom Street
San Francisco, CA 94103
(415) 554-0522
www.roccoscafe.com

❑ **THE ROCK CAFÉ**
114 W. Main Street
Stroud, OK 74079
(918) 968-3990

❑ **ROSIE'S DINER**
4500 14 Mile Road N.E.
Rockford, MI 49341
(616) 866-3663
www.rosiesdiner.com

❑ **RUDY'S CAN'T
FAIL CAFÉ**
4081 Hollis Street
Emeryville, CA 94608-3505
(510) 594-1221
www.rudyscantfailcafe.com

❑ **RUSSIAN RIVER PUB**
11829 River Road
Forestville, CA 95436
(707) 887-7932
www.russianriverpub.com

❑ **RUTH'S DINER**
2100 Emigration Canyon
Salt Lake City, UT 84108
(801) 582-5807
www.ruthsdiner.com

❑ **SAGE GENERAL STORE**
24-20 Jackson Avenue
Long Island City, NY 11101
(718) 361-0707
www.sagegeneralstore.com

❑ **SALSA BRAVA****
2220 E. Route 66
    (Santa Fe Avenue)
Flagstaff, AZ 86004
(928) 779-5293
www.salsabravaflagstaff.com

❑ **SAMMY'S FOOD
SERVICE & DELI**
3000 Elysian Fields
New Orleans, LA 70122
(504) 947-0675
www.sammysfood.com

❑ **SAM LAGRASSA'S**
44 Province Street
Boston, MA 02108
(617) 357-6861
www.samlagrassas.com

❑ **SAM'S NO. 3**
1500 Curtis Street
Denver, CO 80210
(303) 534.1927
www.samsno3.com

❑ **SANTA CRUZ DINER**
909 Ocean Street
Santa Cruz, CA 95060
(831) 426-7151
www.santacruzdiner.com

❑ **SAVARINO'S CUCINA**
2121 Belcourt Avenue
Nashville, TN 37212
(615) 460-9878

❑ **SAVE ON MEATS**
43 W. Hastings Street
Vancouver, BC, V6B 1G4
(604) 250-7779
saveonmeats.ca

❑ **SAVOY CAFÉ & DELI**
24 W. Figueroa Street
Santa Barbara, CA 93101
(805) 962-6611
www.thesavoycafe.com

❑ **SCHELLVILLE GRILL**
22900 Broadway
Sonoma, CA 95476
(707) 996-5151
www.schellvillegrill.com

❑ **SCHOONER
OR LATER****
241 N. Marina Drive
Long Beach, CA 90803
(562) 430-3495
www.schoonerorlater.com

❑ **SCULLY'S TAVERN***
9809 Sunset Drive
Miami, FL 33173
(305) 271-7404
www.scullystavern.net

❑ **THE SHANTY**
38995 N US Highway 41
Wadsworth, IL 60083
www.theshantyrestaurant
.com

❑ **SIDE CAR**
560 Fifth Avenue
Brooklyn, NY 11215
(718) 369-0077
Contact: John DeCoursy
www.sidecarbrooklyn.com

❑ **SILK CITY PHILLY***
435 Spring Garden Street
Philadelphia, PA 19123
(215) 592-8838
www.silkcityphilly.com

❑ **SILVER GULCH
BREWING AND
BOTTLING CO.**
2195 Old Steese Highway
Fox, AK 99712
(907) 452-2739
www.silvergulch.com

❑ **THE SILVER SKILLET**
200 14th Street N.W.
Atlanta, GA 30318
(404) 874-1388
www.thesilverskillet.com

❑ **SINGLETON'S SEAFOOD SHACK**
4728 Ocean Street
Atlantic Beach, FL 32233
(904) 246-4442

❑ **THE SINK**
1165 13th Street
Boulder, CO 80302
(303) 444-7465
www.thesink.com

❑ **SIP & BITE RESTAURANT**
2200 Boston Street
Baltimore, MD 21231
(410) 675-7077
www.sipandbite.com

❑ **THE SKYLARK FINE DINING AND LOUNGE**
Route 1 and Wooding Avenue
Edison, NJ 08817
(732) 777-7878
www.skylarkdiner.com

❑ **SLIM'S LAST CHANCE CHILI SHACK**
5606 1st Avenue South
Seattle, WA 98108
(206) 762-7900
www.slimslastchance.com

❑ **SMACK SHACK AT THE 1029 BAR**
1029 Marshall Street
    Northeast
Minneapolis, MN 55413
(612) 379-4322
the1029bar.com/smack_
    shack.html

❑ **SMALLEY'S CARIBBEAN BARBEQUE**
423 Main Street
Stillwater, MN 55082
(651) 439-5375
www.smalleyspiratebbq.com/
    home.html

❑ **SMOKEY VALLEY TRUCK STOP**
40 Bond Court
Olive Hill, KY 41164
(606) 286-5001

❑ **SMOKIN' GUNS BBQ**
1218 Swift Avenue
North Kansas City, MO
(816) 221-2535
www.smokingunsbbq.com

❑ **SMOQUE***
3800 N. Pulaski Road
Chicago, IL 60641
(773) 545-7427
www.smoquebbq.com

❑ **SOL FOOD**
811 4th Street
San Rafael, CA 94901
(415) 451-4765
www.solfoodrestaurant.com

❑ **SONNY'S FAMOUS STEAK HOGIES**
1857 N. 66th Avenue
Hollywood, FL 33024
(954) 989-0561
www.sonnysfamoussteak
    hogies.com

❑ **SOPHIA'S PLACE**
6313 4th Street N.W.
Albuquerque, NM 87107
(505) 345-3935

❑ **SOPHIA'S RESTAURANT**
749 Military Road
Buffalo, NY 14216
(716) 447-9661

❑ **SOUTH 21 DRIVEIN**
3101 East Independence
    Boulevard
Charlotte, NC 28205
(704) 377-4509
www.south21drivein.com

❑ **SOUTH SIDE SODA SHOP AND DINER***
1122 S. Main Street
Goshen, IN 46526
(574) 534-3790
www.southsidesodashop
    diner.com

❑ **SOUTHERN KITCHEN**
1716 6th Avenue
Tacoma, WA 98405
(253) 627-4282
www.southernkitchen-
    tacoma.com

❑ **SOUTHERN SOUL BARBEQUE**
2020 Demere Road
St. Simons Island, GA 31522
(912) 638-7685
www.southernsoulbbq.com

❑ **THE SPARROW TAVERN**
24-01 29th Street
Astoria, NY 11102
(718) 606-2260
thesparrowtavern.com

❑ **SQUEEZE INN***
7916 Fruitridge Road
Sacramento, CA 95820
(916) 386-8599
www.thesqueezeinn.com

❑ **STANDARD DINER**
320 Central Avenue S.E.
Albuquerque, NM 87102
(505) 243-1440
www.standarddiner.com

❑ **STARLITE LOUNGE**
364 Freeport Road
Blawnox, PA 15238
(412) 828-9842

❑ **STERLE'S SLOVENIAN COUNTRY HOUSE**
1401 East 55th Street
Cleveland, OH 44103
(216) 881-4181
www.sterlescountryhouse
    .com

❑ **STEUBEN'S FOOD SERVICE**
523 E. 17th Avenue
Denver, CO 80203
(303) 830-1001
www.steubens.com

❑ **STONEY CREEK INN**
8238 Fort Smallwood Road
Baltimore, MD 21226
(410) 439-3123
www.stoneycreekinn
    restaurant.com

❑ **STUDIO DINER****
4701 Ruffin Road
San Diego, CA 92123
(858) 715-6400
www.studiodiner.com

❑ **SUNFLOWER CAFFE**
421 1st Street West
Sonoma, CA 95476
(707) 996-6645
www.sonomasunflower.com

❑ **SUPER DUPER WEENIE****
306 Black Rock Turnpike
P.O. Box 320487
Fairfield, CT 06825
(203) 334-3647
www.superduperweenie.com

SUPINO PIZZERIA
2457 Russell Street
Detroit, MI 48207
(313) 567-7879
www.supinopizza.com

SURREY'S CAFÉ AND JUICE BAR
1418 Magazine Street
New Orleans, LA 70130
(504) 524-3828
www.surreyscafeandjuicebar.com

SWAGGER FINE SPIRITS AND FOOD
8431 Wornall Road
Kansas City, MO 64114
(816) 361-4388
www.swaggerkc.com

SWEETIE PIE'S
4270 Manchester Avenue
St. Louis, MO 63110
(314) 371-0304

TACO BUS
913 E Hillsborough Avenue
Tampa, FL 33603
(813) 232-5889
tampatacobus.com

T-BONE TOM'S STEAKHOUSE
707 Highway 146
Kemah, TX 77565
(281) 334-2133
www.tbonetoms.com

TACO TACO CAFE
145 E. Hildebrand Avenue
San Antonio, TX 78212
(210) 822-9533
www.tacotacosa.com

THE TAMALE PLACE
5226 Rockville Road
Indianapolis, IN 46224
(317) 248-9771
www.thetamaleplace.com

TAMPA BAY BREWING CO.
1600 E. 8th Avenue
Tampa, FL 33605
(813) 247-1422
www.tampabaybrewing
        company.com

TAP TAP HAITIAN RESTAURANT
819 5th Street
Miami Beach, FL 33139
(305) 672-2898
www.taptaprestaurant.com

TASTE OF PERU
6545 North Clark Street
Chicago, IL 60626
(773) 381-4540
www.tasteofperu.com

TATTOOED MOOSE
1137 Morrison Drive
Charleston, SC 29403
(843) 277-2990
tattooedmoose.com

TAYLOR'S AUTOMATIC REFRESHER*
933 Main Street
St. Helena, CA 94574
(707) 963-3486
www.taylorsrefresher.com

TECOLOTE CAFÉ
1203 Cerrillos Road
Santa Fe, NM 87505
(505) 988-1362
www.tecolotecafe.com

TED PETERS*
1350 Pasadena Avenue South
South Pasadena, FL 33707
(727) 381-7931

TEE OFF BAR AND GRILL
3129 Clement Street
San Francisco, CA 94121
(415) 752-5439
www.teeoffbarandgrill.com

10TH AVE BURRITO
817 Belmar Plaza
Belmar, NJ 07719
(732) 280-1515
www.tenthaveburrito.com

TERRY'S TURF CLUB
4618 Eastern Avenue
Cincinnati, OH 45226
(513) 533-4222

THEE PITTS AGAIN*
5558 W. Bell Road
Glendale, AZ 85308
(602) 996-7488
www.theepittsagain.com

13 GYPSIES
887 Stockton Street
Jacksonville, FL 32204
(904) 389-0330
www.13gypsies.com

3 SISTERS CAFÉ
6360 Guilford Avenue
Indianapolis, IN 46220
(317) 257-5556
www.3sisterscafein.com

TICK TOCK DINER*
281 Allwood Road
Clifton, NJ 07012
(973) 777-0511
www.ticktockdiner.com

TIOLI'S CRAZEE BURGER
4201 30th Street (near
        El Cajon Boulevard)
San Diego, CA 92104
(619) 282-6044
www.crazeeburger.com

TOCABE: AN AMERICAN INDIAN EATERY
3536 W. 44th Avenue
Denver, CO 80211
(720) 524-8282
www.tocabe.com

TOMAHAWK RESTAURANT
1550 Philip Avenue
North Vancouver, BC V7P 2V8
(604) 988-2612
www.tomahawkrestaurant
        .com

TOM'S BAR-B-Q*
4087 New Getwell Road
Memphis, TN 38118
(901) 365-6690
www.tomsbarbq.com

TOMMY'S JOYNT**
1101 Geary Boulevard
San Francisco, CA 94109
(415) 775-4216
www.tommysjoynt.com

TORTILLA CAFÉ
210 7th Street SE
Washington, DC 20003
(202) 547-5700
www.tortillacafe.com

TORTILLERIA NIXTAMAL
10405 47th Avenue
Corona, NY 11368
(718) 699-2434
www.tortillerianixtamal.com

TOWN TALK DINER
2707 E. Lake Street
Minneapolis, MN 55406
(612) 722-1312
www.towntalkdiner.com

TRAFFIC JAM & SMUG
511 West Canfield Street
Detroit, MI 483201
(313) 831-9470
www.trafficjamdetroit.com

TRE KRONOR
3258 West Foster Avenue
Chicago, IL 60625
(773) 267-9888
www.trekronorrestaurant.com

❑ TRIPLE XXX FAMILY RESTAURANT*
2 N. Salisbury Street
West Lafayette, IN 47906
(765) 743-5373
www.triplexxxfamily
    restaurant.com

❑ TUFANO'S VERNON PARK TAP
1073 W. Vernon Park Place
Chicago, IL 60607
(312) 733-3393

❑ TUNE INN RESTAURANT & BAR
331 Pennsylvania Avenue S.E.
Washington, DC 20003
(202) 543-2725

❑ TUNE-UP CAFÉ**
1115 Hickox Street
Santa Fe, NM 87505
(505) 983-7060
www.tuneupcafe.com

❑ TWISTED ROOT BURGER CO.
2615 Commerce Street
Dallas, TX 75226
www.twistedrootburgerco
    .com

❑ UNCLE LOU'S FRIED CHICKEN**
3633 Mill Ranch Road
Memphis, TN 38116
(901) 332-2367
www.unclelousfriedchicken
    .com

❑ UNION WOODSHOP
18 S. Main Street
Clarkston, MI 48346
(248) 625-5660
www.unionwoodshop.com

❑ UNLV
4505 S. Maryland Parkway
Las Vegas, NV 89154
(702) 895-3011
www.unlv.edu

❑ VALENCIA LUNCHERIA**
172 Main Street
Norwalk, CT 06851
(203) 846-8009
www.valencialuncheria.com

❑ VICTOR'S 1959 CAFÉ**
3756 Grand Ave South
Minneapolis, MN 55409
(612) 827-8948
www.victors1959cafe.com

❑ VILLAGE CAFÉ
1001 W. Grace Street
Richmond, VA 23220
(804) 353-8204
www.villagecafeonline.com

❑ VIRGIL'S CAFÉ
710 Fairfield Avenue
Bellevue, KY 41073
(859) 491-3287
www.virgilscafe.com

❑ VIRGINIA DINER*
322 W. Main Street
Wakefield, VA 23888
(888) 823-4637
www.vadiner.com

❑ VOULA'S OFFSHORE CAFÉ*
658 N.E. Northlake Way
Seattle, WA 98105
(206) 634-0183
www.voulasoffshore.com

❑ WADDELL'S PUB AND GRILLE
4318 South Regal
Spokane, WA 99223
(509) 443-6500
www.waddellspubandgrill
    .com

❑ WESTSIDE DRIVE IN
1939 West State Street
Boise, ID 83702
(208) 342-2957
www.cheflou.com

❑ THE WHALE'S RIB RESTAURANT
2031 NE 2nd Street
Deerfield Beach, FL 33441
(954) 421-8880
www.whalesrib.com

❑ WHITE MANNA*
358 River Street
Hackensack, NJ 07601
(201) 342-0914

❑ WHITE PALACE GRILL
1159 S. Canal Street
Chicago, IL 60607
(312) 939-7167
www.whitepalacegrill.com

❑ WHITNER'S BBQ
869 Lynnhaven Parkway
Virginia Beach, VA 23452
(757) 689-8215
www.whitnersbbq.com

❑ THE WIENERY
414 Cedar Avenue South
Minneapolis, MN 55467
(612) 333-5798
www.wienery.com

❑ WILLIE BIRD'S
1150 Santa Rosa Avenue
Santa Rosa, CA 95404
(707) 542-0861
www.williebirdsrestaurant
    .com

❑ WILSON'S BARBEQUE**
1851 Post Road
Fairfield, CT 06824
(203) 319-7427
www.wilsons-bbq.com

❑ WOODYARD BAR-B-QUE
3001 Merriam Lane
Kansas City, KS 66106
(913) 236-6666
www.woodyardbbq.com

❑ W.O.W—WORTH OUR WEIGHT
1021 Hahman Drive
Santa Rosa, CA 95405
(707) 544-1200
www.worthourweight.com

❑ YJ'S SNACK BAR*
128 W. 18th Street
Kansas City, MO 64108
(816) 472-5533

❑ ZEST
1134 E. 54th Street
Indianapolis, IN 46220
(317) 466-1853
www.zestexcitingfood.com

❑ ZIA'S DINER
326 South Guadalupe Street
Santa Fe, NM 87501
(505) 988-7008
www.ziadiner.com

❑ ZYDECO'S
11 E. Main Street
Mooresville, IN 46158
(317) 834-3900
www.zydecos.net